Palgrave Studies in Impact Finance

Series Editor
Mario La Torre, Department of Management,
Sapienza University of Rome, Rome, Italy

The *Palgrave Studies in Impact Finance* series provides a valuable scientific 'hub' for researchers, professionals and policy makers involved in Impact finance and related topics. It includes studies in the social, political, environmental and ethical impact of finance, exploring all aspects of impact finance and socially responsible investment, including policy issues, financial instruments, markets and clients, standards, regulations and financial management, with a particular focus on impact investments and microfinance.

Titles feature the most recent empirical analysis with a theoretical approach, including up to date and innovative studies that cover issues which impact finance and society globally.

Shika Saravanabhavan · Meenakshi Rajeev

Moving Beyond Barriers

India's Financial Inclusion Journey

palgrave
macmillan

Shika Saravanabhavan
Entrepreneurship Development
Institute of India
Ahmedabad, Gujarat, India

Institute for Social and Economic
Change
Bengaluru, Karnataka, India

Meenakshi Rajeev
Indian Institute of Technology
Jammu, Jammu and Kashmir, India

Institute for Social and Economic
Change
Bengaluru, Karnataka, India

ISSN 2662-5105 ISSN 2662-5113 (electronic)
Palgrave Studies in Impact Finance
ISBN 978-981-95-1065-8 ISBN 978-981-95-1066-5 (eBook)
https://doi.org/10.1007/978-981-95-1066-5

Cover illustration: amtitus/GettyImages

This Palgrave Macmillan imprint is published by the registered company Springer Nature Singapore Pte Ltd.
The registered company address is: 152 Beach Road, #21-01/04 Gateway East, Singapore 189721, Singapore

Dedicated to our parents & parents-in-law-
Your blessings, strength, and support have made this possible.

Foreword

Financial inclusion ensures that all individuals, especially those from socially and economically disadvantaged groups, have access to a wide range of appropriate and affordable financial services. Such inclusion brings widespread benefits to both the economy and society by promoting equitable economic growth, alleviating poverty, and offering broad-based advantages across various population groups. This book offers a timely and insightful examination of the major dimensions of financial inclusion, viz., credit, savings, insurance, and remittances, within the Indian context, highlighting the key challenges and opportunities in providing financial services to the underserved.

Financial inclusion in India has come a long way, from the credit-centric policies of the pre-liberalisation era to the present framework, which is inclusive and broad in its outlook, recommending a wide range of financial services be made available to all. The Reserve Bank of India (RBI) has played a crucial role in shaping this transformation. Its historically proactive policy measures, such as encouraging branch expansion in unbanked areas, launching the Business Correspondent model, supporting the introduction of Basic Savings Bank Deposit Accounts, and fostering digital payment systems, have significantly enhanced financial access across the country. This book offers a critical and in-depth examination of India's financial inclusion journey, assessing both the progress achieved and the gaps that persist. The chapters combine empirical evidence with policy analysis, exploring ways to improve access to and usage of financial services in India.

At a time when financial inclusion is central to economic development policy, this book underscores the need for genuinely inclusive strategies that leave no one behind. It highlights that financial inclusion is not just about opening bank accounts, but about enabling meaningful participation in the financial system and enhancing dignity through financial empowerment.

I commend the authors for their commitment to this subject. I trust that their work will not only lay a strong foundation for future research in the field, but also offers valuable insights for policymakers, enabling them to take meaningful steps towards building a more inclusive and equitable financial system for all.

Dr. C. Rangarajan
Former Chairman of the Prime
Minister's Economic Advisory
Council, Former Governor
of the Reserve Bank of India
Madras School of Economics
Chennai, India

Preface

As we set out to write this book, our primary objective was to provide a comprehensive analysis of financial inclusion in India. Financial Inclusion, as we understood it, was more than just opening new bank accounts; it was about dismantling social, geographic, and structural barriers to ensure that all individuals, particularly the traditionally disadvantaged, could gain access to a wide range of suitable financial services at affordable costs.

This understanding drove our inquiry as to why, despite decades of policies and programmes, so many people in India still remain outside the financial mainstream. While access to financial services has improved substantially in recent years, active and sustained usage continued to remain low, particularly in rural areas. To examine this overarching issue, we realised the need to adopt both macro and micro perspectives. The macro perspective allowed us to analyse the institutional and policy frameworks and their impact on financial inclusion. At this level, we developed a comprehensive index which subsumed supply-side indicators from scheduled commercial banks as well as co-operatives, presenting a more representative measure of the real extent of financial inclusion, especially in rural areas, where cooperative banks play a central role in financial inclusion.

The micro perspective, based on nationally representative household-level data, allowed us to explore in depth the demand-side factors that shape financial inclusion. Variables such as education, social category, income, and occupation could be understood far more clearly when examined at the micro-level. Guided by the Rangarajan Committee Report (2008) which identifies four basic financial services: credit, deposit facilities, insurance, and remittance products, as the core components of financial inclusion, we undertook a detailed demand-side analysis of each of these components to better understand the factors that enable access and usage. We carried out the analysis separately for the urban and rural regions, recognising that the challenges of financial inclusion are different in the rural and urban regions.

Thus, this book is our attempt to bring together data-backed evidence and analysis to paint a fuller picture of financial inclusion in India: where we stand, how we got here, and what it will take to ensure that every citizen can be a part of the financial system. We hope this book becomes a valuable resource for researchers, students, and policy makers who are committed to building an inclusive financial system.

Bengaluru, India

Shika Saravanabhavan
Meenakshi Rajeev

Acknowledgements

We owe our deepest gratitude to the many individuals who made this book possible. Their wisdom, guidance, and thoughtful suggestions are woven throughout these pages. First of all, we are deeply honoured that Dr. C. Rangarajan, former Governor of the Reserve Bank of India, has graciously agreed to write the foreword for this work. We are equally grateful to Dr. N. R. Bhanumurthy and Dr. Sugata Marjit for reading the manuscript and expressing their observations through their endorsements. We are thankful to Dr. R. S. Deshpande, Dr. Manojit Bhattacharjee, Ms. B. P. Vani, Dr. Indrajit Bairagya, Dr. Malini Tantri, and Dr. Abdul Aziz, whose insights were invaluable at every stage of this work. Their constructive criticism and thoughtful feedback played a crucial role in shaping the final manuscript. Meenakshi Rajeev gratefully acknowledges the institutional support received from the Institute for Social and Economic Change (ISEC), Bengaluru and the Indian Institute of Technology (IIT), Jammu. The support extended by the Indian Council of Social Science Research (ICSSR) and the Reserve Bank of India (RBI) to ISEC is also sincerely acknowledged.

Lastly, we extend our heartfelt thanks to our parents, spouses and all other family members for their unwavering support and encouragement throughout this journey.

Contents

Abbreviations

AIDIS	All India Debt and Investment Survey
AIRCS	All India Rural Credit Survey
ATM	Automated Teller Machines
FI	Financial Inclusion
FIAP	Financial Inclusion Action Plan
GPFI	Global Partnership for Financial Inclusion
IRDA	Insurance Regulatory and Development Authority
MFI	Microfinance Institutions
MGNREGA	Mahatma Gandhi National Rural Employment Guarantee Act
NABARD	National Bank for Agriculture and Rural Development
NAFSCOB	National Federation of State Co-operative Banks Limited
NBFC	Non-Banking Financial Company
NSS	National Sample Survey
OBC	Other Backward Castes
OTC	Over-the-Counter
PACS	Primary Agricultural Credit Societies
PMJDY	Pradhan Mantri Jan Dhan Yojana
RBI	Reserve Bank of India
RRB	Regional Rural Banks
SAS	Situation Assessment Survey
SC/ST	Scheduled Castes and Scheduled Tribes
SHG	Self-Help Groups
UPI	United Payments Interface

List of Figures

List of Tables

CHAPTER 1

Theory and Practice of Financial Inclusion: A Focus on India

1.1 Introduction

The financial sector plays a central role in a country's development. It comprises institutions that mobilise and allocate financial resources across various sectors of the economy, thereby contributing to the development of the country in several ways. To begin with, it improves the productive capacity of the economy by providing essential financing to entrepreneurs and businesses. This stimulates technological changes and innovations in the economy, bringing about economic modernisation and growth (Claessens, 2006; King and Levine 1993; Mckinnon 1973; Schumpeter 1934; Shaw, 1973).

At a micro level, financial institutions provide access to various financial services, thereby connecting ordinary people to the financial mainstream and promoting financial inclusion. This is especially important in a developing country like India, where households routinely face numerous risks in their daily life. For such households, access to financial services acts as a buffer against unforeseen contingencies (Ray 1998). In addition, it enables them to invest in education and skill development, thereby expanding opportunities to engage in income-generating activities (Banerjee and Newman 1993). Ultimately, these individual-level benefits contribute to broader economic welfare and prosperity.

S. Saravanabhavan and M. Rajeev, *Moving Beyond Barriers*, Palgrave Studies in Impact Finance,
https://doi.org/10.1007/978-981-95-1066-5_1

1.1.1 *Financial Inclusion and its Various Aspects*

Financial inclusion can broadly be defined as a process that ensures that there is no involuntary exclusion of eligible individuals from the financial system. Rajan (2014) defines financial inclusion as "a process of ensuring access to appropriate financial products and services needed by all sections of the society in general and the weaker sections and lower-income groups in particular at an affordable cost in a fair and transparent manner by mainstream institutional players". In line with this, the current financial inclusion drive focuses on providing access to a wide range of financial services, and it endorses active participation of people in the financial sector. Furthermore, the Dr. Rangarajan committee report highlights that mere possession of a bank account or access to a government credit programme is no longer sufficient for true financial inclusion.

1.1.2 *Credit Access*

In a country with a large majority of self-employed population, which includes both agricultural households and small businesses, access to credit is crucial. The ability to access credit reduces poverty, encourages human capital development, widens a person's occupational choice, boosts economic productivity and facilitates the adoption of new technologies (Banerjee and Newman 1993; Burgess and Pande 2005; Karlan and Zinman 2010; Zeller et al. 1998). In India, access to agricultural credit has been given a lot of emphasis by the Government since the pre-liberalisation era.

In the decades following independence, development planning placed strong emphasis on the agricultural sector, with credit delivery emerging as an important part of this plan. Although the emphasis on credit delivery resulted in significant improvements in the outreach and availability of agricultural credit, a large majority of the population continued to remain out of the purview of formal finance and this was especially the case with the socially and economically disadvantaged groups and women (Fletschner 2009; Kumar 2013; Rajeev et al. 2011; Rajeev and Saravanabhavan 2019).

While access to credit enhances welfare, particularly that of the poor, other financial services are also equally important. In times of financial shocks, credit may not be easily accessible, making it essential for households to have access to savings instruments as well. This brings us to the second aspect of financial inclusion-formal savings.

1.1.3 Access to Formal Savings

The ability to save in a formal financial institution is a fundamental aspect of personal financial management. For low-income households, savings act as a precautionary measure to manage financial shocks and uncertainties (Deaton 1990). This role becomes even more critical in developing countries like India, where credit market failures are common and social security nets are either weak or absent (Bhattacharjee and Rajeev 2014). In such contexts, savings function as a vital self-insurance mechanism, offering households a buffer against income volatility and unforeseen expenses.

Bank accounts provide a safe place for storing money. In contrast, informal saving methods such as keeping cash at home, relying on friends, or participating in chit funds, expose the poor to significant risks such as theft or fraud (Collins et al. 2010; Tiwari et al. 2011). In addition, saving money in the bank prevents the temptation to spend frequently and unnecessarily, as the money is out of immediate reach (Prina 2015). Having adequate savings in formal institutions also reduces a household's reliance on informal or high-cost credit during emergencies, thereby enhancing financial stability (Aportela 1999). Despite these advantages, many individuals do not actively use their bank accounts, and savings balances often remain low. Common barriers to formal saving include knowledge gaps, lack of trust, behavioural biases, and high transaction costs (Karlan et al. 2014).

Beyond credit and savings, insurance schemes also play a crucial role in safeguarding households against economic shocks. Insurance products—whether life insurance, health insurance, or crop insurance—allow households to cope with emergencies without falling into debt or depleting their life savings. Therefore, expanding access to insurance for better financial resilience, particularly for low-income households, is crucial for encouraging comprehensive financial inclusion and long-term economic stability.

1.1.4 Access to Insurance

Insurance is the third important aspect of financial inclusion, as mentioned by the Rangarajan Committee report on financial inclusion (RBI 2008). By paying a small amount as a premium at regular intervals, an individual can insure themselves against a range of risks. Some of the common risks that a household may face are the death of an earning member, health issues, accidents, and crop losses in the case of farmers. Having insurance allows a household to reduce the impact of these shocks and improve its resilience during adverse situations. Apart from providing a safety net to individual households, insurance contributes significantly to broader development goals, including enhanced food security, better health outcomes, and improved access to education (Martínez et al. 2019).

Without the adoption of insurance, financial emergencies can easily have severe negative impacts on low-income households, exacerbating their existing vulnerabilities. This issue is particularly acute for agricultural households, who face high levels of income uncertainty. Studies have shown that a lack of agricultural insurance often results in households resorting to inefficient ways of coping, such as non-adoption of technology, avoiding innovative methods of production, or engaging in excessive crop diversification (Hazell et al. 1986; Wright and Hewitt 1994). These forgone opportunities end up curtailing long-term productivity and growth. In times of crisis, uninsured households are forced to make compromises such as reducing spending on health, nutrition, and education (Binswanger-Mkhize 2012; Dercon 2002). These trade-offs perpetuate poverty and force them to remain in a state of vulnerability. Given the high costs of non-insurance, expanding access to inclusive and affordable insurance should be an important goal of financial inclusion.

While insurance, savings, and credit provide funds during financial distress or shocks, another key strategy a household uses to cope with such distress is diversifying economic activities. Increasingly, we observe a large number of households where family members migrate to different locations to earn additional income. The money that they send home enables such households to cope with emergencies, stabilise consumption, and maintain their standard of living. For such households, having access to formal and reliable channels of money transfer is especially important, as it ensures timely, secure, and cost-effective remittance flows.

1.1.5 Access to Remittance Services

The fourth aspect of financial inclusion, as highlighted by the Rangarajan committee report, is remittance services (RBI 2008), which are particularly crucial for internal migrants. For many such low-income migrant households, migration serves as a risk diversification strategy, with household members moving to areas with better employment opportunities (Lucas and Stark 1985). Generally, these migration flows happen from less developed regions to more developed regions, and the majority of these migrants belong to the poorer segments of the population (Deshingkar 2006; GOI 2011).

Remittances from migrants play a vital role in supporting recipient households. These funds are used for essential needs such as human capital development-improving education and skill development, or for paying off existing debts (Harttgen and Klasen 2011). Usually, a portion of the remittances sent to the bank accounts may even be saved in the account itself for future uses (Anzoategui et al. 2014; Tiwari et al. 2011). Thus, given the importance of remittances in enhancing the well-being of low-income households, it is necessary to ensure that they have access to convenient formal channels for money transfers. However, despite the expansion of fast and efficient banking services, certain sections of the population continue to rely on informal and often unreliable methods of sending money (Demirgüç-Kunt et al. 2018).

Recognising the benefits of access to different financial services, countries across the globe are promoting financial inclusion to drive inclusive economic development, alleviate poverty, and promote sustainable progress. A synergy of technological innovation, global support, and collaborative initiatives has helped place financial inclusion at the centre of global development strategies.

1.2 Global Efforts to Improve Financial Inclusion across the Developing World

Financial inclusion has been identified as an enabler for seven of the 17 sustainable development goals adopted by the United Nations. The global expansion of technology and mobile banking has also played an important role in accelerating financial inclusion in emerging economies by providing affordable and accessible financial services. International organisations, like the World Bank and the International Monetary Fund

(IMF), are also actively supporting financial inclusion initiatives. Most importantly, over the last decade, there have been collective endeavours by country groups to advance financial inclusion through collaborative efforts.

1.2.1 The Agenda of Financial Inclusion and the G20 Summit

The G20 (Group of Twenty) serves as a platform for dialogue and cooperation between developed and developing countries. It comprises 19 individual nations and the European Union. The G20 presidency rotates annually among its member countries, and India held the presidency from 1 December 2022 to 30 November 2023. Although the G20 does not have a permanent secretariat, the country holding the current presidency, along with its predecessor and successor, forms a G20 troika. The troika ensures the continuity of the agenda from one presidency to the next. The country holding the presidency has the opportunity to highlight and prioritise issues of current global relevance.

One such issue that gained prominence within the G20 agenda is financial inclusion. In 2010, at the G20 (Group of 20) summit in Seoul, financial inclusion was formally acknowledged as a crucial channel through which the larger goals of development can be met. In line with this, the G20 leaders drew up the Financial Inclusion Action Plan (FIAP) and established the Global Partnership for Financial Inclusion (GPFI) to implement the action plan.

1.2.2 Financial Inclusion Action Plan (FIAP) and the Global Partnership for Financial Inclusion (GPFI)

The initiation of the FIAP and GPFI represents one of the earliest attempts to advance financial inclusion at a global level. Though not an institution, per se, GPFI serves as an inclusive forum for G20 member countries, non-G20 countries interested in financial inclusion, and other pertinent stakeholders to enable and enhance development through financial inclusion strategies. GPFI is not just committed to increasing the outreach of financial institutions, but also to improving the quality of services available to the excluded and the underserved. The idea behind establishing this platform was to encourage mutual learning, knowledge sharing, and active advocacy among participant countries to address financial inclusion challenges.

Various international organisations such as the World Bank Group, the SME Finance Forum, the International Fund for Agricultural Development (IFAD), and the Organisation for Economic Co-operation and Development (OECD) became implementing Partners of the GPFI. They are involved in capacity building, technical assistance, project implementation, and research. Also, the World Bank maintains a database of G20 financial inclusion indicators based on information from the Global Findex data and enterprise surveys. Additionally, the International Monetary Fund (IMF) also collects and publishes the Financial Access Surveys (FAS), which provide information on access to financial institutions, usage of financial services, payment system infrastructure, and related metrics. These are important sources of data for Governments and researchers who are working on financial inclusion, enabling them to undertake data-driven policy reforms aimed at improving financial inclusion in participating countries.

1.2.3 Financial Inclusion Action Plans since 2010

Since the inception of the first FIAP in 2010, several revisions have been made in the consecutive plans of 2014, 2017, and 2020. The 2017 plan was particularly notable, as it aligned GPFI's work with that of the 2030 Agenda for Sustainable Development. This revision also identified two important focus areas—Digital Financial Inclusion (DFI) and SME finance. In addition to these, other areas such as the financial Inclusion of vulnerable and underserved groups, women's economic empowerment, financial consumer protection, and financial literacy were emphasised as cross-cutting themes.

In earlier Financial Inclusion Action Plans (FIAPs), implementation was through different subgroups, namely—Regulation and Standard-Setting Bodies (SSBs), SME finance, Financial Consumer Protection and Financial Literacy, and Markets and Payment Systems. However, starting with the 2018 FIAP, it was agreed to eliminate the subgroups and appoint two long-term Co-Chairs, who would manage and maintain the work of the GPFI. The 2020 FIAP was planned for the years 2020 to 2023, which was a time of crisis for the global community. This plan reaffirmed the previous plan's commitment to digital finance and SMEs while placing increased emphasis on the needs of vulnerable and underserved groups.

The latest, 2023 G20 FIAP, emphasises its commitment to advancing digital finance through new strategies and innovations. It recognises the importance of harnessing technology to enhance access to financial services. Most importantly, a core aspect of this plan is the call for a common, interoperable digital public infrastructure framework to improve the use of digital services for service delivery to the underserved.

1.2.4 *Main Achievements under the G20 India Presidency*

India assumed the G20 presidency from Indonesia in December 2022, and during the 2023 summit, one of the key focal areas was technological transformation & Digital Public Infrastructure (DPI). By prioritising these areas, India steered the summit discussions in such a way that the member countries of G20 agreed to adopt a common framework of DPI, and this resulted in the DPI framework being integrated into the 2023 G20 FIAP.

DPI refers to "a set of shared digital building blocks, such as applications, systems, and platforms, powered by interoperable open standards or specifications" (Alonso et al. 2023a). The framework is such that it can be institutionalised into the user country's system for improving governance and delivery of public utilities and services. The 2023 G20 summit marked the first attempt to achieve a global consensus on digitisation, and India played a significant role in initiating this venture. The success of India, as a developing country, in implementing the framework helped in advancing the idea of adopting a common framework for all participating countries.

India's success and commitment towards development through harnessing new technology have been well appreciated by policymakers across the world. India has also announced the launch of two India-led initiatives—the Global Digital Public Infrastructure Repository and a Social Impact Fund aimed at advancing Digital Public Infrastructure (DPI) in the Global South during the Virtual G20 Leaders' Summit.[1] Also, it needs to be noted that India has shared its willingness to share its DPI capabilities with other developing member countries so that they benefit through the sharing of ideas and technology.

[1] https://pib.gov.in/PressReleasePage.aspx?PRID=1979113

1.2.5 *Digital Public Infrastructure—A Paradigm Shift in the Delivery of Utilities*

The DPI framework serves as the underlying infrastructure for the delivery of public services, including financial services. The idea is similar to the general public infrastructure built by the Government and used by individuals. For instance, infrastructure like schools and colleges are accessed by the citizens, often at subsidised rates. As a consequence, public education infrastructure contributes to a more educated society, which in turn produces innovative products and services for general consumption. On similar lines, the DPI acts as the backbone on which private agents build innovative services to meet the increasing needs of the population. However, the responsibility for the success and integrity of the system does not lie solely with the Government. It is equally important for market participants who build and leverage the framework to adhere to the common principles on which it is developed (Massally et al. 2023). By doing so, DPI empowers users to integrate the infrastructure into their applications, promoting responsible usage, inclusion, and interoperability (Alonso et al. 2023a).

While a simple idea, DPI represents a paradigm shift, a departure from isolated problem-specific solutions towards a broad framework, which can be adapted and improvised to suit and solve various issues. Traditionally, systems were developed to tackle individual problems, resulting in compartmentalised systems that can be used only for a single issue. DPI, however, offers a versatile structure that provides solutions well beyond digital finance. For instance, it allows citizens to access and use various Government interfaces while allowing the Government authorities to securely store and manage data such as health records and tax payments. Additionally, DPI serves as a powerful platform for information dissemination, addressing one of the most deficient areas in the country. Furthermore, DPI acts as an enabler in expanding access to essential services, such as educational resources for students and efficient delivery of social support schemes.

As a foundational layer of digital infrastructure, DPI provides a platform upon which various agents can build smaller systems tailored to their objectives. This adaptability of the DPI framework is made possible by its various built-in features, such as interoperability, scalability, compliance with rules (Governance), and a strong emphasis on inclusion.[2]

Interoperability and Scalability of the Design: The DPI framework is interoperable, ensuring seamless data exchange and communication between components of the system without encountering compatibility issues. Also, the design of the DPI is modular, allowing individual parts of the system to be built independently while the parts can also be integrated to form a larger system (Massally et al. 2023). This allows easy replication of the individual as well as the whole system. Thus, apart from being interoperable, it is scalable and aids the provision of public and private services to a large population.

Governance: While DPI ensures that the policies and institutions are in place, it also guarantees compliance with laws by embedding legal obligations into the system itself. This means that individuals using the system automatically adhere to the legal requirements, and as a consequence, there is no requirement for external compliance checks (Massally et al. 2023). As a result, the system promotes accountability while also safeguarding user autonomy, safety, and privacy. The design of the system itself is such that it takes care of the privacy and safety of the individual who is using it.

Inclusion of Private Sector and Community: DPI encourages the active participation of the private sector, recognising that the involvement of the market ensures healthy competition and innovation in building and sustaining the DPI framework. By encouraging the participation of private players in designing, building, and operating the system, DPI promotes user-centric solutions. Furthermore, it also allows and encourages growth in tandem with the latest updates in technology. Most importantly, its design idea itself is built around open-source collaborations that ensure innovations for low-cost services.

1.2.6 *The Framework of Digital Public Infrastructure (DPI) in India*

DPI in India consists of three main foundational layers. First, the identity layer (Aadhar, eKYC, GSTN, etc.) provides an identity for all citizens. Second, the payments layer, or the Unified Payments Interface, is an

[2] https://carnegieendowment.org/research/2023/05/what-is-the-dpi-approach?lang=en

instant, real-time payments system owned and operated by the National Payments Corporation of India. Third, the data layer allows paperless storage and safe retrieval of data. For instance, the Digi Locker—a cloud-based document storage system, allows users to authenticate themselves using their Aadhaar identity and download digitally signed copies of their documents across departments from one app (Alonso et al. 2023b).

1.3 Progress in Financial Inclusion across the World and where we Stand

Since the inception of the GPFI in 2010, considerable progress has been made across the world. The latest Findex data (2021) shows that around 76 per cent of the adults had an account in a regulated financial institution (banks or regulated institutions such as a credit union, microfinance institution, or mobile money service provider.), which is an impressive improvement from just 50 per cent in 2011 (Demirgüç-Kunt et al. 2022). One of the main reasons for this improvement in financial inclusion is the use of digital technology to overcome the last-mile gap. Especially in Sub-Saharan African countries, where infrastructure development is one of the lowest in the world, 33 per cent of those who had an account were using a mobile account. This is the highest usage of mobile banking anywhere in the world. Also, digital payments in the region improved from just 35 per cent in 2014 to 57 per cent in 2021 (Demirgüç-Kunt et al. 2022). The example of Sub-Saharan Africa is a shining example of how technology can transform lives, even in the absence of minimal physical infrastructure.

The impressive growth in the use of digital payments can be observed across the world. A portion of this growth, however, can be attributed to the COVID-19 pandemic, during which most people started using digital payments for the first time, especially in developing countries like India and China. Though the spread of mobile money and digital payments has improved financial inclusion in several ways, around 1.4 billion people still lack access to financial services, and most of these individuals live in developing economies (Demirgüç-Kunt et al. 2022). Most importantly, the disadvantaged sections of the population, such as women and the less educated, are still lagging, and some of them remain completely out of the financial mainstream.

Furthermore, there exists a large demand-supply gap in loan access for small businesses in developing countries. Lack of access to financial capital is one of the biggest constraints for the growth of SMEs (Banerjee et al.

2018; Banerjee and Duflo 2005). According to a World Bank report, around forty per cent of formal small businesses in developing countries have unmet funding needs, with women-owned enterprises accounting for a significant portion of this gap (The World Bank 2023). With more than 50 per cent of the households in developing countries like India engaged in self-employment, suitable finance is essential for such households to grow and sustain their businesses as well as for the overall growth of the economy.

1.3.1 Financial Inclusion in India—A Brief History of Reforms

India has a long history of financial inclusion, and the Government has initiated and implemented several policies over time. These measures, including the nationalisation of banks, the introduction of regional rural banks (RRB), and the 1:4 bank licensing policy, were landmark financial inclusion measures during the pre-liberalisation period. These policies were responsible for substantial improvements in financial access (mainly credit delivery) before liberalisation.

After the financial sector reforms of 1991, however, the Indian financial system underwent radical changes, resulting in a pronounced shift away from the restrictive policies of the earlier decades. In this period, the focus was on improving the efficiency of banks, and as a result, financial inclusion efforts took a backseat. But since then, the Reserve Bank of India (RBI) has recognised the relevance of financial inclusion in improving economic development as well as in building a strong and sustainable financial sector. Thus, in 2005, as per the recommendations of the Khan Committee Report, several important changes came into being, such as relaxing the Know Your Customer (KYC) norms and the introduction of basic bank accounts. Later in 2014, financial inclusion efforts got an even greater push with the launch of the Jan Dhan Yojana, and consequently, access to bank accounts improved substantially in India.

This was also the period when financial inclusion was being discussed in a big way across the developing world. Policymakers across the world acknowledged the importance of financial inclusion in development. In line with this, financial sector developments in India also got more focussed on financial inclusion. In all, a new approach to financial development came into being during the early 2000s, and with this, the new phase of the financial inclusion policies, which were technology-assisted, unfurled in India as well as across the world.

1.3.2 Unleashing Digital Transformation: India's Experience with United Payments Interface

The greatest transformation in the context of financial inclusion came with the advent of India Stack or Digital Public Infrastructure. In the context of a developing country like India, the DPI framework has manifested both efficiency in time and money. Around 90 per cent of the Indian population has a registered Aadhar number, which accounts for around 1.3 billion individuals. In 2014, only 36 per cent of adults had bank accounts, but by 2021, around 80 per cent of households had access to bank accounts (Demirguc-Kunt et al. 2022).

The second layer of DPI, the United Payments Interface (UPI), enabled substantial improvement in the volume of digital transactions. Since its launch in 2016, UPI has grown exponentially, becoming an integral part of daily life across India. From small roadside vendors to large retail stores, all accept payments through various mobile applications, and it is common in India to see even roadside pedlars displaying QR codes for digital payments. This widespread adoption (particularly in urban areas) has significantly streamlined the payment system, making transactions faster, more efficient, and highly accessible in recent years.

In the fiscal year 2019, UPI accounted for only 17 per cent of the 3.1 billion digital transactions. In FY 2022, UPI accounted for nearly 52 per cent of the overall 8.84 billion digital financial transactions (GOI 2022). On average, between FY19 and FY22, growth in UPI-based transactions in value and volume terms has been 121 per cent and 115 per cent (GOI 2022). India's UPI currently facilitates the largest volume of daily transactions that are happening on a similar platform anywhere in the world.

1.3.3 Still, some Distance to Cover ...

The financial inclusion narrative in India has rapidly changed in the last few years. While India stands as a beacon of rapid progress and effectiveness in financial inclusion and digital finance, there is still scope for improvement. Indeed, the Government has set in motion the wheels of progress; still, certain regions of the country and population categories continue to remain backward and underserved. Though it can now be asserted that access to bank accounts has improved substantially, the actual usage of these services has not kept pace. Therefore, understanding the barriers to access and usage is important in addressing the remaining gaps and reaching out to the excluded populations in the most efficient manner.

Given this, the purpose of this book is to provide an in-depth analysis of financial inclusion in India through two key levels of examination. First, we present a macro perspective of financial inclusion. As a first step towards examining the various issues, we develop a comprehensive index incorporating supply-side indicators from both scheduled commercial banks and cooperative banks. Unlike previous studies, which often focus solely on commercial banks, our index of financial inclusion acknowledges the importance of cooperative banks and their role in improving financial inclusion within India's rural financial landscape. This approach makes our index more representative of the actual level of financial inclusion in the country.

Many localised studies show that the new accounts that are opened are just channels for receiving Government welfare payments. This is one of the crucial problems faced by the financial programme in the country, and there is an urgent need to examine such trends. Though there are small field studies that provide local insights, a comprehensive study using a nationally representative household survey is noticeably missing.

Taking heed of these issues and many more, this book highlights the considerable achievements of India's financial inclusion policies and also examines the various demand-side challenges and constraints that affect the use of different financial services. Key demand-side factors such as education, gender, the social category of the household, and access to physical infrastructure are explored through household-level analyses. We draw on extensive datasets such as the All-India Debt and Investment Survey, the Situational Assessment Survey, and the Findex survey to help us understand the constraints in access and use of the four important components of financial inclusion—Credit, savings, insurance, and remittances. Recognising that financial inclusion issues differ between urban and rural areas, the analysis is conducted separately for rural and urban areas. This approach, alongside an in-depth study on both access to and use of fundamental financial services, makes this book one of the most comprehensive assessments of financial inclusion to date in India.

References

Ray, Debraj. 1998. *Development economics*. Princeton: Princeton University Press.

Banerjee, Abhijit V., and Andrew F. Newman. 1993. Occupational choice and the process of development. *Journal of Political Economy* 101 (2): 274–298. https://doi.org/10.1086/261876.

King, Robert G., and Ross Levine. 1993. Finance and growth: Schumpeter might be right. *The Quarterly Journal of Economics* 108 (3): 717–737. https://doi.org/10.2307/2118406.

Mckinnon, Ronald. 1973. *Money and Capital in Economic Development*. Washington, D.C.: Brookings Institution.

Schumpeter, Joseph A. 1934. *The theory of economic development: An inquiry into profits, capital, credit, interest, and the business cycle*. Cambridge: Harvard University Press.

Karlan, Dean, and Jonathan Zinman. 2010. Expanding credit access: Using randomized supply decisions to estimate the impacts. *Review of Financial Studies* 23 (1): 433–464. https://doi.org/10.1093/rfs/hhp092.

Zeller, Manfred, Aliou Diagne, and Charles Mataya. 1998. Market access by smallholder farmers in Malawi: Implications for technology adoption, agricultural productivity and crop income. *Agricultural Economics* 19:219–229.

Burgess, Robin, and Rohini Pande. 2005. Do rural banks matter ? Evidence from the Indian social banking experiment. *American Economic Review* 95 (3): 780–795. https://doi.org/10.1257/0002828054201242.

Fletschner, Diana. 2009. Rural women's access to credit: Market imperfections and Intrahousehold dynamics. *World Development* 37 (3): 618–631. https://doi.org/10.1016/j.worlddev.2008.08.005.

Rajeev, Meenakshi, and Shika Saravanabhavan. 2019. Has access to formal credit improved? A study of rural cultivator households in India. In *Contemporary issues in Indian agriculture*, ed. Meenakshi Rajeev. Bangalore: ISEC Monograph series.

Rajeev, Meenakshi, B.P. Vani, and Manojit Bhattacharjee. 2011. "Credibility of Equal Access to Credit:Does Gender Matter?" Economic & Political Weekly 46 (33): 76–79.

Kumar, Sunil Mitra. 2013. Does access to formal agricultural credit depend on caste? *World Development* 43 (March): 315–328. https://doi.org/10.1016/j.worlddev.2012.11.001.

Deaton, Angus. 1990. Savings in developing countries theory and review. In *Proceedings of the World Bank annual conference on development economics 1989, World Bank economic review supplement*, 61–96. Washington, D.C.: The World Bank.

Bhattacharjee, Manojit, and Meenakshi Rajeev. 2014. Accessibility to credit and its determinants: A state-level analysis of cultivator households in India. *Margin: The Journal of Applied Economic Research* 8 (3): 285–300. https://doi.org/10.1177/0973801014531137.

Demirguc-Kunt, A., Klapper, L., Singer, D., Ansar, S., and Hess, J. 2018. The Global Findex Database 2017: Measuring Financial Inclusion and the Fintech Revolution. Washington, DC: World Bank. https://doi.org/10.1596/978-1-4648-1259-0.

Collins, Daryl, Jonathan Morduch, Stuart Rutherford, and Orlanda Ruthven. 2010. *Portfolios of the poor: How the world's poor live on $2 a day*. Princeton: Princeton University Press.

Prina, Silvia. 2015. Banking the poor via savings accounts: Evidence from a field experiment. *Journal of Development Economics* 115:16–31. https://doi.org/10.1016/j.jdeveco.2015.01.004.

Aportela, Fernando. 1999. "Effects of Financial Access on Savings by Low-Income People." *MIT Department of Economics Dissertation Chapter 1.*

Karlan, Dean, Aishwarya Lakshmi Ratan, and Jonathan Zinman. 2014. Saving by and for the poor: A research review and agenda. *Review of Income and Wealth* 60 (1): 36–78. https://doi.org/10.1111/roiw.12101.

RBI. 2008. *Report of the committee on financial inclusion-chairman: Dr. C. Rangarajan*. Mumbai: Reserve Bank of India.

Lucas, Robert E. B., and Oded Stark. 1985. Motivations to remit: Evidence from Botswana. *Journal of Political Economy* 93 (5): 901–918. https://doi.org/10.1086/261341.

GOI. 2011. *Key indicators of employment and unemployment in India 2009–10, NSS 60th round*. New Delhi: NSSO.

GOI. 2022. "The Economic Survey of India 2021–22." https://www.indiabudget.gov.in/budget2022-23/economicsurvey/doc/eschapter/echap09.pdf.

Deshingkar, Priya. 2006. Internal migration, poverty and development in Asia: Including the excluded. *IDS Bulletin* 37 (3): 88–100. https://doi.org/10.1111/j.1759-5436.2006.tb00272.x.

Harttgen, Kenneth, and Stephan Klasen. 2011. A human development index by internal Migrational status. *Journal of Human Development and Capabilities* 12 (3): 393–424. https://doi.org/10.1080/19452829.2011.576819.

Anzoategui, Diego, Asli Demirgüç-Kunt, and María Soledad Martínez Pería. 2014. Remittances and financial inclusion: Evidence from El Salvador. *World Development* 54 (February): 338–349. https://doi.org/10.1016/j.worlddev.2013.10.006.

Tiwari, Akhand, Akhilesh kumar Singh, Anurodh Giri, Minakshi Ramji, Sachin Bansal, and Alphina Jos. 2011. "Understanding Remittance Networks In Gujarat, Orissa and Bihar." Microsave. http://www.microsave.net/files/pdf/Understanding_Remittance_Networks_In_Gujarat_Orissa_and_Bihar.pdf.

Alonso, Cristian, Tanuj Bhojwani, Emine Hanedar, Dinar Prihardini, Gerardo Una, and Kateryna Zhabska. 2023a. "Stacking up the Benefits Lessons from India's Digital Journey e." 23/78. *IMF Working Paper No. 23/78*. IMF Working Paper. Washington, D.C.

Alonso, Cristian, Tanuj Bhojwani, Emine Hanedar, Dinar Prihardini, Gerardo Uña, and Kateryna Zhabska. 2023b. Stacking up the benefits: Lessons from India's digital journey. *IMF ELibrary* 202 (78): https://doi.org/10.5089/9798400240416.001.

Massally, Keyzom Ngodup, Rahul Matthan, and Rudra Chau. 2023. "What Is the DPI Approach?". https://carnegieindia.org/2023/05/15/what-is-dpi-approach-pub-89721.

Banerjee, Abhijit V., and Esther Duflo. 2005. Chapter 7 Growth theory through the lens of development economics. In *Handbook of economic growth*, 473–552. Cambridge, MA. https://doi.org/10.1016/S1574-0684(05)01007-5.

Banerjee, Abhijit, Emily Breza, Esther Duflo, and Cynthia Kinnan. 2018. "Do Credit Constraints Limit Entrepreneurship? Heterogeneity in the Returns to Microfinance." *NBER Working Paper No. 26346*.

The World Bank. 2023. "G20 Policy Recommendations for Advancing Financial Inclusion and Productivity Gains through Digital Public Infrastructure." https://doi.org/https://www.g20.org/content/dam/gtwenty/gtwenty_new/document/G20_POLICY_RECOMMENDATIONS.pdf.

Martínez, Christiane Ströh de, Martina Wiedmaier Pfister, Corinna Müller, and Ariane Schoen. 2019. *Inclusive Insurance in National Financial Inclusion Strategies—Survey Report*. Kuala Lumpur: Alliance for Financial Inclusion (AFI). https://www.afi-global.org/sites/default/files/publications/2018-08/afi_a2ii_report_view.pdf.

Wright, B. D., and J. A. Hewitt. 1994. "All-Risk Crop Insurance: Lessons from Theory and Experience." In *Economics of Agricultural Crop Insurance: Theory and Evidence*, edited by Darrell L. Hueth and William H. Furtan, 4:73–112. Natural Resource Management and Policy. Dordrecht: Springer. https://doi.org/10.1007/978-94-011-1386-1_4.

Hazell, P., C. Pomareda, and A. Valdes. 1986. *Crop Insurance for Agricultural Development: Issues and experience*. London: Johns Hopkins University Press.

Binswanger-Mkhize, Hans P. 2012. Is there too much hype about index-based agricultural insurance? *Journal of Development Studies* 48 (2): 187–200. https://doi.org/10.1080/00220388.2011.625411.

Dercon, Stefan. 2002. Income risk, coping strategies, and safety nets. *The World Bank Research Observer* 17 (2): 141–166. https://doi.org/10.1093/wbro/17.2.141.

Demirgüç-Kunt, Asli, Leora Klapper, Dorothe Singer, Saniya Ansar. 2022. The Global Findex Database 2021: Financial Inclusion, Digital Payments, and Resilience in the Age of COVID-19. Washington, DC: World Bank. http://documents.worldbank.org/curated/en/099818107072234182

Rajan, Raghuram G. 2014. Financial inclusion: Technology, institutions and policies. Keynote address at NASSCOM India Leadership Forum, RBI Documents. Reserve Bank of India.

Claessens, Stijn. 2006. "Access to Financial Services: A Review of the Issues and Public Policy Objectives." *World Bank Research Observer* 21 (2): 207–40.
Shaw, Edward. 1973. Financial Deepening in Economic Development. New York: Oxford University Press.

CHAPTER 2

Financial Sector Development in India: Historical Insights

2.1 Introduction

As discussed in the previous chapter, financial inclusion (FI) has four major components: deposit mobilisation, credit disbursement, insurance provision, and remittance facilities. Achieving true financial inclusion implies that these core services are made accessible to low-income people at a reasonable cost, enabling them to improve their financial security and well-being. To realise this idea of an inclusive financial sector, the government has introduced several institutional innovations and policy initiatives over the years.

Before 1990, financial sector development focussed on expanding the network of banks, especially in the rural regions. During this period, there was significant Government focus on credit disbursal to the priority sectors, leading to some of the landmark initiatives such as differential interest rates, the establishment of Regional Rural Banks, bank licensing policy, and the nationalisation of banks. Despite these efforts, a large majority of the population continued to lack access to formal financial services, especially in rural areas.

After financial sector reforms, post-1991, the focus was more on financial depth than financial inclusion. While this led to the deepening of the financial system, it also resulted in reduced access for low-income and marginalised groups. Recognising these shortcomings, the government

S. Saravanabhavan and M. Rajeev, *Moving Beyond Barriers*, Palgrave Studies in Impact Finance,
https://doi.org/10.1007/978-981-95-1066-5_2

initiated a targeted financial inclusion initiative, beginning with a major financial inclusion drive in 2006 and later the flagship Jan Dhan Yojana in 2014, aiming to bridge the gaps in access to formal banking services.

This chapter discusses these changes in the Indian banking sector over time, focusing on the major initiatives that were brought out to strengthen the financial sector and improve financial inclusion (A detailed discussion is beyond the scope of this book and one can refer to RBI (2008); Sen and Vaidya (1997)).

The chapter unfolds as follows. Section 2 gives an outline of the Indian banking system and its structure. Section 3 discusses, in brief, the development of the banking sector during the pre-independence era and the changes in the system after independence. Section 4 concludes.

2.2 The Structure of the Banking System in India

The Indian financial system is largely dominated by the banking sector, which accounted for around 50 per cent of the total flow of financial resources directed towards the commercial sector in 2017–18, primarily through bank credit. In addition to providing credit, banks play a significant role in mobilising a significant share of the country's gross domestic savings. This section provides a brief description of the structure and role of the banking sector in India.

Figure 2.1 illustrates the structure of India's banking system, which comprises two main institutions: the commercial and cooperative banking systems. The Reserve Bank of India, under the Banking Regulation Act of 1949, oversees all commercial banks. These commercial banks are categorised by their ownership pattern into public sector banks and private sector banks. The public sector banks include nationalised banks, State banks and their associates, and Regional Rural Banks (RRBs). Private sector banks include private Indian and foreign banks. Collectively, these institutions comprise the Scheduled commercial banks.

The cooperative institutions were established and promoted with the specific objective of providing credit to the agricultural sector. The banking-related functions of cooperative banks are regulated by the RBI, and the management function is regulated by the respective state Government/Central Government. Cooperative credit institutions are broadly classified into rural cooperative credit institutions and urban cooperative credit institutions. Of these, the rural cooperatives are further classified

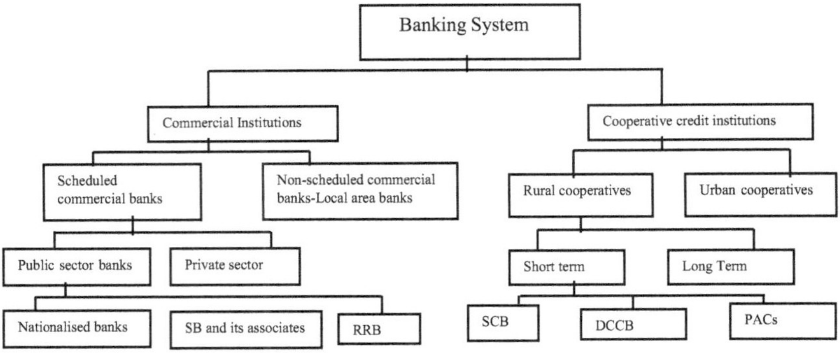

Fig. 2.1 Structure of the Banking System in India
Source Reserve Bank of India

into short-term and long-term credit institutions. The short-term cooperative credit structure is organised into a three-tier system consisting of the state cooperative Banks at the top tier, District Central Cooperative Banks at the intermediary level and the Primary agricultural credit societies (PACS) at the grassroots level.

2.3 Development of the Banking Sector in India

The story of financial sector development in India is a long one, as banking in some form has existed in the country for several centuries. However, we begin our narrative from the eighteenth century as it is generally considered that modern banking started to take form during this period.

2.3.1 Pre-Independence Period

In the eighteenth century, towards the end of the Mughal period, merchant moneylenders served as banks, providing credit to the small princely states and also acting as a channel for safe money transfer (D. Tripathi 2004). With the rise of British power, English Agency houses came into existence to finance the British traders, playing dual roles as trading and financial institutions. They functioned as banks where the Company servants could deposit their money and use it as a means for remitting money to families back home (Muranjan 1952; Tripathi 2004).

These agency houses remained prominent in much of the eighteenth and early nineteenth centuries.

An important development in banking during the nineteenth century was the establishment of the three presidency banks—the Bank of Bengal, the Bank of Bombay, and the Bank of Madras—each receiving support from the state. These state-backed institutions were established to reduce the Government's dependence on local moneylenders and English agency houses. Further, the enactment of the 1860 law saw the introduction of limited liability, which increased the number of private banks and foreign banks in India (Banerjee et al. 2004; RBI 2008). By the end of the nineteenth century, there were several Indian Joint-stock banks such as Allahabad Bank and Punjab National Bank.

The number of Indian Joint-stock banks grew further with the strengthening of the *Swadeshi* movement at the beginning of the twentieth century. In 1921, the presidency banks were merged to form the Imperial Bank, which functioned as the central bank till the formation of the Reserve Bank in 1935. However, the period that followed was not a good time in Indian banking history. The aftermath of the great depression, the Second World War that followed, and the unstable domestic situation weakened the banking sector, leading to numerous bank failures.

2.3.2 Post-Independence Period

At the time of independence, India had a fragmented banking landscape consisting of around 97 scheduled commercial banks, 557 non-scheduled banks, and 395 cooperative banks. However, most of the banks were situated in the major cities of Calcutta, Bombay, and Madras, with limited banking presence in other regions (RBI 2008).

Even after independence, bank failures continued, particularly among smaller banks, and as a result, many of these banks were merged or amalgamated with larger banks to protect public deposits and stabilise the financial system. Throughout the 1950s and 1960s, the unhealthy banks were systematically removed from the system, as part of the process of strengthening the financial system. During this period, the RBI was selective in issuing bank licenses, taking care to issue new licenses only to well-functioning banks. Consequently, the number of non-scheduled bank branches dropped significantly, from 1504 in 1951 to just 203 by 1967.

In the first two decades after independence, cooperatives became the primary vehicle for credit disbursal, particularly in rural areas. With the national development agenda rooted in a socialistic pattern, financial development also followed a similar route, with policymakers prioritising cooperative expansion to improve financial access. The 1951 All-India Rural Credit Survey, commissioned to assess rural financial needs, recommended a central role for the Reserve Bank of India in controlling and overseeing the function of the cooperative banks. At that time, the share of cooperatives in rural credit was only 3 per cent, prompting the Government to adopt strong measures to ensure the success of the cooperative banks. These efforts increased the share of cooperative banks in rural credit to over 20 per cent by 1971 (Chakravarthy 2005).

To assess the effectiveness of the various measures, the All-India Rural Credit Review Committee (Venkatappa Committee) was set up in 1966. However, the committee found that the progress of the cooperative banks was not as expected and recommended that, along with cooperatives, commercial banks should play a more active role in the agricultural credit market (Chakravarthy 2005). In response, the RBI adopted a multi-agency approach to financial development, involving both commercial banks and cooperative banks.

However, there was growing concern that the commercial banks, of which most belong to the private sector, were not contributing to the development of the country and that the financial resources were not reaching the weaker sections and the poorer populations. A significant share of the credit was flowing towards the industrial sector while the agriculture and allied sectors, which employed the majority of the population-were constrained for funds. To address this imbalance, Prime Minister Smt. Indira Gandhi implemented bank nationalisation, with the aim of directing the financial resources of the banks for the planned development of the country.

2.3.3 *Nationalisation of Banks and Afterwards*

Nationalisation was the most decisive point in the history of Indian banking and can rightly be regarded as the beginning of banking development in the country. This move brought fourteen large banks under the control of the central bank in 1969, followed by the nationalisation of six more banks in 1980. By the end of 1980s, the majority of banks in India were under Government control. The main intent of bank nationalisation was to promote balanced economic growth, with a strong emphasis on expanding financial access in the rural areas and directing resources to the priority sectors.

Another important milestone in Indian banking was the establishment of the Regional Rural Banks (RRBs) in 1975. These banks were created to specifically develop rural areas and provide crucial banking services to small farmers, cottage industries, small traders, and agricultural labourers. The Government envisaged these institutions as hybrids, accommodating the scale and efficiency of commercial banks and the community focus of the cooperative banks to better address the issues at the grassroots level (RBI 2007).

The RRBs were designed to operate on a local scale and were to cover not more than two or three districts. Though it started with just five RRBs, by 1990, there were 196 RRBs with more than 14,000 rural branches. Also, the purpose-wise advances of the RRBs reveal that the majority of their loans are disbursed to priority sectors such as agriculture and allied services and retail trade.

This period saw several other policies aimed at improving financial inclusion across the country. One notable initiative was the implementation of the Lead Bank scheme by the RBI. Under this scheme, each district was allotted to a particular bank, designated as the Lead Bank, which played a supervisory role and was responsible for improving the banking services in that region. Furthermore, in 1977, the Government introduced the 1:4 bank licensing policy, which required banks to open four branches in unbanked areas to obtain a branch license in an already banked area. This policy facilitated significant branch expansion, especially in rural areas. Research has shown that these policies have indeed reduced rural poverty by promoting savings mobilisation and credit provision in underserved areas (Burgess and Pande 2005).

Additionally, policies for directed lending to the priority sector were introduced, with a formal definition of the priority sector laid down in 1972. Initially, public sector banks were mandated to give at least one-third of their total credit to priority sectors. Later, the definitions and requirements were further refined, and by the 1980s, banks were required to provide 40 per cent of their total credit to the priority sector. Within this allocation, 18 per cent was earmarked for the agricultural sector and 10 per cent for weaker sections of the society.

Another key initiative to support the needy was the 'Differential Interest Rate' scheme, under which the weaker sections such as the low-income populations, scheduled castes and tribes, and women-headed households were provided credit at a concessional interest rate, which was justified on the grounds of improving production and income levels for these disadvantaged groups (Dasgupta 2001; Pawar and Sutar 1982).

As a result of these initiatives, moneylenders gradually lost their foothold as the dominant source of credit. In 1961, 85 per cent of all credit was taken from non-institutional sources, and it decreased to 39 per cent in 1981.[1] Furthermore, Table 2.1 shows a substantial increase in the percentage of bank offices, particularly in the rural sector, over the period of 1972 to 1992, and this corresponds to the social banking policies that were vigorously pushed by the Government during the 1970s and the 1980s.

Table 2.1 Selected indicators of financial inclusion over the years—Before financial reforms (amount rupees in million)

Year	*Number of rural bank offices*	*% to Total*	*Credit Amount Outstanding (Mn)*	*% to Total*	*Deposit Amount (Mn)*	*% to Total*
Rural						
1972	5274	36	257	5	539	7
1982	20,310	51	3749	13	6313	14
1992	35,254	57	20,692	15	35,750	15
Semi-urban						
1972	4607	31	783	14	1869	22
1982	9240	23	5324	17	10,500	23
1992	11,606	19	21,599	16	46,591	20
Urban						
1972	2637	18	1193	21	2087	25
1982	6034	15	6926	23	11,467	25
1992	9023	14	29,643	22	55,289	23
Metropolitan						
1972	2132	15	3381	60	3864	46
1982	4596	11	14,908	48	17,545	38
1992	6238	10	64,771	47	99,477	42

Source Authors' calculations using RBI data

[1] All India Debt and Investment Survey Reports, Various issues.

This expansion is mirrored in other indicators as well, such as the rise in total credit amount outstanding and total deposit amount, reflecting the gradual formalisation of financial services. However, the rapid expansion of such policies, with overemphasis on social development, had its downside too. Many commercial banks experienced a decline in their profitability, and by the end of the 1980s, several banks became inefficient and incompetent, struggling to sustain their operations (Patra and Roy 2000).

2.3.4 Banking Sector Reforms and FI

As a result of the numerous challenges faced by the financial sector, the Narasimham Committee in 1991 proposed several recommendations for structural reforms in the economy and the banking system. However, the focus of the banking reforms was on increasing financial depth, with financial inclusion receiving limited attention. The changes during this time were more market-oriented, moving away from the socialistic approach of the earlier period.

The first phase of banking reforms (1991 to 1998) introduced several liberal measures aimed at improving the efficiency of the banking sector. Out of these, the deregulation of interest rates was a significant step. Until then, the interest rates were pegged, with the RBI prescribing a ceiling rate, to keep the rates artificially low. Many argued that such interest rate ceilings resulted in inefficient allocation and mobilisation of resources, below optimal investments and savings, and a weakening of the monetary system (Bhole 1985; Rakesh and Ray 2016).

The liberalisation efforts also included measures such as reductions in Statutory Liquidity Ratio (SLR) and Cash Reserve Ratio (CRR) to allow banks more liquidity and flexibility in lending. Another important change from the previous era was the abolition of the 1:4 bank licensing policy. Additionally, the committee recommended doing away with the priority sector loans; however, this was not implemented.

The non-performing assets (NPA) of public sector banks had risen significantly due to the emphasis on lending to priority sectors and the mandatory social obligations that had to be followed before the 1990s (Rajeev and Mahesh 2010). Most of the reforms introduced after 1991 were driven by 'efficiency considerations' (Ahluwalia 2000) and therefore, the focus was on improving and strengthening performance, profitability, and the financial stability of the banking system. As a result,

Table 2.2 Gross NPAs and percent to gross advances of public sector banks after financial reforms

	1993	*1994*	*1995*	*1996*	*1997*	*1998*	*2000*
Gross NPAs	39,253	41,041	38,385	41,661	43,577	45,653	53,294
% to gross advances	23	25	20	18	18	16	14

Source Authors' calculations using RBI data

the percentage of NPAs has reduced over time. Table 2.2 reveals that the percentage of NPAs to gross advances has declined from 23 per cent in 1993 to 14 per cent in 2000.[2]

Following financial liberalisation, banks had less incentive to serve the poor due to the high costs involved. As a result, indicators of financial inclusion showed a decreasing trend over subsequent years. For instance, comparing Tables 2.1 and 2.3, we observe that the number of rural bank offices as a percentage of the total was 57% in 1992, and it decreased to 35% in 2022. One contributing factor was the discontinuation of the 1:4 bank licensing policy in 1990, which had previously required banks to open four rural branches for every urban branch. Although banks could not close down rural branches if they were the only banking facility in the area, new branches were now opened based on the potential profitability and viability of the region (Burgess and Pande 2005). Consequently, many rural bank branches which were considered unviable were shut down.

A comparison of Tables 2.1 and 2.3 reveals that the number of rural bank branches declined from 35,254 in 1992 to 32,443 in 2002—an approximate 8 per cent decrease over the decade, while the number of urban branches increased substantially. Similarly, there was little improvement in total credit outstanding and deposit amount over the period. User-side data from the All-India Debt and Investment Survey also shows that the credit from institutional services had decreased from 64 per cent in 1991 to 56 per cent in 2013. In contrast, the reliance on informal services increased during the same period.

[2] https://rbidocs.rbi.org.in/rdocs/Publications/PDFs/50T_13092024BC37474D6C9345888728EA263BAB3818.PDF

https://rbidocs.rbi.org.in/rdocs/Publications/PDFs/55T_1309202433CB921563F34D6282EB48DB4B720D9E.PDF

Table 2.3 Selected indicators of financial inclusion over the years—After financial reforms

Year	*Number of Rural bank offices*	*% to Total*	*Credit Amount Outstanding (₹ in million)*	*% to Total*	*Deposit Amount (₹ in million)*	*% to Total*
Rural						
2002	32,443	48	66,681	11	159,423	14
2012	35,936	36	493,266	9	493,266	9
2022	52,263	35	1,039,340	9	1,966,609	10
Semi-urban						
2002	14,910	22	73,814	11	214,990	19
2012	22,725	25	716,831	13	716,831	13
2022	42,106	28	1,494,898	13	2,955,114	16
Urban						
2002	11,252	17	108,254	17	255,478	23
2012	18,997	21	1,110,513	21	1,110,513	21
2022	26,816	18	1,766,359	16	4,029,828	22
Metropolitan						
2002	9292	14	407,243	62	493,501	44
2012	17,028	19	3,068,941	57	3,068,941	57
2022	27,500	18	6,777,454	61	9,790,760	52

Source Authors' calculations using RBI data-Basic Statistical Returns of SCBs in India—Various issues
Note The number of bank branches does not include rural administrative offices

In response to low financial inclusion, there was a renewed interest in expanding financial access from the 2000s onward. This effort aligned with the global push to reduce poverty and inequality by improving people's access to financial services. Reflecting this renewed effort, between 2002 to 2012, the number of rural branches grew by 11 per cent, and from 2012 to 2022, the number of rural branches increased by 45 per cent. Several initiatives were brought out during this period to support the expansion of rural banking infrastructure. Notably, the guidelines brought out by the RBI in 2013 made it mandatory that 25% of the total number of branches opened during a year should be in unbanked rural centres.

2.3.5 *Refocussing on Financial Inclusion—The Financial Inclusion Drive Period*

In the earlier phases of financial inclusion, policies were directed towards improving credit delivery; however, the financial Inclusion drive has shifted its emphasis from credit-centric strategies to ensuring universal access to a broader range of financial services—including savings, credit, basic insurance, and payment systems, offered at an affordable cost (Rajan 2009).

In 2005, the Khan Committee brought out several important recommendations, most notably the introduction of Business Correspondents (BCs) and Business Facilitators (BFs) (Khan 2005). Acting on these suggestions, the RBI in 2006 encouraged banks to use private agents (BC/BF) to provide doorstep delivery of services to overcome the last-mile problem.

Beginning in 2005, there was a strong policy push towards providing bank accounts for all. To facilitate this, the RBI introduced the "no frills account" for the unbanked poor, where the account can be maintained even with zero balance. Later in 2010, the RBI introduced Basic Savings Bank Deposit Accounts (BSBDAs), and the existing "no frills accounts" were converted into BSBDAs. This strategy of focusing on opening new bank accounts is driven by several motives.

Firstly, the Governments wanted to replace product subsidies with direct cash transfers, as a strategy to reduce corruption and minimise leakages in the delivery of welfare benefits (Barua et al. 2016). Implementing this required the recipients to have their own bank accounts. A second reason was to counter the fall in the rate of savings (Barua et al. 2016). Thirdly, owning a bank account would act as the entry point for the unbanked into the formal financial system and would give them the confidence to make use of other services like credit and money transfer services from a formal bank.

As part of the financial inclusion drive policies, the RBI also simplified the procedures for applying for new bank accounts by relaxing some of the earlier Know Your Customer (KYC) requirements. Especially in rural areas, the educational level of the people is low, and therefore, people find it difficult to approach a bank for their various financial needs. Therefore, simplification of procedures was done to include individuals with low levels of education and poor financial literacy.

Despite the efforts since 2005, the real breakthrough in accelerating financial inclusion came with the launch of the Pradhan Mantri Jan Dhan Yojana (PMJDY) in 2014. This flagship programme marked a turning point by bringing financial inclusion to the forefront of the national development agenda.

2.3.6 *The Jan Dhan Yojana*

The Jan Dhan Yojana was launched as part of the Jan Dhan-Aadhar-Mobile (JAM) trinity initiative. The Aadhar linkage has simplified the Know your Customer (KYC) verification norms and has enabled a phenomenal increase in bank account ownership. Studies indicate that customers are indeed finding it easier to conduct banking transactions because of Aadhar enrolment (Sharma et al. 2016). Furthermore, the joint initiative (JAM trinity) has also strengthened the Government's strategy to implement direct benefit transfers while progressively doing away with product subsidies, which were riddled with corruption and inefficiencies.

The Jan Dhan Yojana is aimed at bringing universal access to bank accounts. The basic bank account holders are provided with a Rupay debit card which can be used for transactions at Automated Teller Machines (ATMs) and point-of-sale (POS) terminals, and each account has an inbuilt accidental insurance cover of Rupees one Lakh and a life insurance cover of 30,000 which is payable on death of the beneficiary.

Together, the financial inclusion drive, which started in 2005, and the subsequent PMJDY have brought remarkable changes in the level of financial inclusion in Indian states. The latest data shows that around 492,961,410 bank accounts have been opened as of 21 June 2023, with a balance of 1,98,086.26 crore rupees in these accounts. Out of this, 67 per cent were rural accounts. Furthermore, 335,906,870 Rupay debit cards have been issued to the account holders as of June 2023.

Figure 2.2 shows that since 2014, there has been a significant improvement in the number of bank accounts being opened. Public sector banks and Regional Rural Banks have the highest share in opening new bank accounts under PMJDY. Furthermore, it is notable that private sector banks opened relatively few accounts, which indicates their passive role in the financial inclusion drive. This limited participation suggests that private sector banks may view the strategy of maintaining a large number of small accounts as unprofitable. By March 2019, the private banks had opened 13,337,962 (3%) bank accounts as compared to 376,874,834 (79%) by public sector banks and 88,183,836 (18%) by Regional Rural Banks. This disparity persists despite private banks making up 18.2% of all bank branches in India.[3]

In India, the rural regions have historically lagged behind in terms of banking infrastructure, and as discussed earlier the number of rural financial inclusion efforts declined during the post-liberalisation period. However, the launch of the Pradhan Mantri Jan Dhan Yojana (PMJDY) marked a turning point, giving a significant boost to rural financial inclusion. Figure 2.3 shows the percentage of rural accounts opened across various states under PMJDY. It is encouraging to observe that in the majority of states, over 50% of the total accounts opened are located in rural areas.

Despite the increased bank account ownership, a major concern is the usage of these bank accounts. It is often claimed that many of

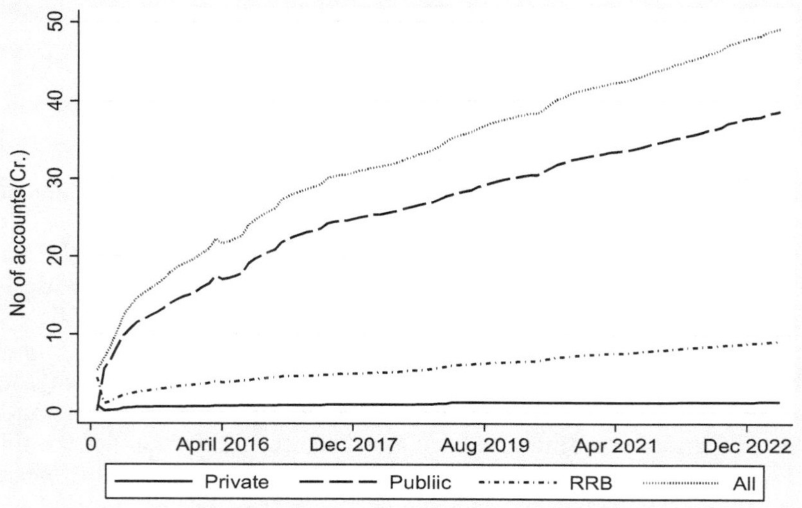

Fig. 2.2 Trend of bank accounts opened as part of PMJDY
(*Source* Authors' calculations using data from online archives of PMJDY)

[3] Basic Statistical Returns of SCBs in India-2018.

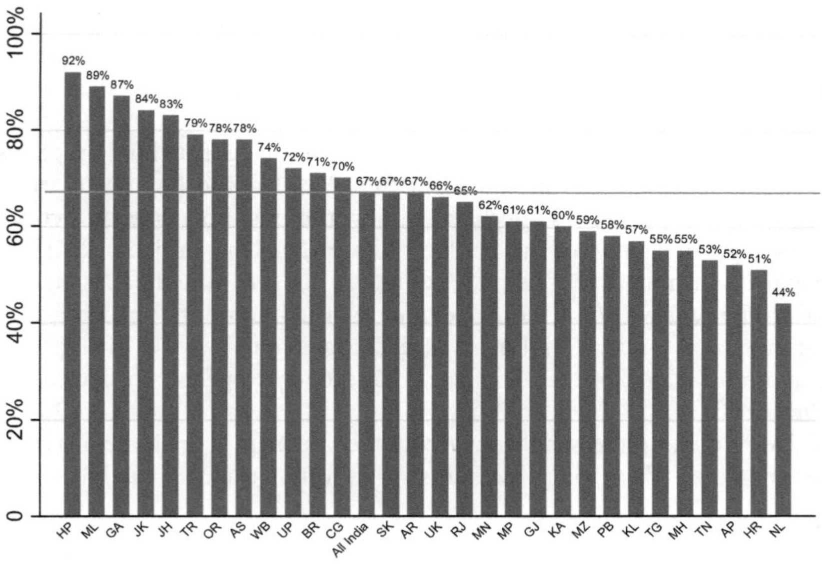

Fig. 2.3 Rural PMJDY accounts as a percentage of PMJDY accounts across various states (as of 21-06-2023).
(*Source* Authors' calculations using data from online archives of PMJDY)

these accounts remain dormant, with little to no savings or financial transactions taking place (Sharma et al. 2016). Fig. 2.4, illustrates the trend in zero-balance accounts since the launch of PMJDY. The reduction in zero balance accounts coincides with the increase in Aadhaar seeding of accounts, which facilitated the Direct Benefit Transfers through these accounts resulting in the beneficiaries having money in their JDY accounts. For instance, the Government mandated that MGNREGA payments should be routed through the bank accounts, which contributed to increased account balances. However, despite this improvement in balances, the challenge of ensuring regular and meaningful usage of these accounts remains a concern (Asli Demirgüç-Kunt et al. 2018).

The government has not published data on dormant accounts under the Pradhan Mantri Jan Dhan Yojana (PMJDY) since 2017. The latest information we have is from a written reply to a Rajya Sabha question dated 26–12-18, which states that there are 33.66 crore bank accounts

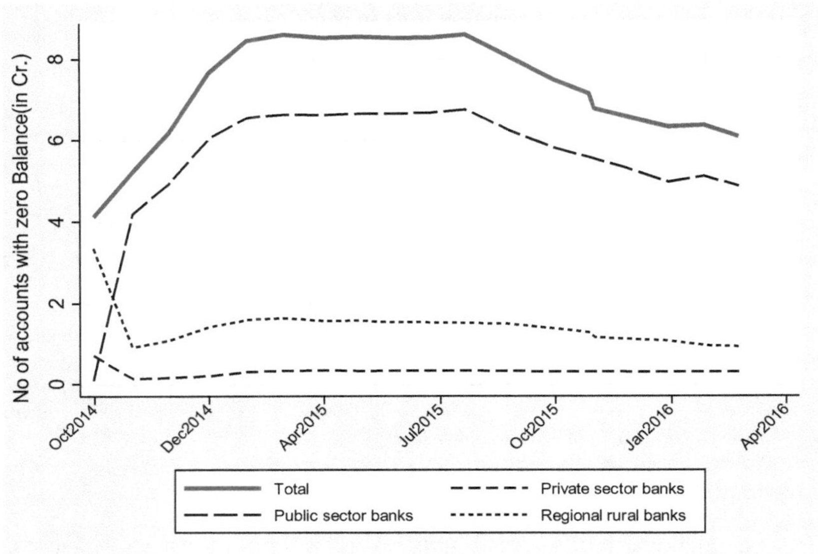

Fig. 2.4 Number of bank accounts with zero balance. (*Source* Authors' calculations using data from online archives of PMJDY)

under the Pradhan Mantri Jan Dhan Yojana (PMJDY) and out of this 28.16 crore bank accounts are operative.[4]

2.3.7 *Credit Scenario in the Context of the Financial Inclusion Drive and the Jan Dhan Yojana*

The traditional approach to financial inclusion was centred on improving credit access. Efforts taken by the Government in the 1970s and 1980s, such as the expansion of rural branches, the reservation for the priority sectors and the differential interest schemes, were instrumental in improving overall credit access, especially for the agricultural sector. However, there is a prevalent view that subsidised credit has disproportionately helped the better-off, with the disadvantaged sections seeing only limited gains (Gonzalez-Vega 1984). Studies have shown that credit constraints of the weaker sections, which include small and marginal

[4] http://pib.nic.in/newsite/PrintRelease.aspx?relid=187339

Table 2.4 Share of small borrowers (SB) in total credit-2021

Population	*Total Credit*		*Of which: Credit to SB*			
	No of accounts	*Amount (Mn)*	*No of account*	*Amount (Mn)*	*Share of SB in the total number of accounts (%)*	*Share of SB in total credit amount (%)*
Rural	86,138	10,393,396	72,766	3,926,527	84	38
Semi-urban	76,383	14,948,976	58,028	3,275,124	76	22
Urban	48,280	17,663,588	33,850	1,476,393	70	8
Metropolitan	87,534	67,774,538	62,756	1,440,316	72	2
All India	298,335	110,780,498	227,401	10,118,360	76	9

Note SB—Small borrowers, Mn—Amount in Millions
Source Authors' calculations using RBI data

farmers, village artisans, small traders and micro industries, have not improved much (Rajeev et al. 2012; Rajeev and Vani 2017). Table 2.4 presents the share of small borrowers in total credit for 2021.

Around 84 per cent of the rural accounts are small accounts, however, the share in the total credit amount is only 38 per cent. For the urban and metropolitan areas, the shares of small borrowal accounts are comparatively lower. The RBI defines a small borrowal account as one with a credit limit of up to 2 Lakh Rupees, a definition that has been in place since 1999. Prior to 1999, a small borrowal account was defined as an account with a credit limit of up to Rs 25,000. Due to definitional change, there has been an increase in the number of accounts since 1999 (See Fig. 2.5 & Appendix Fig. A1).

Figure 2.5 presents the trend in the share of small borrowal accounts in the post-liberalisation period. It shows that while the majority of the borrowal accounts are small accounts, the amount in these accounts is less than 20 per cent of the total credit amount for most years. Notably, a decline in the share of these accounts has been observed since 1999, which is true for all individual states too.

To help ease credit constraints for small borrowers, the Jan Dhan Yojana (JDY) bank account provides an overdraft facility of Rs 5000 as an add-on, available to account holders who have maintained an active account for at least six months. The overdraft facility is given to only one member of the family, preferably a female member, with the aim of empowering the poor to have access to some form of formal credit and

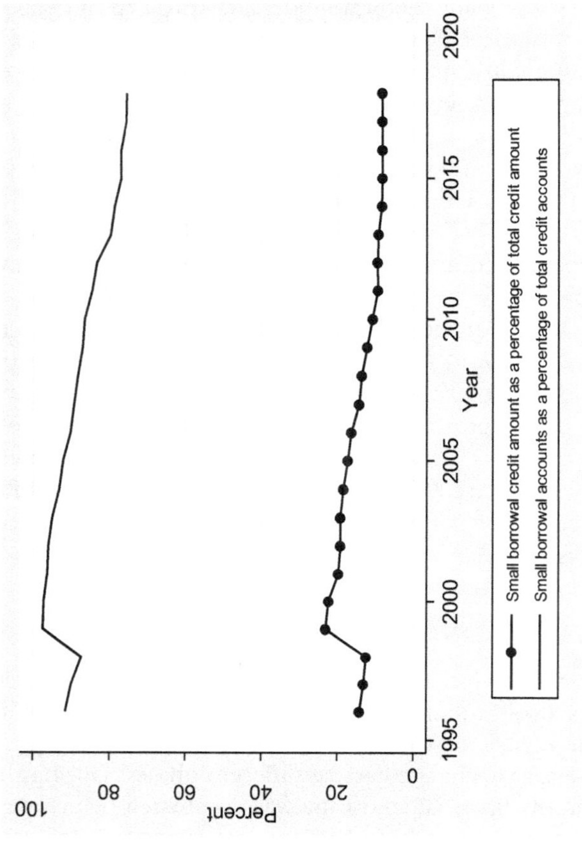

Fig. 2.5 Share of small borrowal accounts—after liberalisation. (*Source* Authors' calculations using RBI data)

thereby lessen dependence on moneylenders and other informal sources. The overdraft amount may be small, but in an emergency, it could be of great help to low-income households. In 2018, the limit of the overdraft amount was increased to Rupees 10,000.[5]

However, the overdraft scheme has seen limited uptake among Jan Dhan account holders. Moreover, the Government does not provide relevant statistics as to how many account holders have availed of this scheme. According to an unstarred Lok Sabha question dated 15-12-2017, only 2.4 per cent of the Jan Dhan bank accounts have used the overdraft facility.[6] Two key factors contributing to this low usage may be the following. First. The lack of awareness about the scheme among beneficiaries. Secondly, there is a common misconception that the overdraft amount provided through this scheme is free money from the Government, which need not be paid back (Swain 2018). Addressing these informational gaps is crucial to improving the uptake and effective use of the overdraft facility.

As per the guidelines of the scheme, the rate of interest should not be more than 2 per cent over the bank's base rate. Also, it is subjective for the banks to decide whether the account holder should be given an overdraft, depending on the person's transactions as well as the balance in the account. Therefore, banks are also uninterested in providing the overdraft amount. There is a perceived risk that account holders may withdraw the money and not repay it, which in effect would add to the non-performing assets of the banks (ibid.).

2.4 Concluding Observations

This chapter provides a historical overview of financial development in India, tracing its evolution from the pre-independence period to the present day. Our review of the different periods shows that the main agents in the system have changed across different phases. During the pre-independence era, the financial landscape was dominated by private banks and joint stock companies, which had minimal incentive for servicing the poor. However, the situation changed after independence, especially after the nationalisation of banks, which was aimed at expanding banking services to rural and low-income populations.

[5] Pradhan Mantri Dhan Jan Yojana Brochure, 22-August-2014, Dept of Financial services, Ministry of Finance

[6] http://164.100.47.194/Loksabha/Questions/QResult15.aspx?qref=58052&lsno=16

Furthermore, we have reviewed the various policies implemented during the financial inclusion period, with a particular focus on the PMJDY. The PMJDY represents a significant shift in strategy compared to earlier financial inclusion programmes. Earlier programmes were credit-centric, and they failed to produce the type of phenomenal change that the PMJDY has achieved. PMJDY places primary emphasis on opening bank accounts for the unbanked, thereby establishing a foundation for broader financial inclusion. Credit facilities, micro insurance, pension schemes, and other financial products are add-on services which account holders can access over time as they continue transactions and become familiar with banking procedures. This approach encourages gradual and sustainable integration into the financial mainstream.

From our analysis of the Jan Dhan Yojana, we see that it has made a substantial impact on the financial inclusion scenario in India, particularly with its focus on the rural sector. Overall, the scheme has made considerable progress in bringing the unbanked into the formal financial mainstream by facilitating the widespread opening of bank accounts. However, certain Northeastern states such as Manipur, Nagaland, and Mizoram show a low percentage of JDY rural bank accounts despite their predominantly rural demographics. This suggests the need for more targeted and region-specific strategies to address the challenges faced by these areas.

To build on the foundations laid by PMJDY, it is essential to inculcate banking habits in people through financial literacy and outreach programmes. These initiatives are especially necessary for the success of add-on services like overdraft facilities. Unlike the subsidised loans of earlier schemes, the overdraft facility provides a sustainable business case for the banks if implemented judiciously. Educating the account holders about the interest rates and the benefits of timely repayment is a priority, as timely repayment would make them eligible for higher credit amounts over time. Furthermore, consistent repayment helps build their creditworthiness, enhancing their future credit opportunities. While the RBI has already undertaken efforts to promote financial literacy, there remains significant scope for expanding and deepening these initiatives, particularly in underserved regions.

Appendix

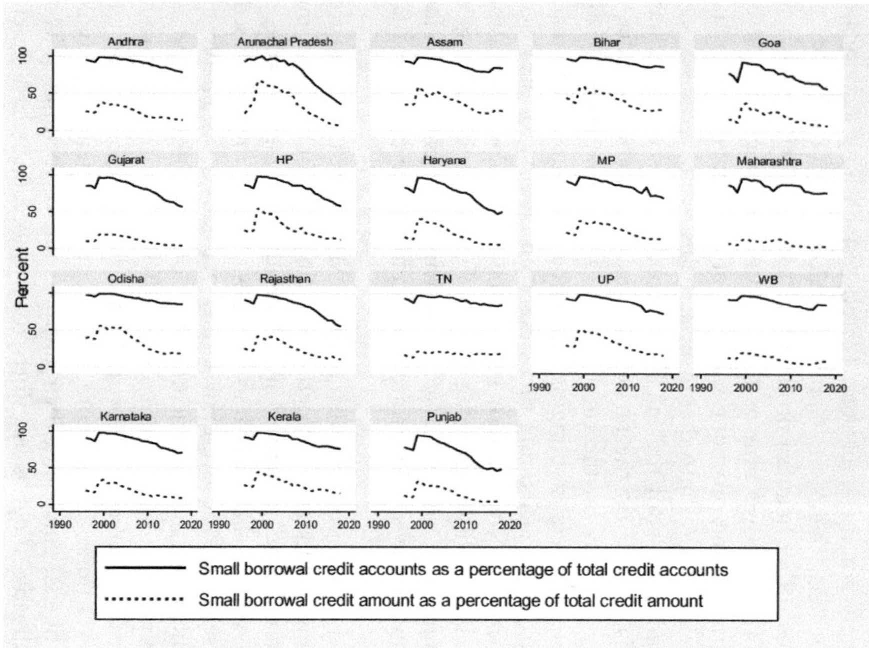

Fig. A1 Share of small borrowal accounts in selected states

References

Ahluwalia, M. S. 2000. *Reforming Indias financial sector: An overview*. Planning commission.

Banerjee, Abhijit, Shawn Cole, and Esther Duflo. 2004. Banking reform in India. In *India policy forum*, vol. 1, 277–332. Global Economy and Development Program, The Brookings Institution.

Barua, Abheek, Rajat Kathuria, and Neha Malik. 2016. "The Status of Financial Inclusion, Regulation, and Education in India." 568. ADBI Working Paper Series. Tokyo: Asian Development Bank.

Bhole, L. M. 1985. Administered interests rates in India. *Economic & Political Weekly* 20 (25/26): 1089–1104.

Burgess, Robin, and Rohini Pande. 2005. Do rural banks matter ? Evidence from the Indian social banking experiment. *American Economic Review* 95 (3): 780–795. https://doi.org/10.1257/0002828054201242.

Chakravarthy, Tapas Kumar. 2005. *The share of cooperatives in rural credit*. RBI Publications.

Dasgupta, Rajaram. 2001. Priority sector lending-Yesterday, today and tomorrow. *Economic & Political Weekly* 37 (41): 4239–4245.

Demirgüç-Kunt, Asli, Leora Klapper, Dorothe Singer, Saniya Ansar, and Jake Hess. 2018. *Asli Demirgüç-Kunt The Global Findex Database*.

Gonzalez-Vega, Claudio. 1984. Cheap agricultural credit:Redistribution in reverse. In *Undermining rural development with cheap credit*, ed. Dale W. Adams, Douglas H. Graham, and J. D. Von Pischke, 1984th ed., 120–143. Colorado: Westview Press.

Khan, H R. 2005. "Report of the Internal Group to Examine Issues Relating to Rural Credit and Microfinance." Mumbai.

Muranjan, S. K. 1952. *Modern banking in India. Third edit*. Bombay: Kamal Publishing House.

Patra, Michael Debabrata, and Sunando Roy. 2000. Financial stability: A survey of the Indian experience. *Reserve Bank of India Occasional Papers* 21 (1):

Pawar, Jagannathrao R., and Subhash R. Sutar. 1982. Impact of lower interest rate finance on economic conditions of rural weaker section. *Indian Journal of Agricultural Economics* 37:265–272.

Rajan, Raghuram G. 2009. *A Hundred Small Steps: Report of the Committee on Financial Sector Reforms*. https://www.jrvarma.in/reports/Raghuram-Rajan/cfsr_all.pdf.

Rajeev, Meenakshi, and HP Mahesh. 2010. "Banking Sector Reforms and NPA: A Study of Indian Commercial Banks." *ISEC Working Paper 252*. ISEC.

Rajeev, Meenakshi, and B. P. Vani. 2017. *Financial access of the urban poor in India: A story of exclusion*. New Delhi: Springer India. https://doi.org/10.1007/978-81-322-3712-9.

Rajeev, Meenakshi, B. P. Vani, and Manojit Bhattacharjee. 2012. "Nature and Dimensions of Farmers' Indebtedness in India." ISEC Working Paper 267. ISEC.

Rakesh, Mohan, and Partha Ray. 2016. "Indian Financial Sector: Structure, Trends, and Turns." WP/17/7. IMF Working Papers.

RBI. 2007. "Report of the Task Force on Empowering RRB Boards for Operational Efficiency." Mumbai.

RBI. 2008. *Evolution of Banking in India. RBI Publications*. Mumbai: Reserve Bank of India. https://rbidocs.rbi.org.in/rdocs/Publications/PDFs/86727.pdf.

Sen, Kunal, and Rajendra R. Vaidya. 1997. *The process of financial liberalization in India*. Delhi: Oxford University Press.

Sharma, Manoj, Anurodh Giri, and Sakshi Chadha. 2016. "Pradhan Mantri Jan Dhan Yojana Wave III Assessment." Microsave. https://www.microsave.net/files/pdf/PMJDY_Wave_III_Assessment_MicroSave.pdf.

Swain, Bijay Kumar. 2018. "A Research Study Report on Evaluating Implementation of Jan Dhan Yojana." Hyderabad.

Tripathi, Dwijendra. 2004. *The Oxford history of Indian business*. New Delhi: Oxford University Press.

CHAPTER 3

Measuring Financial Inclusion: A State-Level Analysis

3.1 Introduction

In the previous chapter, we briefly examined the history of India's financial policies. We next advance this discussion further by developing a comprehensive index of financial inclusion, which allows us to assess the status of financial inclusion in different states of the country over time.

Financial inclusion is a multi-dimensional concept, and relying on individual indicators need not accurately portray its true status. To address this, we have developed a comprehensive index to assess the status of financial inclusion in India over the period 1994–2017. A novelty of this index is its separate evaluation of financial inclusion in rural and urban areas. The nature and problems of financial inclusion differ significantly between rural and urban regions, necessitating distinct assessments. Notably, existing literature has not focused on this distinction in any substantive manner. In most studies, we find a combined assessment of the rural and urban areas. So our approach aims to fill this gap by providing a more nuanced understanding of financial inclusion through these separate assessments.

This separate assessment of rural and urban areas necessitates examining the different financial institutions operating in the rural and urban areas. In rural areas, both scheduled commercial and cooperative banks are relevant, while in urban areas, scheduled commercial banks are more

S. Saravanabhavan and M. Rajeev, *Moving Beyond Barriers*, Palgrave Studies in Impact Finance,
https://doi.org/10.1007/978-981-95-1066-5_3

prominent. Current literature also focuses much on commercial banks because the net worth of commercial banks is much higher, and their data is also readily available (For example, Chakravarty and Pal, 2010; Sarma, 2012).

Another important distinction of our index is that it incorporates indicators of both cooperative banks and scheduled commercial banks[1] to calculate the financial inclusion Index. Cooperative banks in India are local financial institutions that were initially established to facilitate credit access to poor farmers, especially in rural areas, where the outreach of commercial banks was limited. Over time, the cooperative system has developed an extensive network of small institutions known as Primary Agricultural Credit Societies (PACSs) at the grassroots level in rural areas. Due to their proximity to the community, PACSs are uniquely positioned to have better access to customer information, which may not be readily available to larger commercial banks (Besley 1994). As a result, smaller financial institutions are more effective in assessing the needs and financial capacity of their clients, enhancing their ability to serve poorer households and small businesses. Moreover, cooperative banks have played a critical role in overcoming the 'last-mile problem' in financial inclusion, especially in certain states. Recognising the significance of Primary Agricultural Credit Societies (PACSs), we have incorporated their indicators alongside those of scheduled commercial banks to construct the rural financial inclusion index. We believe this is an important contribution as it helps in building a more comprehensive measure of rural financial inclusion in India.

Thus, the Index that we develop is unique in several ways. First, it addresses the rural–urban disparity in financial inclusion by constructing separate indices for rural and urban areas, incorporating appropriate indicators for rural and urban regions. Second, the measure that we develop is more representative of India's financial system, as it incorporates data from cooperative banks, which play a significant role in promoting rural financial inclusion. Third, unlike most existing studies that rely on arbitrary weighting schemes, we use factor analysis to arrive at the weighting

[1] The main banking system in India consists of commercial and cooperative banking systems. The commercial banks include nationalised banks, State bank and its associates, Regional Rural Banks (RRB) and also private sector banks. These together comprise the Scheduled commercial banks.

scheme for the indicators, ensuring more robust results (For more details, see: Saravanabhavan and Rajeev 2024).

The remainder of the chapter is organised as follows: Sect. 3.2 provides a brief discussion on the importance of building a comprehensive financial inclusion index. Section 3.3 outlines the data sources and methodology. Section 3.4 presents the analysis based on the constructed indices. Section 3.5 explores the relationship between financial inclusion and dependence on moneylenders. The final section concludes.

3.2 Importance of a Comprehensive Financial Inclusion Index

As discussed in the previous chapter, the Government of India introduced several initiatives to improve financial inclusion since independence, recognising the benefits of a well-functioning financial system at both micro and macro levels. The level of financial inclusion, however, has not improved as expected and is not uniform across regions.

Improving financial inclusion in underserved areas requires a clear understanding of its current status. While there have been a few attempts to develop a suitable measure for financial inclusion across Indian states, most existing indices rely on indicators related to scheduled commercial banks. Sarma (2008) has grouped bank indicators into three dimensions: banking penetration, availability, and usage. The indicator for banking penetration is the number of bank accounts per 1000 adult persons. The indicator for availability is the number of bank branches per 1000 adult persons, and finally, the indicators for the usage dimension are the volume of deposits and volume of credit as a proportion of GDP. Similar indicators have been used in most other studies (Chakravarty and Pal 2010; Nitish Kumar 2014; Arora 2012; Bhavani and Bhanumurthy 2012; Mehrotra et al. 2009).

At the global level, several efforts have been made to construct financial inclusion indices using the Findex database for cross-country comparisons (Camara et al. 2014; Yorulmaz 2018; Van et al. 2021; Tram et al. 2023). Additionally, a few studies have developed gender-based financial inclusion indices to analyse the gender disparities in financial inclusion (Tripathi and Rajeev 2023; Morsy 2020).

3.2.1 The Role of PACs in Rural India

Primary agricultural credit societies (PACSs) have played a significant role in promoting financial inclusion by serving small farmers, rural artisans, and the traditionally oppressed castes. According to NAFSCOB data, PACS covered around 79 per cent of the total number of villages in India as of 2017.[2] In states such as Andhra Pradesh, Kerala, Bihar, Haryana, Himachal Pradesh, Uttar Pradesh, Manipur, Mizoram, and Sikkim, PACSs provide complete coverage, reaching 100 per cent of the villages (Saravanabhavan and Rajeev 2024).

This indicates the wide presence of cooperative societies in rural India and the vital role that the cooperatives could play in improving financial inclusion in these regions. The Government of India has long supported the cooperative banking system by providing subsidised financial support and has used it to "channel its development programmes" to the poor, as these institutions have a strong network in the rural areas.

Though cooperative banks are primarily supported by state governments, which are stakeholders, the cooperative system has not been performing well in recent years because of poor governance, inefficient internal processes, and non-recovery of loans (RBI 2012). Despite this, the proportion of households accessing credit from cooperative banks is exceptionally high for states such as Tamil Nadu, Kerala, Karnataka, Andhra Pradesh, Maharashtra, and Punjab.

3.3 Data and Methodology

We develop the financial inclusion indices to measure the extent of financial inclusion over the period 1994–2017 for 17 major states of India. Together, these states account for around 94 per cent of the total land area of the country (census, 2011). The data for the indicators of Scheduled commercial banks are taken from various issues of the Basic Statistical Returns of Scheduled Commercial Banks published by the RBI. The data on Primary Agricultural Societies is obtained from the various issues of the Statistical Statements relating to the Co-operative movement in India, published by NABARD (National Bank for Agriculture and Rural Development) and NAFSCOB (National Federation of State Co-operative

[2] Performance of Primary Agricultural Credit Societies, 2016–17, National federation of State Cooperative Banks Ltd. http://nafscob.org/pacs_f.htm.

Banks). Adult population data (above 14 years) from the census have been used for all calculations.

3.3.1 Financial Inclusion Index

As mentioned earlier, we have constructed two separate indices for rural and urban regions over the period 1994–2017 for 17 major states of India. These indices are made using several indicators of commercial banks and cooperatives (PACSs) and are further aggregated to form the comprehensive financial inclusion index using a weighted geometric mean.

Methodology for Construction of Indices

In most of the existing Indian studies, the weights assigned to the indicators are arbitrarily set, primarily assigning equal weights to all the indicators (Chakravarty and Pa, 2010; Pal and Vaidya 2011). In our study, we arrive at the weighting scheme for aggregation using factor analysis, following the method used by Nicoletti et al. (2000). Their study statistically grouped the variables into intermediate composite indicators, and these intermediate indicators are further aggregated to form the final measure. First, we construct the rural index and label the intermediate indices as the Rural Banks Index and the Rural Cooperatives Index. The bank indicators are grouped under the Rural Banks Index, and the PACSs' indicators are grouped under the Rural Cooperatives Index. Secondly, we construct the urban index using the indicators of the urban scheduled commercial banks. The weights from the factor analysis are provided in the Appendix (Tables A1 and Table A3).

As a prerequisite to conducting the Factor analysis, we carry out Barlett's (Bartlett 1950) and Kaiser–Meyer–Olkin's (Kaiser 1958) tests for appropriateness of factor analysis. We find that Bartlett's test is significant, and the Kaiser–Meyer–Olkin Test shows acceptable values greater than 0.6, indicating that factor analysis is appropriate. The number of factors extracted is based on Kaiser's criterion, where factors with eigenvalues of more than one are considered for the analysis (for further details, see Appendix Tables A2 and A4).

We have used the weighted geometric mean ($\exp(\frac{\sum_{i=1}^{n} W_i \mathrm{Ln}(X_i)}{\sum_{i=1}^{n} W_i})$) to calculate the rural and urban indices where W_i is the set of weights obtained and X_i is the specific indicator. Before calculating the indices, the indicators have been normalised using the min–max method. Also, to achieve comparability of the index over the years, we have normalised the indicators using the global maxima and minima. These two indices are then analysed separately for different states. Finally, the rural and urban indices are aggregated into the final composite Financial Inclusion Index using a simple geometric mean. We assume equal importance to rural and urban financial inclusion, and therefore, we have used equal weights for the final aggregation of the index.

Indicators Used to Construct the Index

We have 14 indicators in total, eight for the rural index and six for the urban index. For the rural index, we have rural demographic outreach, rural geographic outreach, rural deposit account penetration, rural deposit services usage, rural bank credit account penetration, rural bank credit services usage, rural cooperatives (PACSs) demographic outreach, and rural cooperatives (PACSs) credit usage. The indicators for the urban index are urban demographic outreach, urban geographic outreach, urban deposit account penetration, urban deposit services usage, urban bank credit account penetration, and urban bank credit services usage.

Demographic outreach (rural and urban) represents the average number of banks available for a person, and it is a critical measure of financial accessibility. When this number is too high, meaning a branch serves a large population, low-income individuals are more likely to be crowded out. Our study constructed the rural/urban demographic indicator by dividing the total number of rural/urban bank branches in each state by the total rural/urban adult populations of each state. Similarly, the rural/urban banks' geographic outreach is obtained by dividing the total number of bank branches by the rural/urban areas. We construct the PACS demographic outreach indicator by dividing the total number of PACSs by the total rural population. The outreach indicator is crucial, as one of the most cited reasons for people in developing countries not having banking accounts is the distance to the banks, particularly in rural areas.

Ideally, the penetration of banking services should be measured by the number of individuals availing these services (for instance, the number of people with bank accounts). But in the absence of such data, deposit account penetration and credit account penetration are used. Account penetration is the number of bank accounts (deposit/credit) divided by the total adult population. We have also included indicators that proxy for the use of financial services. The deposit services usage gives us an average of how much is deposited by each, which is the total volume of deposits divided by the total adult population for rural and urban areas. Similarly, we have credit services usage of banks for rural/urban areas and credit services usage of PACSs for rural areas. Other studies have used the credit-income and the deposit-income ratios to measure actual usage. But here, we argue that since these ratios measure the credit and deposit volume in terms of per-rupee value, it is not an apt measure of usage. Instead, the average volume per head would give us a better estimate, as it also captures the depth and width of financial inclusion. Our indicators provide us with an average of "how much" goes to each.

3.4 Analysis—The Financial Inclusion Index

The urban and rural indices for the year 2022 are presented in Fig. 3.1. It shows how the level of financial inclusion of the various states changes with per capita income (per capita net state domestic product (NSDP)). Both the rural and urban indices show improvement with an increase in income. However, this increase is more prominent for the urban index, particularly for the states having per capita income above Rupees 0.1 million, implying a large rural–urban divide (See Fig. 3.1). Thus, our analysis of these indices reveals a noteworthy pattern: while there is a sharp increase in urban as well as rural financial inclusion, rural inclusion is advancing relatively at a slower pace even in the presence of the massive financial inclusion drive (also see Saravanabhavan and Rajeev 2024).

To better understand the rural scenario, we graphically examined the intermediate indices of the rural index, namely, the Rural Banks Index and Rural Cooperatives Index, in Fig. 3.2. Our findings highlight the disparities across the different states, particularly the differences between relatively higher-income states and lower-income states. Higher-income states (states with per capita income between Rupees 0.10 and 0.15 million) such as Kerala, Punjab, Maharashtra, and Gujarat have performed better under the Rural Cooperatives Index as compared to the Rural Banks Index. The lower-income states have better performance under the Rural Banks Index (also see Saravanabhavan and Rajeev 2024).

This observation reveals two distinct strategies followed by states to improve rural financial inclusion. While some states emphasise commercial banking, others emphasise a good mix of commercial and cooperative banking. Interestingly, it appears that the rural regions of the richer states

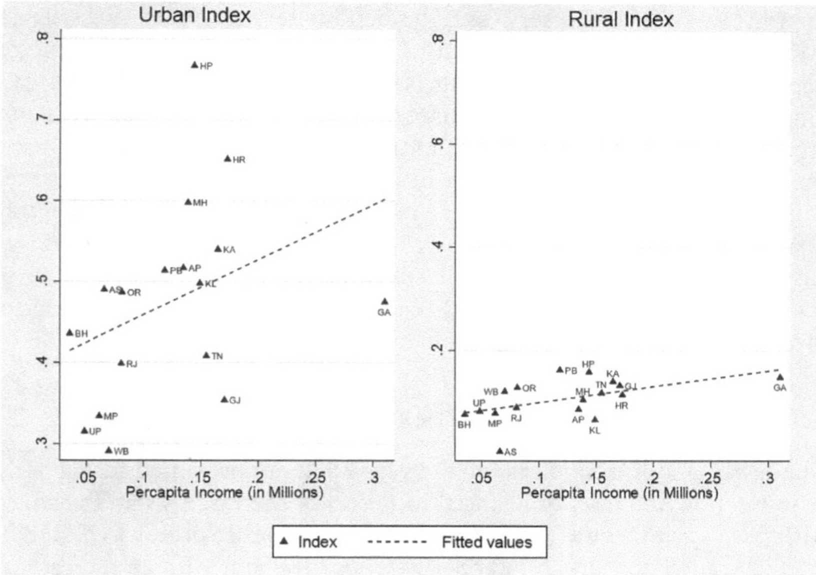

Fig. 3.1 Urban and rural index: Performance of major states in India—2022. *Note* AS-Assam, BR-Bihar, MP-Madhya Pradesh, WB-West Bengal, OR-Odisha, UP-Uttar Pradesh, RJ-Rajasthan, AP-Andhra Pradesh, PB-Punjab, TN-Tamil Nadu, KA-Karnataka, HP-Himachal Pradesh, HR-Haryana, GJ-Gujarat, MH-Maharashtra, KL-Kerala, GA-Goa
(*Source* Author's analysis using RBI data)

have better utilised the local-level cooperative institutions for financial inclusion. Notably, some of the higher-ranking states on the Rural Cooperative Index—such as Kerala, Karnataka, Gujarat, and Maharashtra also have a strong history of community engagement.

After constructing the rural and urban indices, we aggregate them to form the comprehensive financial inclusion index. Figure 3.3 presents all three indices of the various states for the year 2022. The figure reveals significant variation across states, with Himachal Pradesh ranking the highest in overall financial inclusion and Assam ranking the lowest. Figure 3.4 presents the trend of financial inclusion over the period 1994–2022 for a few major states, categorising them based on their State GDP per capita. The high-income states show higher index values, while the low-income states show lower index values. For almost all the categories

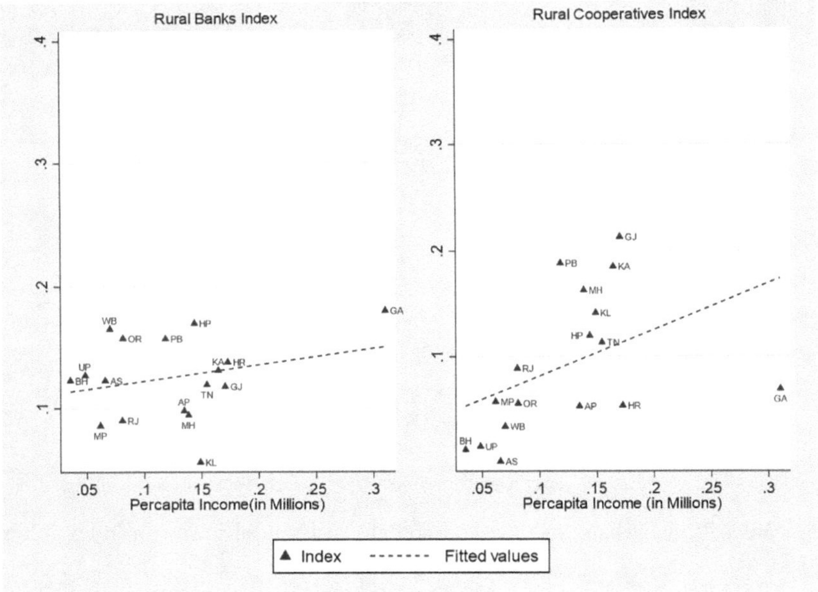

Fig. 3.2 Rural banks and rural cooperatives index: Performance of major states in India—2022.
Note AS-Assam, BR-Bihar, MP-Madhya Pradesh, WB-West Bengal, OR-Odisha, UP-Uttar Pradesh, RJ-Rajasthan, AP-Andhra Pradesh, PB-Punjab, TN-Tamil Nadu, KA-Karnataka, HP-Himachal Pradesh, HR-Haryana, GJ-Gujarat, MH-Maharashtra, KL-Kerala, GA-Goa
(*Source* Author's analysis using RBI data)

of states—high, mid, and low—the rural–urban gap has widened since 2008[3] (See Appendix Tables A5, A6, and A7 for the index values).

Seeking an explanation for this trend, we examined the individual indicators comprising the index. We find that, while the urban indicators show a smooth increase during the drive period, the rural indicators exhibit more modest gains. For instance, the rural deposit account penetration shows improvement during the drive period, however, deposit

[3] Though the FI drive was first initiated in 2005–06, the actual implementation and take-off of the policies have taken some time and so the impact of the drive is felt mostly after 2008, after the recommendations of the Rangarajan Committee-2008. (Fig. 3.4).

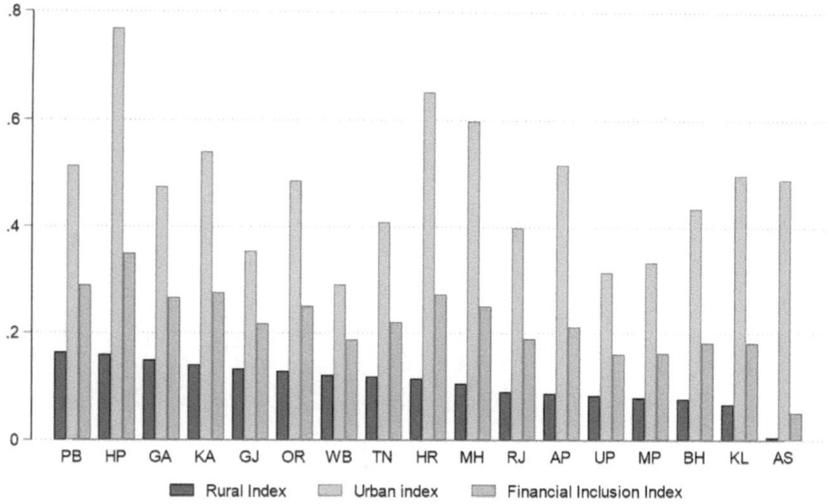

Fig. 3.3 Rural, urban, and the comprehensive financial inclusion index values for 2022
Note AS-Assam, BR-Bihar, MP-Madhya Pradesh, WB-West Bengal, OR-Odisha, UP-Uttar Pradesh, RJ-Rajasthan, AP-Andhra Pradesh, PB-Punjab, TN-Tamil Nadu, KA-Karnataka, HP-Himachal Pradesh, HR-Haryana, GJ-Gujarat, MH-Maharashtra, KL-Kerala, GA-Goa; RI-Rural Index, UI-Urban Index, FII-Financial Inclusion Index
(*Source* Author's analysis using RBI data)

volume does not show corresponding improvement. This implies that even though new accounts are being opened, they are not actively used. We also observe that the improvement in rural credit usage is comparatively lower and that the improvement falls short of the progress seen in urban regions. One main reason for this disparity is the better infrastructure and economic situation in urban regions. Commercial banks generally find it lucrative to open new branches in urban areas due to higher levels of economic activity in urban regions. Consequently, after liberalisation, with the termination of strict bank licensing policies, more branches are being opened in urban regions, and some of the unviable rural branches are being closed down by the banks. As a result, over the period 1992 to 2002, there was a reduction in the number of

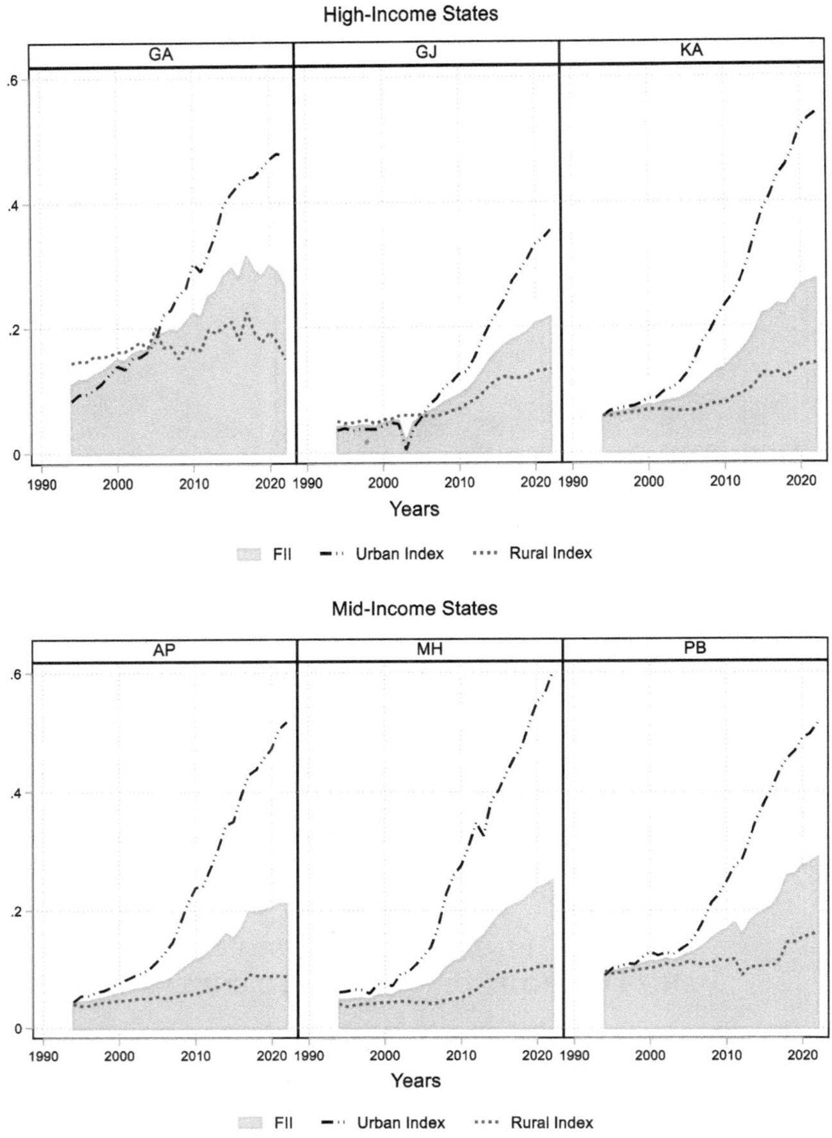

Fig. 3.4 Trend of financial inclusion 1994–2022—A few major states (*Source* Authors' analysis using RBI data)

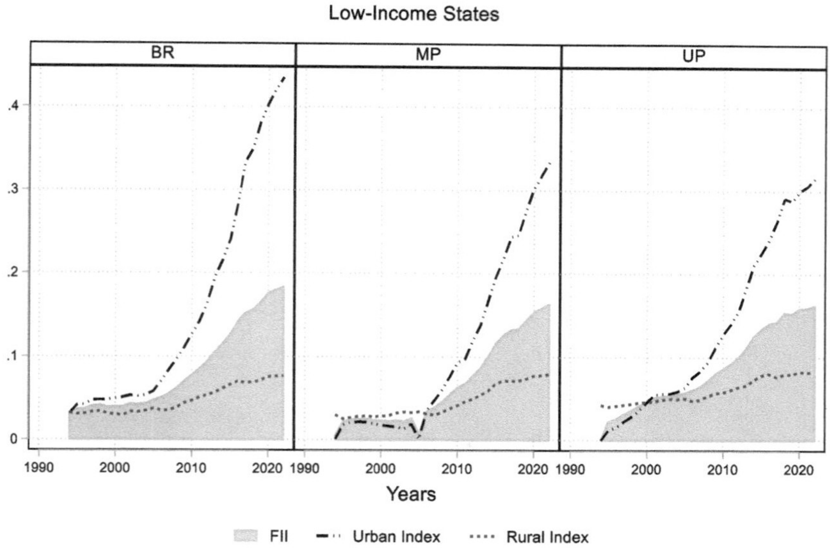

Fig. 3.4 (continued)

rural bank branches.[4] This suggests that the geographic and demographic penetration has also not improved for the rural regions after liberalisation.

Overall, we observe increasing rural–urban differences within the states; however, states such as Goa and Gujarat show notable improvements in both rural and urban financial inclusion indices. Other states should also aim to improve financial inclusion by simultaneously strengthening banking infrastructure and promoting financial knowledge.

3.5 Financial Inclusion and Dependence on Moneylenders

An important question that arises in this context is whether improvements in financial inclusion have contributed to a decline in people's dependence on moneylenders. This question is important as the interest rates charged by moneylenders are often much higher, trapping borrowers into cycles of debt. A recent study by Saravanabhavan and Rajeev (2024)

[4] Basic Statistical Returns of SCBs in India-Various issues.

provided empirical evidence suggesting that greater access to formal financial services is associated with a reduction in the reliance on informal credit sources such as moneylenders.

Using a double-hurdle model, the study found a statistically significant negative relationship between the financial inclusion index they developed and reliance on moneylenders, indicating that financial inclusion is associated with reduced dependence on informal credit sources. While this result is consistent across cooperative as well as commercial banks, the nature and extent of reduction differ. For cooperative banks, an increase in the FI index leads to a decrease in dependence on moneylenders from the start. In contrast, commercial banks exhibit a threshold effect, meaning that a certain level of financial inclusion must be achieved before a significant reduction in dependence occurs. This threshold is notably higher in urban areas, indicating that greater penetration of urban commercial banks is required to meaningfully reduce reliance on moneylenders. It is, however, heartening to observe that the dependence on moneylenders reduced over time (between the 70th and 77th Rounds of the NSSO-AIDIS surveys), perhaps due to various financial inclusion drives. But there is still scope for reducing this dependence further.

3.6 Discussion

In this chapter, we have undertaken a comprehensive analysis of the level of financial inclusion across the major states in India over the period 1994 to 2017. To accomplish this, we constructed a Financial Inclusion Index by considering indicators from both scheduled commercial banks and cooperative banks. This inclusion is significant because cooperative banks and societies, despite being an integral part of the rural financial system, do not get due emphasis in current policy discourse.

Only a limited number of studies emphasise its importance. For instance, a previous study conducted by Saravanabhavan and Rajeev (2024) brings out the positive impact of cooperatives on financial inclusion. The study emphasises the importance of small institutions in catalysing development processes. However, it was also observed that the cooperative banking system in India is plagued by several problems, prominent amongst those being the non-performing loans. Thus, improving the overall health of the cooperative banking system is essential to make it sustainable and useful to the population at large.

The analysis from this chapter shows that despite the significant improvement in financial inclusion across the country, driven largely by initiatives such as the Jan Dhan Yojana, our financial inclusion indices show that the rural areas are still lagging behind. Notably, the year 2014, which marked the launch of PMJDY, corresponds with a sharp rise in the urban financial inclusion index. However, the rural index does not reflect a similar upward trend. This highlights the need for targeted efforts to strengthen rural financial inclusion by enhancing economic opportunities, improving financial infrastructure, and promoting financial awareness in rural regions. A closer examination of state-wise trends during the drive period shows that the improvement in the urban and rural indices is comparable only in states like Goa and Gujarat, while in all the other states, we see that the rural index is much below the urban index. To further validate these observations, we had done a careful examination of individual indicators, which also confirmed that the urban indicators have improved during this period, while the rural indicators showed only modest gains.

Appendix

Table A1 Calculation of weights for rural index using factor analysis

Components			*Squared value*		*Summed to unity*	
Variables	*1*	*2*				
Rural banks' geographic outreach	0.700	–0.065	0.490	0.004	0.105	0.004
Rural banks' demographic outreach	0.922	0.206	0.850	0.042	0.181	0.037
Rural banks' deposit account penetration	0.965	0.065	0.931	0.004	0.199	0.004
Rural banks' deposit services usage	0.943	0.061	0.889	0.004	0.190	0.003
Rural banks' credit account penetration	0.819	–0.138	0.671	0.019	0.143	0.017
Rural banks' credit usage	0.921	–0.089	0.848	0.008	0.181	0.007
Rural PACSs' demographic outreach	–0.056	0.786	0.003	0.618	0.001	0.542
Rural PACSs' credit usage	–0.041	–0.663	0.002	0.440	0.000	0.386
Explained variance	4.684	1.139				
Explained variance/total	0.804	0.196				

Table A2 KMO and Bartlett's test for rural indicators

KMO and Bartlett's Test		
Kaiser–Meyer–Olkin Measure of Sampling Adequacy		0.84
Bartlett's Test of Sphericity	Approx. Chi-Square	3.346E+03
	df	28

Table A3 Calculation of weights for urban index using factor analysis

Variables	*Components* *1*	*Squared values*	*Summed to unity*
Urban banks' geographic Outreach	0.772	0.596	0.1445
Urban banks' demographic outreach	0.757	0.573	0.1389
Urban banks' deposit penetration	0.925	0.856	0.2074
Urban banks' deposit services usage	0.911	0.830	0.2012
Urban banks' credit penetration	0.764	0.584	0.1415
Urban banks' credit usage	0.829	0.687	0.1666
Explained variance	4.13		

Table A4 KMO and Bartlett's test for urban indicators

KMO and Bartlett's Test		
Kaiser–Meyer–Olkin Measure of Sampling Adequacy		0.771
Bartlett's Test of Sphericity	Approx. Chi-Square	2.47E+03
	df	15

Table A5 Urban index values 1994–2022

1994			*2004*			*2014*			*2022*		
State	*UI*	*Rank*	*State*	*UI*	*Rank*	*State*	*UI*	*Rank*	*State*	*UI*	*Rank*
KL	0.13	1	KL	0.22	1	HP	0.49	1	HP	0.77	1
PB	0.09	2	GA	0.16	2	GA	0.40	2	HR	0.65	2
GA	0.08	3	HP	0.15	3	MH	0.38	3	MH	0.60	3
HR	0.06	4	PB	0.13	4	HR	0.37	4	KA	0.54	4
MH	0.06	5	KA	0.11	5	PB	0.35	5	AP	0.52	5
KA	0.06	6	MH	0.11	6	KL	0.35	6	PB	0.51	6
TN	0.05	7	HR	0.10	7	KA	0.35	7	KL	0.50	7
HP	0.05	8	AP	0.10	8	AP	0.34	8	AS	0.49	8
AS	0.05	9	AS	0.06	9	OR	0.26	9	OR	0.49	9
WB	0.05	10	TN	0.06	10	AS	0.26	10	GA	0.48	10
AP	0.04	11	UP	0.06	11	TN	0.26	11	BH	0.44	11
GJ	0.04	12	BH	0.05	12	BH	0.21	12	TN	0.41	12
BH	0.03	13	RJ	0.05	13	UP	0.21	13	RJ	0.40	13
RJ	0.02	14	WB	0.05	14	RJ	0.21	14	GJ	0.35	14
OR	0.02	15	OR	0.04	15	GJ	0.20	15	MP	0.33	15
MP	0.00	16	GJ	0.04	16	MP	0.17	16	UP	0.32	16
UP	0.00	17	MP	0.02	17	WB	0.16	17	WB	0.29	17

Table A6 Rural index values 1994–2022

1994			*2004*			*2014*			*2022*		
State	*RI*	*Rank*	*State*	*RI*	*Rank*	*State*	*RI*	*Rank*	*State*	*RI*	*Rank*
GA	0.14	1	GA	0.17	1	GA	0.20	1	GA	0.21	1
HP	0.10	2	HP	0.12	2	HP	0.16	2	HP	0.16	2
PB	0.10	3	PB	0.11	3	TN	0.12	3	KA	0.13	3
HR	0.07	4	HR	0.07	4	KA	0.11	4	TN	0.12	4
KA	0.06	5	TN	0.07	5	GJ	0.11	5	GJ	0.11	5
TN	0.05	6	KA	0.06	6	PB	0.10	6	PB	0.11	6
GJ	0.05	7	WB	0.06	7	OR	0.09	7	OR	0.10	7
UP	0.04	8	OR	0.06	8	WB	0.09	8	WB	0.10	8
WB	0.04	9	GJ	0.06	9	HR	0.09	9	HR	0.09	9
MH	0.04	10	UP	0.05	10	MH	0.08	10	MH	0.09	10
AP	0.04	11	AP	0.05	11	KL	0.08	11	KL	0.08	11
RJ	0.03	12	MH	0.04	12	AP	0.08	12	UP	0.08	12
BR	0.03	13	RJ	0.04	13	UP	0.07	13	RJ	0.07	13
OR	0.03	14	BR	0.03	14	RJ	0.07	14	MP	0.07	14
MP	0.03	15	MP	0.03	15	BR	0.06	15	AP	0.07	15
KL	0.03	16	KL	0.02	16	MP	0.06	16	BR	0.07	16
AS	0.01	17	AS	0.02	17	AS	0.03	17	AS	0.03	17

Table A7 Financial inclusion index values 1994–2022

1994			*2004*			*2014*			*2022*		
State	*FI*	*Rank*	*State*	*FI*	*Rank*	*State*	*FI*	*Rank*	*State*	*FI*	*Rank*
GA	0.11	1	GA	0.16	1	GA	0.28	1	HP	0.35	1
PB	0.09	2	HP	0.13	2	HP	0.28	2	PB	0.29	2
HP	0.07	3	PB	0.12	3	KA	0.19	3	KA	0.28	3
HR	0.07	4	HR	0.09	4	PB	0.19	4	HR	0.27	4
KL	0.06	5	KA	0.08	5	HR	0.18	5	GA	0.27	5
KA	0.06	6	AP	0.07	6	MH	0.18	6	MH	0.25	6
TN	0.05	7	MH	0.07	7	TN	0.17	7	OR	0.25	7
MH	0.05	8	KL	0.07	8	KL	0.17	8	TN	0.22	8
WB	0.04	9	TN	0.06	9	AP	0.16	9	GJ	0.22	9
GJ	0.04	10	WB	0.05	10	OR	0.16	10	AP	0.21	10
AP	0.04	11	UP	0.05	11	GJ	0.15	11	RJ	0.19	11
BR	0.03	12	OR	0.05	12	UP	0.12	12	WB	0.19	12
RJ	0.03	13	GJ	0.05	13	WB	0.12	13	BR	0.18	13
OR	0.03	14	BR	0.04	14	RJ	0.12	14	KL	0.18	14
AS	0.02	15	RJ	0.04	15	BR	0.11	15	MP	0.16	15
MP	0.01	16	AS	0.03	16	MP	0.10	16	UP	0.16	16
UP	0.00	17	MP	0.02	17	AS	0.09	17	AS	0.05	17

References

Arora, Rashmi Umesh. 2012. "Financial Inclusion and Human Capital in Developing Asia: The Australian Connection." *Third World Quarterly* 33 (1): 177–97. https://doi.org/10.1080/01436597.2012.627256.

Bartlett, M. S. 1950. "Tests of Significance in Factor Analysis." *British Journal of Statistical Psychology* 3 (2): 77–85. https://doi.org/10.1111/j.2044-8317.1950.tb00285.x.

Besley, Timothy. 1994. "How Do Market Failures Justify Interventions in Credit Markets?" *The World Bank Research Observer* 9 (1): 27–47.

Bhavani, T A, and N R Bhanumurthy. 2012. *Financial Access in Post-Reform India*. New Delhi: Oxford University Press. https://doi.org/10.1093/acprof:oso/9780198076650.003.0002.

Camara, Noelia, Ximena Pena, and David Tuesta. 2014. "Factors That Matter for Financial Inclusion: Evidence from Peru." BBVA Bank, Economic Research Department, Working Papers: 1409, no. 14: 23. https://doi.org/10.5605/IEB.10.1.

Chakravarty, Satya R., and Rupayan Pal. 2010. "Measuring Financial Inclusion : An Axiomatic Approach." WP-2010–003. Indira Gandhi Institute of Development Research Working Papers. Mumbai: IGIDR. http://www.igidr.ac.in/pdf/publication/WP-2010-003.pdf.

Kaiser, Henry F. 1958. The Varimax Criterion for Analytic Rotation in Factor Analysis. *Psychometrika* 23 (3): 187–200.

Kumar, Nitish. 2020. "Political Interference and Crowding out in Bank Lending." *Journal of Financial Intermediation* 43 (July): 100815. https://doi.org/10.1016/j.jfi.2019.02.001.

Mehrotra, N., V. Puhazhendhi, G. Nair, and Sahoo B.B. 2009. "Financial Inclusion: An Overview." 48. NABARD Occasional Papers. Mumbai: NABARD.

Morsy, Hanan. 2020. Access to Finance—Mind the Gender Gap. *The Quarterly Review of Economics and Finance* 78 (November): 12–21. https://doi.org/10.1016/j.qref.2020.02.005.

Nicoletti, Giuseppe, Stefano Scarpetta, and Oliver Boylaud. 2000. "Summary Indicators of Product Market Regulation with an Extension to Employment Protection Legislation." 226. OECD Economics Department Working Papers. Paris. https://doi.org/10.2139/ssrn.201668.

Pal, R., and R. Vaidya. 2011. "Outreach of Banking Services Across Indian States: 1981–2007 Converging or Diverging?" In *India Development Report*. New Delhi: Oxford University Press.

RBI. 2012. "Strengthening and Revitalising Rural Cooperative Credit Delivery System." In *RBI Documents-Speech Delivered by Dr Deepali Pant Joshi, Executive Director, Reserve Bank of India*. Mumbai: Reserve Bank of India. https://rbidocs.rbi.org.in/rdocs/Speeches/PDFs/SRRCDS250314.pdf.

Saravanabhavan, Shika, and Meenakshi Rajeev. 2024. "Financial Inclusion in India: How Far Do Grassroots Institutions Matter?" *Journal of International Development* 36 (5): 2318–41. https://doi.org/10.1002/jid.3897.

Sarma, Mandira. 2012. "Index of Financial Inclusion—A Measure of Financial Sector Inclusiveness." 07/2012. School of International Studies Working Paper. Delhi.

Tram, Thi Xuan Huong, Tien Dinh Lai, and Thi Truc Huong Nguyen. 2023. "Constructing a Composite Financial Inclusion Index for Developing Economies." *The Quarterly Review of Economics and Finance* 87 (February): 257–265. https://doi.org/10.1016/j.qref.2021.01.003.

Tripathi, Sabyasachi, and Meenakshi Rajeev. 2023. "Gender-Inclusive Development through Fintech: Studying Gender-Based Digital Financial Inclusion in a Cross-Economy Setting." 1397. ADBI Working Paper Series. https://doi.org/10.56506/ZWGS6876.

Van, Loan Thi-Hong., Anh Vo, Nhan Thien Nguyen, and Duc Hong Vo. 2021. "Financial Inclusion and Economic GROWTH: An International Evidence." *Emerging Markets Finance and Trade* 57 (1): 239–63. https://doi.org/10.1080/1540496X.2019.1697672.

Yorulmaz, Recep. 2018. "An Analysis of Constructing Global Financial Inclusion Indices." *Borsa Istanbul Review* 18 (3): 248–58. https://doi.org/10.1016/j.bir.2018.05.001.

CHAPTER 4

Financial Inclusion and Credit Access: A Case of Rural India

4.1 Introduction

In the previous chapter, we developed a novel measure of financial inclusion (FI) using commercial and cooperative bank-related indicators. This approach allowed us to gain an overview of the state of financial inclusion across the different regions of the country. Our analysis revealed several insights, notably that, despite the government's push for financial inclusion, the utilisation of financial services has not improved as significantly as anticipated.

Other studies and anecdotal evidence also reveal that the scope of financial services has not significantly improved for the average individual. While a majority of people now possess bank accounts, many seldom access or utilise other financial instruments. True financial inclusion means that individuals not only own a bank account but also actively access and use various other essential banking services such as credit, savings, insurance, and remittance services. However, people face several constraints that limit their ability to use these services effectively. To explore these constraints in greater depth, this book examines the demand-side aspects of financial inclusion using household-level data from the All-India Debt and Investment Survey (AIDIS) data provided by NSSO.

This chapter focuses on credit for the rural sector, a critical area for the Indian economy given its heavy reliance on the agriculture sector.

S. Saravanabhavan and M. Rajeev, *Moving Beyond Barriers*, Palgrave Studies in Impact Finance,
https://doi.org/10.1007/978-981-95-1066-5_4

Agriculture is widely acknowledged as the backbone of the Indian rural economy, with a significant proportion of the rural population either directly or indirectly engaged in the agricultural sector. According to the latest AIDIS, around 40 per cent of households in India are said to be involved in farming, and around 15 per cent are involved in agricultural labour for their livelihood.

Given the heavy dependence on agriculture for their livelihoods, rural households need access to funds to meet their working capital needs as well as to expand their operations. However, farm incomes are low, making it difficult for farmers to keep up with their expenses (Kannan 2015). On average, agricultural households[1] earn only Rupees 6,426 against an average household consumption expenditure of Rupees 6223 (GOI 2018a). This narrow margin leaves little room for savings or financial stability and hardly enough to sustain a decent living. Even more concerning is the fact that the income of 22.5% of the farmers is below the poverty line (ibid.).

These challenges are compounded by the fact that Indian agriculture is dominated by small and marginal farmers who often lack the savings or assets to sufficiently fund their production expenditure on their own. Moreover, agriculture is highly dependent on weather conditions, which adds to the uncertainty in their output and incomes. For example, inadequate monsoon rains often result in reduced agricultural yields, posing significant hardships for the farmer. Apart from this, the agricultural sector has a long operating cycle, which includes the stages of sowing, harvesting, and monetisation of the crop. This often causes farmers to face financial inadequacies during the interim period. Hence, farmers, particularly those with lower incomes, require access to external financing to sustain their farming activities. As much as it helps the poor farmers to continue their farming activities, external finances can also enable them to adopt new agricultural methods, inputs, and technologies, which in turn can make agriculture a more sustainable and profitable means of livelihood (Wossen et al. 2017; Pitt and Khandkar 1998; Zeller et al. 1998; Kannan 2011).

Given the small land holdings of Indian farmers, it is equally important to ensure access to credit for non-farm activities as part of a broader financial inclusion strategy. Such credit access is crucial not only for farmers but

[1] We make no distinction between agricultural households and cultivator households and they are used interchangeably throughout the book.

also for rural landless households, offering them an opportunity to diversify their income and improve their financial well-being. However, our analysis of NSSO data reveals that such non-farm activities are low in rural India, and credit access is also scant for these households. In comparison to non-agricultural sector credit, agriculture credit is better due to the priority sector lending norms and the various schemes that have existed for the agricultural sector over the years.

Given the lack of access to credit services in rural India, we have undertaken a detailed analysis of the various determinants of access to rural agricultural credit. We utilise data from the 70th and 77th Rounds of the NSSO data for the analysis.

The rest of the chapter unfolds as follows: Sect. 4.2 provides a brief background of the study, emphasising the problems in credit access for the Indian farmer. Section 4.3 discusses the data and methodology. Section 4.4 presents the descriptive analysis of the data. Section 4.5 presents the econometric analysis and results, and the final section concludes and draws implications from the results.

4.2 A Brief Background: Problems in Credit Access for the Indian Farmer

The Government of India has imposed restrictions on the interest rates that banks can charge to specific priority sectors. In the agriculture sector, particularly, banks are obligated to provide loans at subsidised interest rates to support agricultural production. When interest rates are lower than market rates, there is typically a large number of small-amount borrowers. However, banks face substantial transaction costs to monitor and ensure the due diligence of these borrowers, making such lending less profitable. As a result, loan denial is an often-reported outcome in such cases (Feder et al. 1990; Kochar 1997).

4.2.1 Information Asymmetry and Decreased Efficiency

Another critical issue in rural credit markets is the problem of information asymmetry between the lender and the borrower. When information is low, the banks cannot simply raise interest rates to offset the lending risks, as doing so could attract high-risk borrowers—an issue discussed extensively by Stiglitz and Weiss (1981). In such situations, when the risk involved in lending cannot be adequately assessed, banks resort to rationing of credit. Consequently, farmers may face financial constraints that limit their productive capacity. For instance, farmers may be forced to use suboptimal levels of inputs, leading to decreased output and efficiency. This, in turn, can undermine not only farmers' livelihoods but also the broader agricultural industry (Feder et al. 1990; Besley 1994).

4.2.2 *Dependence on Informal Lenders*

In situations where access to formal credit is limited and credit information systems are weak, individuals often turn to informal credit markets (Kochar 1997; Mohieldin and Wright 2000). Informal lenders, being local individuals, often have better information about borrowers due to their proximity to the community. The physical proximity allows them to assess the financial behaviour and repayment capacity of the customers, which in turn leads to lower monitoring costs (Bose 1998). Notably, the local knowledge reduces the risks for the lenders, and they may not demand any security for loans. Additionally, informal financial markets adapt themselves to local needs, making them particularly appealing to the poor (Adams and Fitchett 1992).

Despite these advantages, informal lending is often discouraged due to the high interest rates charged by lenders, making it an unfavourable option for the poor. Given that the lender and the borrower are usually from the same locality, the lender-borrower relationships are long-standing, often involving repeat lending (Bell 1991; Ghosh et al. 2000). Consequently, informal lenders rely on trust and reputation, and even resort to coercion and violence to ensure repayment (Ayyagari et.al. 2010). Thus, the informal credit market has features that make it undesirable in an economy striving to establish an inclusive financial system. However, studies show that barriers to accessing formal credit have led to an increased dependence on moneylenders (Diagne 1999; Deb and Rajeev 2007; Pal 2002). Notably, since the liberalisation of the economy in 1991, this dependence on moneylenders has been increasing (Pradhan 2013; Gill 2016).

4.2.3 *Constraints Faced by Farmers*

Evidence from different parts of the developing world reveals a range of challenges faced by farmers. For example, a study of smallholder farmers in Tanzania highlights that a key barrier to credit access is the lack of awareness about available credit programmes (Kashuliza and Kydd 1996). Similarly, research from Vietnam shows that household characteristics such as the age of the household head, household size and land ownership significantly influence a household's access to credit (Quach and Mullineux 2007). Additionally, a field survey in Pakistan identifies several other important factors, such as the size of land operated by the household, literacy levels, and the level of regional infrastructure development play a crucial role in determining credit access (Amjad and Hasnu 2007).

Focusing on research from India, a study by Kumar (2013a, b) reveals that commercial banks do not discriminate based on caste in the provision of agricultural credit. In contrast, cooperative banks tend to favour higher caste households in the provision of agricultural credit (Kumar 2013a, b). Additionally, studies have also examined the impact of gender on access to credit, finding that women-headed households generally lack access to credit (Fletschner, 2009; Ghosh and Vinod, 2012, 2017; Rajeev et al., 2011).

Low credit access is often attributed to the requirement of collateral by formal financial institutions. Collateral is demanded to gauge the creditworthiness of the borrower and to mitigate the risks for the lender (Zeller 1994). This requirement of collateral can, however, deter the poor, especially the small and marginal farmers, from seeking loans from formal institutions. Most often, these individuals do not have appropriate assets to offer as security, and even when they do possess property, they may not have the right documentation to prove legal ownership (Besley 1994). As a result, the lack of suitable land documentation also stands in the way of the financial inclusion of the poor.

The lack of access to formal financial services has serious negative consequences on the lives of the poor, while access to these services can enhance household welfare, regardless of their economic situation. Overall, research has shown that access to financial services results in reduced poverty, decreased inequality, and improved access to opportunities (Quach and Mullineux 2007; Burgess and Pande 2005; Honohan 2006; Kaboski and Townsend 2012; Pitt and Khandkar 1998). However, despite the ongoing benefits, credit access remains low and highly unequal, even in the current scenario where financial inclusion policies are being pursued and promoted in a big way.

Given this context, this chapter explores the socio-economic and other demand-side factors that constrain access to credit, with the aim of identifying obstacles that must be addressed to enhance financial inclusion.

4.3 Data and Methodology

To provide a brief country-level analysis of the different aspects of financial inclusion, we use the latest Findex database, which is published by the World Bank, with funding from the Melinda Gates Foundation. Four rounds of data have been brought out so far. First in 2011, second in 2014, and the last one in 2017. The 2021 edition, which is the latest survey, is a cross-country survey covering about 128,000 adults aged 15 years and above in 123 countries, and for India, 3000 respondents were surveyed. The survey has been done using telephonic interviews and face-to-face interviews. In countries where telephone coverage is less than 80 per cent, face-to-face interviews have been conducted.

Though Findex gives recent data on access and use of financial services such as credit, savings, and remittances, it does not give information about the various social classes, level of state-wise access, and access to informal sources, which are central issues in this book. Hence, the main analysis in the chapter will be conducted using NSSO household-level data.

The All-India Debt and Investment Survey (AIDIS) provided by NSSO gives comprehensive information on access to credit across India. To provide a comparative analysis, we use data from two consecutive rounds—the 70th and 77th Rounds of NSSO data. AIDIS is one of the large-scale sample surveys which provide information on households' access to formal and informal financial services. These surveys collect information on various aspects, including household characteristics, asset status, transactions, and the credit situation of the households. The 70th Round survey was conducted from January to December 2013, covering a total sample of 110,800 households, of which 62,135 households are from the rural sector and 48,665 households are from the urban sector. The 77th Round survey, carried out from January to December 2019, included 116,461 households with 69,455 households from the rural sector and 47,006 households from the urban sector. Both the 70th and 77th Rounds of the survey were conducted in two visits. We utilise the data from visit one as the data collected from the first visit itself provides comprehensive information on the credit situation of households and is sufficient to address the issues in the chapter.

To examine the different factors that may impact access to agricultural credit, we analyse data from the 70th Round of NSSO-AIDIS. We have restricted our analysis to rural cultivator/agricultural households, which are defined as households that have operated any land for agricultural activities in the past year. These households are further categorised into small, marginal, medium, and large farmers based on the size of the land they operate. The small farmers have less than one hectare, marginal farmers have one to two hectares, medium farmers have two to ten hectares, and large farmers have more than ten hectares. In this study, households are considered to have access to credit if they have borrowed any money at any time during the past year, up to the survey date. It is also worth noting here that the loan amount is recorded in the survey only if there is an existing loan (i.e. credit outstanding).

In the following sections, we begin by exploring the issue of credit accessibility using descriptive methods such as percentage analysis and graphical representation. We particularly examine whether different regions, social classes and wealth classes experience varying levels of access to credit. Such a descriptive analysis indicates the reasons for exclusion and the categories of population that require special attention. To rigorously assess the determinants of credit access, we carry out an econometric analysis using a double-hurdle model. The econometric model is explained in Sect. 4.5.

4.4 Access to Formal Credit to Rural Agricultural Households—Descriptive Analysis

First, to provide a comparison across major Asian countries, we use the Findex database of 2021. Figure 4.1 presents the percentage of respondents who have borrowed from any formal institution in the last year across major Asian countries.

Figure 4.1 reveals that only 13 per cent of the population in India has borrowed from financial institutions, placing India's credit access among the lowest compared to other major Asian countries. In the rural sector, this number drops to just 11 per cent (not shown in the figure). In contrast, China, Cambodia, and Thailand report the highest levels of credit access among the countries analysed.

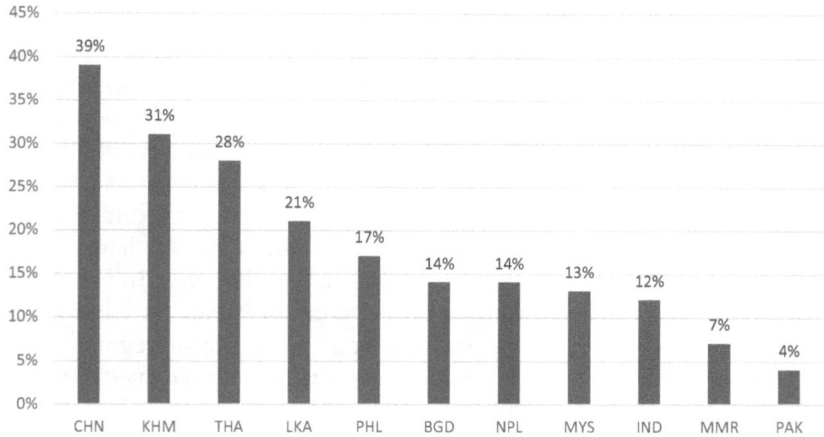

Fig. 4.1 Percentage of respondents (above 15 years) who have borrowed from any formal financial institution in the last year across major countries in Asia. *Note*: MYS-Malaysia, THA-Thailand, PHL-Philippines, KHM-Cambodia, CHN-China, NPL-Nepal, LKA-Sri Lanka, MMR-Myanmar, PAK-Pakistan, IND-India, BGD-Bangladesh. The figures represent the aggregate of both rural and urban regions of each country
(*Source* Authors' calculations using Findex Database 2021)

After providing a broad analysis of the accessibility to credit in India vis-a-vis other developing countries in Asia, we now address the accessibility question in some detail for India, using the NSSO survey, as it provides more information.

4.5 Access to Production Loans in Rural India

As discussed earlier, credit delivery, particularly for the agricultural sector, has been an important policy objective of the Government since independence. During the early days, the Indian population was largely agrarian, and so the agricultural sector played a critical role in developing the country's economy. Several measures were introduced to improve agricultural credit, starting from the nationalisation of banks in 1969 to expanding bank branches through the bank licensing policy.

Recent policies and schemes such as the Kisan Credit Card (KCC) and Pradhan Mantri Jan Dhan Yojana (PMJDY) have made improvements;

however, several challenges remain. The small and marginal farmers, who constitute the majority of the farmers in rural India, continue to have a hard time. Many of them still rely on informal sources of credit from moneylenders, due to various constraints in accessing formal credit. Additionally, studies show that regional disparities persist, with some states and regions seeing better access to credit than others.

To get an idea of how access to production credit is changing over the recent years, we present a comparative analysis of data using the 70th and 77th Round AIDIS. Figure4.2 gives us the percentages of rural cultivator households accessing production loans across the different states. Our analysis reveals that the percentage of households accessing production credit remained low across most states in both 2003 and 2013, with particularly low access observed in states like Bihar and Assam.

The figure also shows that the overall percentage of cultivator households accessing production credit increased modestly from 23 per cent to 26 per cent. For most states, the improvement in the use of production loans remained limited. Notably, states such as Odisha and Telangana

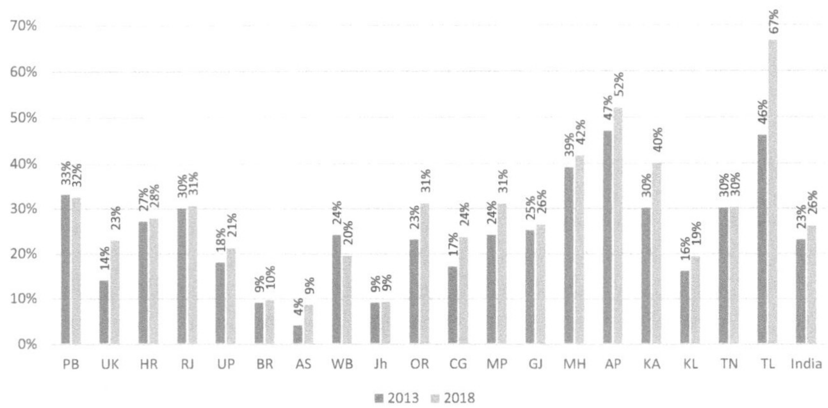

Fig. 4.2 Percentage of rural cultivator households accessing formal production loans across major states.
Note -MH-Maharashtra, KA-Karnataka, HR-Haryana, RJ-Rajasthan, OR-Orissa, GJ-Gujarat, PB-Punjab, BR-Bihar, UP-Uttar Pradesh, MP-Madhya Pradesh, AS-Assam, KL-Kerala, TN-Tamil Nadu, WB-West Bengal, AP-Andhra Pradesh
(*Source* Author's calculations using 70th and 77th Rounds of NSSO-AIDIS data)

Table 4.1 Percentage of indebted cultivator households according to land holdings—NSSO 77th Round

	Incidence of indebtedness(%)	*Average Amount of debt per indebted farmer HH (Rupees)*
Marginal(< = 1HA)	32	₹ 1,28,295
Small(1 < x < = 2A)	41	₹ 1,37,501
Semi Medium(2 < x < = 4HA)	49	₹ 2,14,125
Medium(4 < x < = 10HA)	61	₹ 3,00,398
Large(>10HA)	60	₹ 4,92,874
Total	40	₹ 1,84,359

Source Author's calculations using 77th Round of NSSO-AIDIS data
Note Average amount of debt –includes loans taken for both income-generating as well as non-income-generating purposes. Households are said to be accessing credit if it has outstanding credit as of 30.06.2008

experienced a significant increase in access to production loans from formal sources.

As mentioned earlier, a key concern regarding the agricultural sector is the predominance of small and marginal farmers. Data from the last two agricultural censuses reveal a steady increase in the number of operational landholdings, while the average size of landholdings has been decreasing. In 2005, the number of landholdings was 129 million, which had increased to 138 million in 2011. The average land holdings according to the 2011 agricultural census were around 1.5 hectares. In our sample, we see that 50 per cent of the households are marginal farmers and 22 per cent of households are small farmers (NSSO, 2013).

Table 4.1 clearly shows that large farmers have borrowed significantly more than small and marginal farmers. For instance, the average loan amount outstanding per large farmer household is around ₹ 4.92 lakhs, while for the marginal farmer household, it is around ₹1.3 lakhs. This is expected as the large borrowers have larger land sizes and, due to the established "scale of finance" provisions, they are eligible for larger loans.

4.5.1 *Are Informal Lenders Still Relevant in Rural India?*

As alluded to previously, there has been an increase in dependence on non-institutional credit, especially since the 1990s (Chattopadhyay, 2011; Rajeev and Bhattacharjee, 2012). Non-institutional finance remains an important part of the financial structure in rural India, and, for better or for worse, there is a coexistence of institutional and non-institutional sources of credit. The dependence on non-institutional sources, however, has reduced since 2013. More precisely, the percentage of rural households having money lenders or input trader loans at the all-India level decreased from 20 per cent in 2013 to 13 per cent in 2019.

Most states show a decrease in the dependence on moneylenders; however, some states, such as Punjab, Uttar Pradesh, Orissa, Maharashtra, and Kerala, show an increase in this dependence. Most importantly for states such as Punjab, Andhra Pradesh, Karnataka, Kerala, Orissa, and Tamil Nadu, the percentage of dependence is uncomfortably high. Surprisingly, in the Southern states, there is a high percentage of households which are dependent on non-institutional (excluding friends and relatives) credit. This shows that there is ample credit demand to be met by the formal institutions.

The credit demand for income-generating purposes is for fixed capital expenditures and working capital expenditures. The non-income-generating purposes mainly include housing, consumption expenditure, educational expenditure, medical expenditure, and other such expenditures. From our data, we find that institutional credit is mainly used for income-generating purposes, for current and capital expenditure and non-institutional credit is used for consumption purposes. A careful look at Table 4.2 shows that a larger percentage of households (18% in 2019) take loans for non-income-generating purposes from non-institutional sources, while only 4% of the loans from non-institutional sources are for income-generating purposes.

Table 4.2 Change in percentage of rural agricultural households accessing credit by purpose

	Institutional Credit		*Non-Institutional Credit*	
	2013(%)	*2018(%)*	*2013(%)*	*2018(%)*
Income-generating	16	19	4	4
Non-Income-generating	14	13	16	18

Source Author's calculations using 70th and 77th Rounds of NSSO-AIDIS data

Usually, households borrowing from informal lenders obtain loans through personal security. This is one of the main reasons why moneylenders are thriving in rural areas. Usually, when farmers are not able to obtain formal credit, they approach informal lenders, especially in an emergency (Kochar 1997; Mohieldin and Wright 2014; Chowdhary and Gupta 1996). The urgency of the requirement forces them to accept loans at much higher interest rates.

We observe from our analysis of the 77th Round data that the majority of the agricultural households borrowing from institutional agencies borrow at a rate of less than 12 per cent. However, in the case of non-institutional sources, most of the loans are above 12 per cent. Around 57 per cent of farmers (who borrowed from moneylenders) borrowed at a rate in the range of 12 per cent to 24 per cent, 23 per cent borrowed at rates in the range of 24 per cent to 36 per cent and a further 15 per cent borrowed at rates above 36 per cent.

In the above section, we carried out a preliminary analysis of the credit exclusion of agricultural households in India. These initial results must be tested using rigorous econometric methods to make further conclusions. Therefore, in the following section, we employ a double-hurdle model to explore the various factors that determine access to formal agricultural credit and the extent of formal agricultural credit taken by rural agricultural households. Such an analysis will help us to identify the segments that need special attention.

4.6 Econometric Analysis and Results

In this section, we move on to the core issue of credit access, and we explore the factors that determine access to formal credit and the extent of formal agricultural credit taken, using a double-hurdle model. Mere access is not enough because if the loan amount is small and insufficient, it may lead one to partly depend on the informal sector again. We consider production loans in our analysis, as these loans fall under priority sector lending and are necessary for the livelihood of the farmer community. The following sections discuss the method in detail, the possible determinants, and finally, the results of the analysis.

4.6.1 Econometric Method

In this section, we outline the methodology used for the regression analysis. The dependent variable is the amount of production loans taken by agricultural households. This variable takes a continuous value when a household has obtained a loan and zero when no loan is taken. Considering the structure of the dependent variable, which includes both zero outcomes and continuous values, we use a double-hurdle model for estimation. This model is appropriate as it separately analyses the decision to borrow and the amount borrowed in two stages (Cragg 1971).

In the first hurdle, which is a probit model, we examine whether a household has taken a loan, coded as 1 if the household has a loan, and 0 otherwise. The second hurdle looks at the actual amount of loan taken, recorded as a positive value if the household has borrowed, and 0 if not. We interpret the first hurdle as representing access to loans and the second hurdle as representing the usage or extent of borrowing.

4.6.2 Variables Used

In our analysis, the dependent variable is the logarithm value of total production credit from formal sources. It takes a positive value for households that have accessed a formal loan and zero if no loan has been taken. The loan amount considered here is the total loan taken for income-generating agricultural activities.

The explanatory variables in the model are the following. We have included a dummy variable to represent a small/marginal farmer household. It takes the value of one if the farmer household has an operational land holding of less than one hectare and zero for all others (The classification of farmers has been given in sect. 4.3). Another explanatory variable we have included in the model is the wealth of the household. Since we do not have the income or consumption expenditure of the household from the survey, we have taken the value of total assets as a proxy for it.

Further, we have included the total rural irrigated land area owned by the household in the model, anticipating that this variable will have a positive effect on access to formal agricultural credit. Another variable that we have included is the average interest rate charged by moneylenders. The interest rate is averaged over each of the states, and we expect that as the moneylender interest rates increase, the amount of loans taken from formal institutions will also increase (See Bhattacharjee and Rajeev, 2013).

Other household characteristics such as caste, gender of household head and age of household head have also been included in the analysis. The caste variable comprises three categories, namely scheduled castes and tribes, other backward castes, and the general castes. The gender of the household head is represented by a dummy variable which is equal to one if the head of the household is a female, and zero otherwise.

We have also considered the maximum level of education in the household. One of the reasons for people not accessing banking products is the lack of awareness about products and also unfamiliarity or difficulty with procedures (Cole, Sampson, and Zia 2011). Households with higher educated individuals will have a better understanding of the various procedures involved in procuring a loan, and therefore, households with higher educated members are likely to have better access to credit in comparison to households with lower educational attainment. We have classified households based on the maximum education in the households: below primary, primary, secondary, and tertiary.

The ratio of the number of children to the total household size and the household size has also been accounted for, based on the reasoning that a higher number of dependents is likely to cause more financial deficiency, resulting in higher demand for credit. We have also included the region dummies as control variables to account for the common regional characteristics. The list of variables and summary statistics is provided in the Appendix Table A8.

4.6.3 Analysis and Results

As mentioned in the above section, the dependent variable is the logarithm value of the total agricultural credit amount borrowed from formal sources. Table 4.3 reports the regression results.

The model shows that the wealth status of the household has a significant and positive effect on access as well as the amount of credit. This is consistent with the widely prevalent view that Government subsidies and programmes help the better-off households while the disadvantaged are excluded (Besley 1994; Adams 1992). The better economic position of these households may give them better access to funds from financial institutions.

Table 4.3 Double-hurdle model—Determinants of production credit amount for rural agricultural households

	(Tier 1)	*(Tier 2)*
Variables	Access to credit	Credit Amount
Log of total asset (wealth)	0.1306***	0.3597***
	(0.019)	(0.019)
Small/marginal	−0.6039***	−0.2557***
	(0.054)	(0.048)
Average interest rate-ML		0.0240***
		(0.003)
Total irrigated area	0.1702***	0.0800***
	(0.032)	(0.013)
(Base-SCST)		
OBC	0.0459	0.1146***
	(0.042)	(0.040)
General	0.1534***	0.2649***
	(0.050)	(0.058)
Female head	−0.4898***	−0.1294*
	(0.061)	(0.077)
(Base-Below primary)		
Primary	0.1408***	0.0487
	(0.051)	(0.049)
Secondary	0.1452***	0.1664***
	(0.053)	(0.056)
Tertiary	0.1749**	0.1702***
	(0.075)	(0.059)
Age of household head	0.0184**	0.0120
	(0.009)	(0.009)
Age of household head sq	−0.0001	−0.0001
	(0.000)	(0.000)
Household size	−0.0126	0.0168*
	(0.009)	(0.009)
Ratio of children	−0.2782***	−0.0560
	(0.101)	(0.092)
(Base-North)		
North-East	−0.7619***	−0.4886***
	(0.067)	(0.085)
East	0.0366	−0.8974***
	(0.060)	(0.086)
Central	0.0857	−0.5063***
	(0.053)	(0.064)
West	0.4430***	−0.5333***
	(0.058)	(0.059)

(continued)

Table 4.3 (continued)

	(Tier 1)	*(Tier 2)*
South	0.0070	−0.0350
	(0.060)	(0.071)
Constant	−2.2309***	4.6339***
	(0.328)	(0.364)
Sigma	−0.0980***	
	(0.017)	
Observations	30,155	30,155

Dependent Variable: Amount of total production credit from formal sources
Robust standard errors in parentheses, *** $p < 0.01$, ** $p < 0.05$, *$p < 0.1$

Our analysis also reveals that small and marginal farm households have a significant negative association with access to loans, as well as with the extent of money borrowed, implying that small/ marginal farmers have a disadvantage in accessing formal agricultural loans as compared to others. As expected, the average interest rate charged by the moneylenders is positively and significantly associated with the amount of formal production credit. This suggests that when the interest rates charged by moneylenders are high, the amount of formal loans taken by households also increases.

The caste of the agricultural household also plays a significant role. The coefficients of caste variables are negative and significant, implying that the disadvantaged caste groups, such as SC/STs and OBCs, have a lower probability of accessing credit as compared to the general castes. From the second stage of the model, even after controlling for household assets(wealth), we again see that scheduled castes and tribes (SC/STs) and other backward castes (OBCs) obtain lower amounts of credit compared to general castes.

Our model further reveals that female-headed households have a significantly lower probability of accessing formal credit compared to male-headed households, highlighting a gender-based disparity in access to formal production credit. We also find that households with members having secondary and higher education have a higher probability of accessing formal credit as well as larger loan amounts when compared to below-primary-educated households. Most of the loan agreements may require at least some level of paperwork, which may become an impediment for less-educated individuals. Additionally, other control variables such as age, household size, ratio of children, and regional dummies show expected signs.

4.7 Concluding Observations

This chapter examines credit accessibility for agricultural households in rural India. While the reliance on informal credit sources has declined since 2013, these sources still remain relevant, with dependence on informal credit increasing in certain states. The supply-side data reveals that the southern states have a higher outreach of formal financial institutions as compared to the rest of India, however, analysis from this chapter shows that the dependence on moneylenders is also higher for the southern states. This indicates that there is an unmet credit demand that formal institutions are yet to adequately address. There may be several reasons for this, such as the purpose of the loan and repayment history, which need to be carefully analysed.

Further, we have attempted to understand the differential access to credit among rural cultivator households. We have compared data from two time points using the 70th and the 77th Rounds of the NSSO-All-India Debt and Investment Surveys, and the analysis shows the existence of substantial disparity amongst the states in access to loans. States such as Bihar and Assam show very low access to loans in the latest round, indicating significant scope for improvements.

The econometric analysis reveals that small/marginal farmers have a lower probability of accessing formal production credit compared to larger farmers and tend to receive lower amounts of loans. A part of small and marginal farmers, as well as landless farmers, do not have clear land title records as mutations do not take place automatically in several states, and this becomes a key impediment in accessing formal loans in certain states (Rajeev and Vani 2011). Therefore, improving and updating land ownership records is an urgent priority to ensure equitable access to formal finance.

Further, the results also establish that socially disadvantaged caste groups face similar challenges, with a reduced likelihood of accessing formal credit and receiving smaller amounts of loans than households from the general castes. This indicates that the affirmative policies of the Government have not yet fully removed inequalities in access to formal finance for agricultural households.

Appendix

Table A8 Summary statistics—Agricultural households-rural sector

Variables	*Description of variable*	*Mean*	*Std. Dev*	*Min*	*Max*
Log production loan	Log value of production loan	4.104	5.197	0	15.202
Log total assets (wealth)	Log value of total assets owned	13.452	1.245	0	19.323
Small/Marginal	= 1 if the household belongs to small/ marginal category	0.880		0	1
Average interest rate-ML	Average interest rate of moneylender (state)	34.163	9.924	0	60
Irrigated land	Irrigated land owned (Hectares)	0.412	1.017	0	29.115
Base = SCST	= 1 if the household belongs to the SC/ST category	0.362		0	1
OBC	= 1 if the household belongs to Other backward caste	0.392		0	1
General	= 1 if the household belongs to the general caste	0.245		0	1
Female head	= 1 if the head of household is female	0.091		0	1
Base-Below primary	= 1 if the maximum educational level in the household is below primary	0.203		0	1
Primary	= 1 if the maximum educational level in the household is primary	0.307		0	1
Secondary	= 1 if the maximum educational level in the household is secondary	0.380		0	1
Tertiary	= 1 if the maximum educational level in the household is tertiary	0.111		0	1
Age of household head	Age of household head	48.583	13.090	13	101
Household size	Number of members in the household	5.135	2.389	1	36
Ratio of children	Number of children to total household size	0.262	0.223	0	0.857
Base-North	= 1 if Northern zone	0.138		0	1

(continued)

(continued)

Variables	*Description of variable*	*Mean*	*Std. Dev*	*Min*	*Max*
North-East	= 1 if North-Eastern zone	0.137		0	1
East	= 1 if Eastern zone	0.208		0	1
Central	= 1 if Central zone	0.253		0	1
West	= 1 if Western zone	0.118	0.322	0	1
South	= 1 if Southern zone	0.147	0.354	0	1

References

Adams, Dale W. 1992. "Taking a Fresh Look at Informal Finance." In *Informal Finance in Low Income Countries*, edited by Dale W. Adams and Delbert A. Fitchett, 5–23. Colorado: Westview Press.

Amjad, Shehla, and Saf Hasnu. 2007. "Small Holders' Access to Rural Credit: Evidence from Pakistan." *The Lahore Journal of Economics* 12 (2): 1–25.

Ayyagari, Meghana, Asli Demirguc-Kunt, and Vojislav Maksimovic. 2010. "Formal versus Informal Finance: Evidence from China." *Review of Financial Studies* 23 (8): 3048–3097. https://doi.org/10.1093/rfs/hhq030.

Bell, Clive. 1991. "Interactions between Institutional and Informal Credit Agencies in Rural India." *The World Bank Economic Review* 4 (3): 297–327. http://documents.worldbank.org/curated/en/160931468756339586/Interactions-between-institutional-and-informal-credit-agencies-in-rural-India.

Besley, Timothy. 1994. "How Do Market Failures Justify Interventions in Credit Markets?" *The World Bank Research Observer* 9 (1): 27–47.

Bhattacharjee, Manojit, and Meenakshi Rajeev. 2013. "Modeling Loan Repayment Behavior in Developing Countries." *Applied Economic Perspectives and Policy* 35 (2): 270–295.

Bose, Pinaki. 1998. "Formal—Informal Sector Interaction in Rural Credit Markets." *Journal of Development Economics* 56 (2): 265–280.

Burgess, Robin, and Rohini Pande. 2005. Do Rural Banks Matter ? Evidence From the Indian Social Banking Experiment. *American Economic Review* 95 (3): 780–795. https://doi.org/10.1257/0002828054201242.

Chattopadhyay, Sadhan Kumar. 2011. "Financial Inclusion in India: A Case-Study of West Bengal." 34269. MPRA Working Paper. Munich. https://mpra.ub.uni-muenchen.de/34269/1/Financial_Inclusion_in_India.pdf.

Chowdhary, S., and M. R. Gupta. 1996. "Delayed Formal Credit, Bribing and the Informal Credit Market in Agriculture: A Theoretical Analysis." *Journal of Development Economics* 51 (2): 433–449.

Cole, Shawn, Thomas Sampson, and Bilal Zia. 2011. "Prices or Knowledge? What Drives Demand for Financial Services in Emerging Markets?" *Journal of Finance* 66 (6): 1933–1967.

Cragg, John G. 1971. "Some Statistical Models for Limited Dependent Variables with Application to the Demand for Durable Goods." *Econometrica* 39 (5): 829–844.

Deb, Sharmistha, and Meenakshi Rajeev. 2007. "Banking on ' Baniyas ' for Credit." *Economic and Political Weekly* 42 (4): 280–283.

Diagne, Aliou. 1999. "Determinants of Household Access to and Participation in Formal and Informal Credit Markets in Malawi." *International Food Policy Research Institute* 67 (67): 1–62.

Feder, Gershon, Lawrence J. Lau, Justin Y. Lin, and Xiaopeng Luo. 1990. "The Relationship Between Credit and Productivity in Chinese Agriculture: A Microeconomic Model of Disequilibrium." *American Journal of Agricultural Economics* 72 (5): 1151–1157.

Fletschner, Diana. 2009. "Rural Women's Access to Credit: Market Imperfections and Intrahousehold Dynamics." *World Development* 37 (3): 618–631. https://doi.org/10.1016/j.worlddev.2008.08.005.

Ghosh, Parikshit, Dilip Mookherjee, and Debraj Ray. 2000. "Credit Rationing in Developing Countries: An Overview of the Theory." In *Readings in the Theory of Economic Development*, edited by Dilip Mookherjee and Debraj Ray, ch 11: 283–301. London: Blackwell.

Ghosh, Saibal, and D. Vinod. 2012. "Determinants Of Banking Outreach: An Empirical Assessment of Indian States." *The Journal of Developing Areas* 46 (2): 269–295. https://doi.org/10.1353/jda.2012.0034.

Ghosh, Saibal, and Dharmarajan Vinod. 2017. "What Constrains Financial Inclusion for Women? Evidence from Indian Micro Data." *World Development* 92: 60–81. https://doi.org/10.1016/j.worlddev.2016.11.011.

Gill, Anita. 2016. "Agricultural Credit in Punjab: Have Policy Initiatives Made a Dent in Informal Credit Markets?" In *Economic Transformation of a Developing Economy*, edited by Lakhwinder Singh and Nirvikar Singh, 165–182. Singapore: Springer.

GOI. 2018a. "Doubling Farmers' Income." Report of the Committee on Doubling Farmers' Income. New Delhi.

Honohan, Patrick. 2006. "Household Financial Assets in the Process of Development." WPS 3965. World Bank Policy Research Working Paper. Washington,D.C.

Kaboski, Joseph P., and Robert M. Townsend. 2012. "The Impact of Credit on Villages." *American Journal of Applied Economics* 4 (2): 98–133. https://doi.org/10.1257/app.4.3.98.

Kannan, Elumalai. 2011. "Relationship between Agricultural Credit Policy, Credit Disbursements and Crop Productivity: A Study in Karnataka." *Indian*

Journal of Agricultural Economics 66 (3): 444–56. https://doi.org/10.22004/ag.econ.204767.

Kannan, Elumalai. 2015. "Trends in Agricultural Income: An Analysis at the Select Crop and State Levels in India." *Journal of Agrarian Change* 15 (2): 201–19. https://doi.org/10.1111/joac.12068.

Kashuliza, Anacleti K., and Jonathan G. Kydd. 1996. "Determinants of Bank Credit Access Forn Smallholder Farmers in Tanzania: A Discriminant Analysis Application." *Savings and Development* 20 (3): 285–304.

Kochar, Anjini. 1997. "An Empirical Investigation of Rationing Constraints in Rural Credit Markets in India." *Journal of Development Economics* 53 (2): 339–371. https://doi.org/10.1016/S0304-3878(97)00020-5.

Kumar, Nitin. 2013a. "Financial Inclusion and Its Determinants: Evidence from India." *Journal of Financial Economic Policy* 5 (1): 4–19. https://doi.org/10.1108/17576381311317754.

Kumar, Sunil Mitra. 2013b. "Does Access to Formal Agricultural Credit Depend on Caste?" *World Development* 43 (March): 315–328. https://doi.org/10.1016/j.worlddev.2012.11.001.

Mohieldin, Mahmoud S., and Peter W. Wright. 2014. "Formal and Informal Credit Markets in Egypt." *Economic Development and Cultural Change* 48 (3): 657–670.

Pal, Sarmistha. 2002. "Household Sectoral Choice and Effective Demand for Rural Credit in India." *Applied Economics* 34 (14): 1743–1755. https://doi.org/10.1080/00036840210121228.

Pitt, Mark M., and Shahidur R. Khandkar. 1998. "The Impact of Group-Based Credit Programs on Poor Households in Bangladesh: Does the Gender of Participants Matter?" *The Journal of Political Economy* 106 (5): 958–996.

Pradhan, Narayan Chandra. 2013. "Persistence of Informal Credit in Rural India: Evidence from 'All-India Debt and Investment Survey' and Beyond. WPS (DEPR): 05/2013." RBI Working Paper Series, Reserve Bank of India, India.

Quach, M., and A. Mullineux. 2007. "The Impact of Access to Credit on Household Welfare in Rural Vietnam." *Research in Accounting in Emerging Economies* 7: 279–307.

Rajeev, Meenakshi, and Manojit Bhattacharjee. 2012. "Access to Financial Services : Are Poor Excluded ?" 808. Norwegian Institute of International Affairs Working Paper. Oslo,Norway. https://brage.bibsys.no/xmlui/handle/11250/277551.

Rajeev, Meenakshi, B. P. Vani, and Manojit Bhattacharjee. 2011. Credibility of Equal Access to Credit:Does Gender Matter? *Economic & Political Weekly* 46 (33): 76–79.

Rajeev, Meenakshi, and B. P. Vani. 2011. "Farm Sector in Karnataka: Farmers' Indebtedness and Risk Management." Project Report No. CESP/93." Bangalore: ISEC.

Stiglitz, Joseph E., and Andrew Weiss. 1981. "Credit Rationing in Markets with Imperfect Information." *The American Economic Review* 71 (3): 393–410.

Wossen, Tesfamicheal, Tahirou Abdoulaye, Arega Alene, Mekbib G. Haile, Shiferaw Feleke, Adetunji Olanrewaju, and Victor Manyong. 2017. "Impacts of Extension Access and Cooperative Membership on Technology Adoption and Household Welfare." *Journal of Rural Studies* 54: 223–33. https://doi.org/doi:10.1016/j.jrurstud.2017.06.022.

Zeller, Manfred. 1994. "Determinants of Credit Rationing: A Study of Informal Lenders and Formal Credit Groups in Madagascar." *World Development* 22 (12): 1895–1907.

Zeller, Manfred, Aliou Diagne, and Charles Mataya. 1998. "Market Access by Smallholder Farmers in Malawi: Implications for Technology Adoption, Agricultural Productivity and Crop Income." *Agricultural Economics* 19: 219–229.

CHAPTER 5

Financial Inclusion and Credit Access: A Case of Urban India

5.1 Introduction

In the previous chapter, we examined credit accessibility in the rural sector, and in the current chapter, we extend the discussion to the urban sector. In Chapter 3, we made the observation that financial inclusion in the urban sector has improved substantially over the years. However, the important question remains whether the poorer sections and the disadvantaged categories have access to financial services or not.

Building on this broad concern, this chapter focuses on urban self-employed households, who are in regular need of finance, and examines whether they have adequate access to credit. Most of these households operate as own-account enterprises with little or no savings, and therefore, are in constant need of external funds to meet their fixed and working capital requirements (Rajeev and Vani 2017). Notably, self-employment in urban areas is often adopted not by choice but often as a coping mechanism in the face of high unemployment and lack of formal sector job opportunities (Banerjee and Duflo 2011). Most of these enterprises are small in scale and scope, which constrains their growth potential and long-term sustainability. For instance, our data indicates that 26% of the urban self-employed households in the non-farm sector have assets valued at less than three lakh rupees.

S. Saravanabhavan and M. Rajeev, *Moving Beyond Barriers*, Palgrave Studies in Impact Finance,
https://doi.org/10.1007/978-981-95-1066-5_5

Several studies have pointed out that the main challenge faced by these small enterprises is the difficulty in obtaining timely financial support (Ayyagari et al., 2008; Beck and Demirguc-Kunt 2006). A frequently cited reason for the lack of access to formal credit is the absence of robust financial infrastructure (Demirguc-Kunt et al., 2008; Rajeev et al., 2017). It is worth noting here that urban areas are much better endowed than rural areas in terms of financial infrastructure. For instance, as of March 2018, only 34% of the total bank branches were in rural areas, and the rest were situated in urban, semi-urban, and metropolitan regions (27% in semi-urban, 19% in urban areas, and 20% in metropolitan areas).[1] Conceptually, better infrastructure should lead to higher levels of credit accessibility. Our analysis, however, points out that even in urban areas, credit access for the self-employed remains disproportionately low.

Existing studies on credit access predominantly focus on rural agricultural credit (Kochar 1997; Bell 1991; Rajeev et al. 2012; Rakesh 2006; Binswanger and Khandker 1995; Gadgil 1986), while studies on urban credit are few and far between. This emphasis on rural agricultural credit is rooted in India's historical context, where a majority of households relied on agriculture. Accordingly, Government policies during the 1970s and 1980s were also directed towards improving rural agricultural credit systems. In contrast, the needs of non-agricultural self-employed households received comparatively less attention.[2]

Dynamics, however, are rapidly changing as India is increasingly becoming urban, with rural-to-urban migration fast growing due to agricultural sector problems, lack of jobs, and low income in rural areas. While India's urban sector is expanding, formal sector jobs remain limited, and a large proportion of the urban population lacks the requisite skills or education to secure formal sector jobs (Bhowmik 2005). Consequently, for many individuals, self-employment has become an important means of employment. However, the survival of such businesses is critically dependent on access to finance, and many micro-entrepreneurs depend on informal traders for loans.

[1] RBI bank branch statistics. RBI has classified the centres according to the size of the population: rural with less than 10,000, semi-urban with above 10,000 and less than 1 lakh, urban with above 1 lakh and less than 10 lakh, and metropolitan with 10 lakh and above.

[2] UNDP (2009): India Urban Poverty Report 2009.

Given these issues, this chapter seeks to analyse the barriers to credit access in urban areas, with an emphasis on households engaged in self-employment.[3] Initially, in our analysis, we assess whether or not access to credit for the urban self-employed has shown any improvement over time. Further, we examine the terms and conditions of loans and explore how credit access for the self-employed varies across states and various economic and social classes.

Subsequently, we also subject these observations to rigorous econometric analysis to identify the factors that hinder or aid access to credit. We are particularly interested in understanding whether factors such as financial infrastructure contribute to enhancing credit access to urban self-employed. For our research, we primarily use the data from the 70th and 77th Rounds of the NSSO-All-India Debt and Investment survey. Findings stemming from this analysis have valuable policy implications, as they indicate the challenges faced by formal financial institutions in providing access, as well as indicate the specific groups of the population lacking access to formal credit.

Following the introduction, the rest of the chapter is organised as follows. Section 5.2 provides a brief overview of the existing literature. Section 5.3 describes the data and definitions used in the study. Section 5.4 examines the differential access to credit across the various states and socio-economic categories. Section 5.5 discusses the empirical analysis and results. Section 5.6 concludes the chapter with a summary of insights and implications.

5.2 A Brief Background

This section discusses the different strands of literature on the issue of credit access among the self-employed. To begin with, we discuss the relevance of credit in facilitating productive investment. Next, we delve into the underlying causes of credit rationing, and finally, we focus on the specific attributes of small informal enterprises and how they impact formal credit access.

[3] As demand for credit by others are not certain. But this group needs funds on a regular basis and usually borrows from informal lenders. This fact has been revealed from various field-survey-based studies (Rajeev and Vani 2017).

5.2.1 *Relevance of Credit in Improving Productive Investment*

Numerous scholars have emphasised the role of banks in fostering innovation and enhancing production processes in the economy (McKinnon 1973; King and Levine 1993; Evans and Jovanovic 1989; Schumpeter 1934). The establishment of a new enterprise requires financial capital, however, when external resources are lacking, individuals or households have to depend on their personal funds (Evans and Jovanovic 1989). This is a serious disadvantage for poor households that lack any resources for initial investment. Furthermore, the expansion of existing enterprises also depends on the availability of finance (Paulson and Townsend 2004). A lack of sufficient financial capital often results in growth stagnation. Despite the evident importance of formal finance to small enterprises, we observe a general reluctance on the part of formal institutions to lend to small entrepreneurs or self-employed households (Beck and Demirguc-Kunt 2006).

5.2.2 *Reasons for Credit Rationing by Lenders*

A significant body of literature that addresses the lack of access to bank credit dwells on the concept of information asymmetry and its consequent phenomenon, credit rationing, which leads financial intermediaries to be cautious in lending to certain borrowers (Stiglitz and Weiss 1981). In urban regions, bank branches are usually overburdened with a large number of customers, which makes monitoring the customers a formidable task.

As a result, the banks reduce the credit given to potential customers (usually small borrowers), leading to inadequate investment. Furthermore, due to a lack of borrower information, the banks typically insist on some form of security as a condition for lending, a requirement that is usually a disadvantage for poor households who lack proper property documents[4] (Rajeev and Vani 2011). This may result in relatively richer households or individuals appropriating most of the formal credit services.

[4] Many poor vendors sit on pavements and do not even have a small shop(Rajeev and Vani 2017).

5.2.3 *Characteristics of Informal Enterprises*

In most of the developing countries, including India, self-employment generally means "survival self-employment" (Fields 2013). This is mainly because, for many households, self-employment is more of a necessity than a choice. Many individuals lack the skillset to be employed in the formal sector. Consequently, they are unable to get meaningful jobs, leading to many engaging in small ventures such as running small retail shops and engaging in roadside hawking.

Furthermore, a significant portion of these household enterprises operate within the informal sector, which is characterised by low levels of investment and a reliance on personal, social, or informal networks for financial and operational support. While some individuals may choose to enter the informal sector voluntarily to benefit from weaker regulatory oversight and fewer legal obligations (DeSoto 1989), in the Indian context, it is survival-driven self-employment that predominates (Gurtoo and Williams 2009).

These household enterprises are often seen as the "first unit of micro-entrepreneurship" with the potential to grow into more efficient and sustainable ventures when the economic environment becomes favourable (Das 2003). With appropriate support, these enterprises could transform into reliable sources of income and employment, especially for low-income households (Banerjee and Duflo 2011; Demirguc-Kunt, Klapper, and Panos 2007). However, most of these enterprises lack any savings to fuel such expansion and require external funds for their everyday expenses and long-term investments.

5.3 Data and Definitions

The main data sources for this chapter are the 70th and 77th Rounds of the NSSO-All-India Debt and Investment Survey. These datasets provide detailed information on urban households, their assets, and the household's borrowings from formal/institutional as well as informal/non-institutional sources. A detailed description of this data was provided in Chapter 4.

As mentioned earlier, our analysis focuses exclusively on self-employed urban households. According to the NSSO, a self-employed person is one who "is engaged independently in a profession or trade on own account or with one or a few partners working in household enterprises".

The workers/entrepreneurs are categorised as own-account workers, employers, and helpers (NSSO 2014).

Own-account entrepreneurs are self-employed individuals who operate enterprises with or without partners and without using hired labour. Employers/establishments, on the other hand, work as own-account workers with or without partners and run the enterprise using hired labour. The unpaid helpers assist the household enterprise without receiving any financial compensation (NSSO 2014). For our purposes, if the household has at least one member who is self-employed as an own-account worker or an employer, we define it to be a self-employed household.

With regard to sources of credit, formal credit includes loans from Banks and Cooperative Credit Institutions, Government schemes, self-help groups linked to banks and Non-Banking Financial Companies (NBFCs), and other such entities. According to AIDIS, a household is said to have access to credit if it has an outstanding credit on the date of the survey (with the disbursement date being any time before the survey date).

5.4 Descriptive Analysis: Credit Access to Urban Self-Employed Households

As we observed in the previous chapter, overall access to loans in India remains low compared to other major Asian countries such as China, Cambodia, and Thailand. Over the period from 2017 to 2021, the Findex survey data reveals that the percentage of adults borrowing from formal financial institutions increased marginally from 8% in 2017 to 12% in 2017, which is a modest 4% increase. When we specifically look at urban India, this figure stands at 13%, indicating a challenge in accessing credit even in urban areas.

Given this low rate of urban credit access, we further examine the issue in subsequent sections, using data from the 70th and 77th Rounds of the NSSO-AIDIS, which provide demand-side insights for the years 2013 and 2019, respectively. This data allows us to explore access to production credit across states and socio-economic categories in greater detail.

5.4.1 *A State-Wise Comparative Analysis: Credit Access to Urban Self-Employed Households*

Self-employed households in the non-farm sector engage in a diverse range of activities, including wholesale and retail trade, transport and storage, accommodation and food services, as well as manufacturing of textiles, leather, and related products. Of these different activities, wholesale and retail trade plays a significant role in the livelihoods of urban self-employed households, with approximately 40% of the non-farm sector households involved in this sector (See Fig. 5.1). This sector is predominantly characterised by unorganised retail, which includes small neighbourhood stores (kiranas), pavement vendors, and hawkers. It is important to note here that pavement vendors and hawkers who lack proper commercial spaces may find it particularly difficult to access loans from formal institutions (Rajeev and Vani 2017).

In Fig. 5.2, we present a state-wise analysis of access to production loans among self-employed households in the urban sector, illustrating the variation in access between 2013 and 2019. The figure reveals that only states such as West Bengal, Maharashtra, and Jharkhand have shown comparatively better improvements across the period of study. In West Bengal, access to production loans has improved from 12% to 17%, in

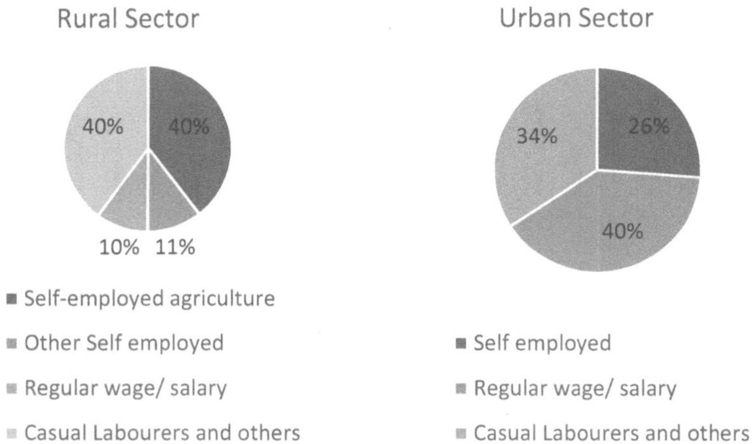

Fig. 5.1 Percentage of self-employed households in rural and urban sectors (*Source* Author's calculations using 77th Round of NSSO-AIDIS data)

Maharashtra access to production loans has improved from 5% to 12%, and in Jharkhand, the increase is from 8% to 12%. The remaining states under examination exhibit relatively modest improvements. Notably, in the Southern states, despite having a higher percentage of self-employed households accessing production loans from formal sources, there is a decrease in access during the study period.

When we investigate the lack of access across socio-economic groups (Table not shown), over time, we find that access to production loans has not improved much for any of the social groups. Overall, we could say that in the case of social categories, we do not observe much difference in access, implying that the variations in access to production loans are not significantly driven by disparities among different caste groups. Instead, it indicates that broader structural factors may be at play, affecting access to production credit in a consistent manner across social categories.

Table 5.1 presents the percentage of self-employed households accessing credit from various sources. Among those who borrow from either formal or informal sources, 36% obtain production credit from banks, while around 19% access through Self-Help groups. Women

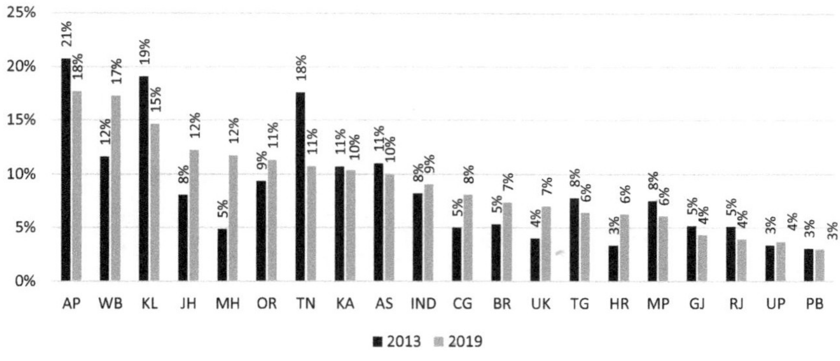

Fig. 5.2 Percentage of non-farm self-employed households in the urban sector who have access to production loans across major states

Note AP-Andhra Pradesh, WB-West Bengal, KL-Kerala, JH-Jharkhand, MH-Maharashtra, OR-Orissa, TN-Tamil Nadu, KA-Karnataka, AS-Assam, CG-Chhattisgarh, BR-Bihar, UK-Uttarakhand, TG-Telangana, HR-Haryana, MP-Madhya Pradesh, GJ-Gujarat, RJ-Rajasthan, UP-Uttar Pradesh, PB-Punjab, IND-India

(*Source* Author's calculations using 70th and 77th Rounds of NSSO-AIDIS data)

Table 5.1 Percentage of indebted urban self-employed households who have access to formal loans from different credit sources

Source of loan	*Percentage of households availing of loans(%)*
Commercial Banks	36
Regional Rural Banks	2
Cooperative societies/Banks	4
Bank-linked SHG/JL & Non-bank-linked SHG/BL	19
NBFC	9
PF/Employer/financial corporation/Others	7
Moneylender/chit funds/agents/traders	12

Note NBFC-Non-Bank Finance Corporations. *Source* Author's calculations using 70th Round of NSSO-AIDIS data

borrowers commonly rely on SHGs, as they often face barriers in accessing formal credit due to lower levels of education and lack of ownership of physical assets, which limits their eligibility for individual loans from formal institutions.

Among the households that access productive loans, a significant percentage—around 12% rely on loans from moneylenders and other informal lenders, who typically charge high interest rates. The persistent reliance on moneylenders likely stems from the challenges in accessing loans from formal financial institutions (see Beck, 2013; Rajeev and Vani, 2017). Most of the households obtaining informal production loans are burdened with annual interest rates of more than 20%. In contrast, the majority of loans from commercial banks and cooperative banks are provided at annual interest rates between 6 and 20%. Instances of very high interest rates in the formal sector may be rare and may arise when loans remain outstanding for a very long time, resulting in accumulated interest charges.

The above analysis reveals the low access to production loans to urban self-employed households. To further examine these preliminary observations, the next section employs a probit model with correction for sample selection to study the various factors that determine access to formal production credit among urban self-employed households.

5.5 Econometric Results and Analysis

Here, we present our analysis in three subsections. First, we explain the methodology used for the econometric analysis. Second, we identify the variables that influence access to production loans for urban self-employed households. In the third sub-section, we present the results of the analysis.

5.5.1 *Econometric Methodology*

The objective of this econometric analysis is to examine the factors that impact production loan access (non-farm) among urban self-employed households. In doing so, we must take care of two issues—modelling the households' decision to become self-employed, and their decision to avail production loans. These decisions are not independent of each other, as self-employment is a prerequisite for the need for a production loan. Since the decision to become self-employed in the non-farm sector is a non-random decision, it is important to account for potential selection bias in the analysis.

In such a scenario when we are modelling two dependent variables whose errors are likely to be correlated, and when sample selection bias is suspected, a probit model with sample selection correction is generally used (In the previous chapter where we had examined access to agricultural credit, we used a double-hurdle model as there is no issue of sample-selection bias. This is because most of the households in the rural sector are agricultural households. In India, agriculture as an occupation is handed down from generation to generation and therefore may not be appropriate to consider agriculture as a choice for these households).

According to Van de Ven and Van Pragg (1981), there is an underlying relationship such that the outcome of interest y_i^p is observed only if

$$y_i^* = x_i\beta + u_{1i}(\text{LatentEquation})$$

Or,

$y_i^p = 1$ if $y_i^* > 0$ (Probit equation/Outcome Equation).

However, the observations for the outcome variable, y_i^p, is not always observed; we observe y_i^p only if the selection variable is greater than zero

$$y_i^s = Z_i\alpha + u_{2i}0\,(Selection\ Equation)$$

where i refers to household i, $u_{1i}, u_{2i} \sim N(0,1)$ and $Cov(u_{1i}, u_{2i}) = \rho$;

When $\rho = 0$ a univariate probit model is sufficient.

We have: y_i^p=1 if a household decides to take a production loan, 0 otherwise;

y_i^s=1 if a household decides to get into self-employment, 0 otherwise. Data for y_i^p is observed only if y_i^s is equal to one. Therefore, we have three types of observations in the sample:

y_i^p is equal to zero when y_i^s is equal to zero;

y_i^p is equal to 1 when y_i^s is equal to 1;

y_i^p is equal to zero when y_i^s is equal to 1.

The likelihood function is built upon these three observations, and the model is estimated using the maximum likelihood estimation technique (Greene 2003). One important criterion for this model is that there should be at least one variable in the selection equation that is not included in the main outcome equation. In the absence of such a variable, the model is identified only by its functional form.

5.5.2 *Variables*

In this analysis, the dependent variable for the main "outcome equation" is access to formal loans for non-farm production purposes, which is a binary variable. This variable assumes a value of one for households that have procured production loans, but zero otherwise. The dependent variable for the "selection equation" is also binary, taking the value of one if the household decides to be self-employed, but zero if it is not.

As outlined in the methodology, this type of regression necessitates the inclusion of an exclusive variable, which is used only in the selection equation and not in the outcome equation. In our analysis, this exclusive variable is the number of unpaid helpers[5] within the household. Literature shows that unpaid workers play an important role in

[5] Here we are discussing access to production loans from banks. The banks are not concerned about the number of unpaid helpers in the enterprise and therefore it will not impact the decision whether the banks lend money to the specific microenterprise or not. However, having unpaid workers can increase chances of households becoming self-employed as the helpers provide free labour which are crucial for microenterprises which lacks capital or funds to hire external help. Literature shows that unpaid workers play an important role in self-employed households and it is a common characteristic of small enterprises in developing countries (Margolis2014; Tambunan 2009).

self-employed households, and are also a common feature of small enterprises in developing countries (Margolis 2014; Tambunan 2009). The other explanatory variables used in the analysis are as follows.

Our primary focus is to understand the influence of financial infrastructure on access to credit. For this, we have used the demographic outreach of bank branches/bank infrastructure as one of the explanatory variables. This variable is calculated by dividing the total number of urban bank branches in each state by the total adult urban population. Next, we have included a binary variable to represent whether or not a household enterprise operates within the service sector. The service sector is the most dominant category and comprises a wide range of activities such as retail and wholesale trade, hotels and restaurants, entertainment, transport, education, health, financial services and insurance.

Another important explanatory variable used in the analysis is the urban land area owned by a household. This variable serves as a proxy for physical property or immovable assets, often used as security to avail loans. Small enterprises generally do not have enough assets that can be offered as security, and often they lack proper financial statements and performance records that banks typically rely on to assess the creditworthiness of borrowers (Nikaido et al. 2015). It is against this backdrop that we use the variable urban land area owned by the household, and we anticipate this variable to have a positive association with access to formal credit. Further, we have used the logarithm of the total value of assets as a measure of the wealth of the household.

Additionally, we have identified several other household characteristics that may have an impact on households' access to production credit. We have included the highest level of education achieved by any member of the household. Education generally equips potential borrowers with the knowledge needed to make well-informed financial decisions. Also, a certain level of education is required for accessing formal loans, given that such loans typically involve paperwork.

We've also incorporated other variables such as the household's caste and the gender of the owner or employer. The caste variable comprises three categories, namely scheduled castes and tribes (SC/ST), other backward castes (OBC), and the general castes. Historically, the disadvantaged castes have faced discrimination and often lacked access to utilities and services. In the previous chapter, in the context of rural credit, we found that SC/ST and OBC categories are likely to have lower access to credit as compared to the general castes. So here we examine whether similar disparities exist in the urban sector. We also examine whether the gender of the enterprise owner affects their access to credit. Here, the gender of the enterprise owner is represented by a dummy variable which is equal to one if it is a female, but zero otherwise.

Additionally, we have included other variables such as the ratio of children to the total household size and the overall household size. These variables are introduced because households with a higher number of dependents are often inclined to seek more credit. To account for unobservable heterogeneity that may arise, we've incorporated regional dummies as control variables in the model. For an overview of the variables used in our analysis, refer to Appendix Table A9.

5.5.3 *Results and Analysis*

The analysis employs a probit model with correction for sample selection. Accordingly, we estimate the model in two stages. The first stage is based on the selection of occupation (self-employment or other). The second stage is based on access to production loans. Consequently, we have two equations to estimate, each associated with a distinct dependent variable: one representing access to loans and the other reflecting the choice of self-employment as an occupation.

The estimated rho between the errors of the two equations in our case is -0.4439, and the Wald test for independent equations is significant, implying the existence of sample selection bias, and thus affirming the appropriateness of employing a probit model with sample selection correction rather than a univariate probit model.

Table 5.2 presents the results of the analysis. First, we explain the second stage of the model. Here, the dependent variable is whether the household accesses production loans or not (conditional on whether the household is self-employed). The results indicate a non-linear relationship between the outreach of bank branches (financial infrastructure) and the outcome variable.

The coefficient of bank infrastructure is negative, and the coefficient of its squared term is positive, indicating a non-linear relationship. This suggests that in regions with a limited number of bank branches, there is a negative impact on access to production loans. Conversely, in areas with a higher density of bank branches, access to loans improves. In regions with a scarcity of bank branches, it's possible that the banking institutions primarily serve larger borrowers, leading to a crowding out of smaller

Table 5.2 Access to credit among urban self-employed households: A probit regression model with correction for sample selection bias

	Outcome	*Selection*
Variables	Access to prod loans	Self-employed
Bank infrastructure	–0.3403*	–0.2435**
	(0.182)	(0.106)
Bank infrastructure(sq)	0.0492*	0.0340**
	(0.028)	(0.016)
Service sector	0.1950***	
	(0.070)	
Log of total asset value	0.0070	0.0573***
	(0.028)	(0.016)
Total land area owned-urban	0.1224**	–0.2786***
	(0.054)	(0.067)
(Base-SCST)		
OBC	0.0392	0.2568***
	(0.077)	(0.043)
General	0.0382	0.2842***
	(0.084)	(0.046)
Women-headed enterprises	0.0429	
	(0.063)	
Women-headed households	–0.0119	–0.1347***
	(0.089)	(0.052)
(Below primary)		
Primary	0.1254	0.2188***
	(0.106)	(0.055)
Secondary	0.2387**	0.2100***
	(0.106)	(0.055)
Tertiary	0.3242***	–0.0206
	(0.111)	(0.060)
Ratio of children	0.2684*	0.0995
	(0.151)	(0.092)
Age of household head	0.0141	0.0186**
	(0.014)	(0.008)
Age of household head square	–0.0001	–0.0002**
	(0.000)	(0.000)
Household size	–0.0249	0.0778***
	(0.015)	(0.009)
(Base-South)		
North	–0.2743***	–0.3619***
	(0.099)	(0.051)
Northeast	0.0092	–0.3236***
	(0.210)	(0.086)

(continued)

Table 5.2 (continued)

	Outcome	*Selection*
East	0.2745***	–0.2739***
	(0.086)	(0.052)
Central	–0.0328	–0.5416***
	(0.095)	(0.047)
West	-0.0799	–0.5515***
	(0.109)	(0.054)
Helpers		0.4302***
		(0.051)
Constant	–0.5406	–2.0156***
	(0.717)	(0.344)
Observations	27,308	27,308
rho	–0.4439	
Wald test of Indep. eqns. (rho = 0): chi2(1) = 11.26 Prob > chi2 = 0.0008		

Note Robust standard errors in parentheses; *** $p < 0.01$, ** $p < 0.05$, * $p < 0.1$. *Source* Analysis based on NSSO-AIDIS 70th Round

borrowers. However, in areas where there is an extensive network of bank branches, larger borrowers are distributed across multiple branches, potentially prompting banks to offer services to smaller borrowers as well.

The analysis further shows that the coefficient of the dummy variable, representing households engaged in the service sector, is positive and statistically significant. This indicates that households that are self-employed in the service sector have a higher probability of accessing formal production credit compared to those in manufacturing. Additionally, the total urban land area owned by a household emerges as a significant and positive predictor of access to formal production credit, highlighting the importance of immovable property as security for obtaining formal credit. This finding also sheds light on why economically disadvantaged households often turn to informal credit sources, as these institutions may not mandate physical security, but instead rely on local knowledge and influence to extend credit.

Notably, caste variables are statistically insignificant, indicating that caste-based differences may not have a substantial effect on access to production credit in urban areas. Education, on the other hand, appears to play an important role. Households with only primary education show no significant advantage over illiterate households in accessing credit.

However, those with secondary or higher levels of education are significantly more likely to obtain production credit, highlighting the positive influence of educational attainment on financial access.

While the primary objective of our analysis is to examine the determinants of access to urban production loans, the insights from the selection equation are also valuable. Here, the dependent variable is whether the household is self-employed or not, or, in other words, it represents the decision to become self-employed.

Bank infrastructure exhibits a non-linear relationship with self-employment. The Bank infrastructure has a negative association with access to production credit, while its squared term shows a positive association. This suggests that in regions where there are more banks (beyond a certain threshold), the negative effect diminishes, and the likelihood of households becoming self-employed increases. The larger the number of banks, the more intense the competition between them, and the more favourable the possibility of securing initial capital and establishing new enterprises may become.

The households belonging to other backward castes and the general caste have a higher probability of becoming self-employed when compared with the scheduled castes and tribes. Interestingly, while women-owned enterprises and social groups do not display any significant relationship with access to production credit, they do, however, have a notable negative impact on the likelihood of pursuing self-employment. Further, as the wealth of the household grows, there is an increasing likelihood of becoming self-employed, indicating the significance of having an initial endowment of resources when starting a business, as discussed by Banerjee and Newman (1993). Also, we find that households with higher educational levels, such as primary and secondary, are more likely to become self-employed as compared to households with below primary level of education. Furthermore, the ratio of helpers to the total household size (which is the exclusion restriction variable) is positive and significant. This means that households with a higher availability of helpers are more likely to become self-employed.

5.6 Concluding Observations

This chapter examined access to production credit among urban self-employed households, drawing on data from the 70th and 77th Rounds of the NSSO-AIDIS. Through a comparative analysis between 2013 and 2019, the findings reveal that access to production loans has remained consistently low over the years, highlighting considerable scope for improvement in addressing the credit needs of the urban self-employed. The state-wise analysis shows that only West Bengal, Maharashtra, and Jharkhand experienced notable improvements in access to production loans during this period. Interestingly, in the Southern states, despite having a higher percentage of self-employed households accessing production loans from formal sources, there is a decrease in access during the study period.

The regression analysis examining the factors influencing access to production loans among self-employed households offers several valuable insights. Most notably, it emphasises the role of financial infrastructure in improving credit accessibility. The analysis reveals a non-linear relationship between the bank infrastructure and access to production credit. In regions with a limited presence of bank branches, there is a negative impact on access to production loans. However, beyond a certain threshold, a greater presence of banks has a positive and significant impact, suggesting that well-developed financial infrastructure facilitates better credit access for self-employed households.

While the government's primary focus has been on enhancing access in rural areas, our findings reveal that urban self-employed individuals also face significant challenges in accessing financial services. Given the fast pace of urbanisation, it is crucial to prioritise improvements in urban financial infrastructure and access mechanisms. Over the years several government initiatives have been brought out to improve access to loans for small and micro enterprises such as the Credit Guarantee Fund Trust for Micro and Small Enterprises (CGTMSE) started in 2000, the establishment of the Small Industries Development Bank of India (SIDBI) in 1999, Micro Unit Development and Refinance Agency (MUDRA) launched in 2014, and SIDBI—Make in India soft loan fund. However, despite the proliferation of such schemes, the supply of credit continues to fall short of the growing demand, pointing to a clear opportunity for strengthening and streamlining financial support for informal and micro businesses in urban India.

Appendix

Table A9 Summary statistics—Urban self-employed households

Variable	*Description of variable*	*Mean*	*Std. Dev*	*Min*	*Max*
Access to a production loan	= 1 if the household accesses production loan	0.123		0	1
Bank infrastructure	Number of urban bank branches divided by urban population	2.516	0.759	1.056	6.279
Services sector	= 1 if the household is self-employed in the services sector	0.316		0	1
Log of total asset value	Log value of total assets owned	13.137	2.557	0	21.338
Urban land area owned	Area of urban land owned(hectares)	0.108	0.509	0	20.055
SCST	= 1 if the household belongs to Scheduled castes/ tribes (SC)	0.219		0	1
OBC	= 1 if the household belongs to Other backward caste	0.384		0	1
General	= 1 if the household belongs to the General caste	0.396		0	1
Female-headed household	= 1 if the household is female-headed	0.124		0	1
Female-headed enterprises	= 1 if the enterprise owned by a female	0.087		0	1
Below primary	= 1 if the highest education in the household is below primary	0.090		0	1
Primary	= 1 if the highest education in the household is primary	0.198		0	1

(continued)

(continued)

Variable	*Description of variable*	*Mean*	*Std. Dev*	*Min*	*Max*
Secondary	= 1 if the highest education in the household is secondary	0.379		0	1
Tertiary	= 1 if the highest education in the household is tertiary	0.333		0	1
Age of household head	Age of household head	47	13.516	6	102
Household size	Number of members in the household	4.525	4.525	1	32
Ratio of children	Number of children to total household size	0.222	0.219	0	1
Number of helpers available	Total number of helpers available for the enterprise	0.164	0.546	0	10
North	= 1 if the household belongs to the Northern region	0.159		0	1
South	= 1 if the household belongs to Southern region	0.243		0	1
Central	= 1 if the household belongs to Central region	0.182		0	1
North-East	= 1 if the household belongs to North-eastern region	0.105		0	1
East	= 1 if the household belongs to eastern region	0.165		0	1
West	= 1 if the household belongs to Western region	0.147		0	1

References

Ayyagari, Meghana, Asli Demirguc-Kunt, and Vojislav Maksimovic. 2008. "How Important Are Financing Constraints? The Role of Finance in the Business Environment." *World Bank Economic Review* 22 (3): 483–516. https://doi.org/10.1093/wber/lhn018.

Banerjee, Abhijit V, and Andrew F Newman. 1993. "Occupational Choice and the Process of Development." *Journal of Political Economy* 101 (2): 274–98. https://doi.org/10.1086/261876.

Banerjee, Abhijit V., and Esther Duflo. 2011. *Poor Economics: A Radical Rethinking of the Way to Fight Global Poverty*. 2011th ed. Delhi: Random House Publishers Private Limited.

Beck, Thorsten, and Asli Demirguc-Kunt. 2006. "Small and Medium-Size Enterprises: Access to Finance as a Growth Constraint." *Journal of Banking and Finance* 30 (11): 2931–43. https://doi.org/10.1016/j.jbankfin.2006.05.009.

Beck, Thorsten. 2013. "Banking Finance for SMEs-Lessons from the Literature." *National Institute Economic Review* 225 (1): R23–38.

Bell, Clive. 1991. "Interactions between Institutional and Informal Credit Agencies in Rural India." *The World Bank Economic Review* 4 (3): 297–327. http://documents.worldbank.org/curated/en/160931468756339586/Interactions-between-institutional-and-informal-credit-agencies-in-rural-India.

Bhowmik, Sharit K. 2005. "Street Vendors in Asia: A Review." *Economic and Political Weekly* 40 (22/23): 2256–64. https://www.epw.in/journal/2005/22-23/review-labour-review-issues-specials/street-vendors-asia-review.html?0=ip_login_no_cache%3D970e446f652ce29bb2dcdd4b471ad5ed.

Binswanger, Hans P, and Shahidur R Khandker. 1995. "The Impact of Formal Finance on the Rural Economy of India." *The Journal of Development Studies* 32 (2): 234–62. https://doi.org/10.1080/00220389508422413.

Das, Maitreyi Bordia. 2003. "The Other Side of Self-Employment: Household Entreprises in India." 27873. Social Protection Discussion Paper Series, Washington, D.C: The World Bank.

Demirguc-Kunt, A, L Klapper, and G Panos. 2007. *The Origins of Self-Employment*. Development Research Group, Washington, D.C.: World Bank.

Demirguc-Kunt, Aslı, T Beck, and P Honohan. 2008. "Access to Finance and Development: Theory and Measurement." *Finance for All? Policies and Pitfalls in Expanding Access-A World Bank Policy Research Report*. Washington, D.C.: The world Bank.

DeSoto, Hernando. 1989. *The Other Path: The Invisible Revolution in the Third World*. New York: Harper and Row.

Evans, David S., and Boyan Jovanovic. 1989. "An Estimated Model of Entrepreneurial Choice under Liquidity Constraints." *Journal of Political Economy* 97 (4): 808–27. https://doi.org/10.1086/261629.

Fields, Gary S. 2013. "Self Employment in the Developing World." Background Research Paper Submitted to the High Level Panel on the Post-2015 Development Agenda, Cornell University and IZA.

Gadgil, M V. 1986. "Agricultural Credit in India: A Review of Performance and Policies." *Indian Journal of Agricultural Economics* 41 (3): 282–309.

Greene, William H. 2003. *Econometric Analysis*. 5th ed. London: Pearson Education.

Gurtoo, Anjula, and Colin C. Williams. 2009. "Entrepreneurship and the Informal Sector." *The International Journal of Entrepreneurship and Innovation* 10 (1): 55–62. https://doi.org/10.5367/000000009787414280.

King, Robert G, and Ross Levine. 1993. "Finance and Growth: Schumpeter Might Be Right." *The Quarterly Journal of Economics* 108 (3): 717–737. https://doi.org/10.2307/2118406.

Kochar, Anjini. 1997. "An Empirical Investigation of Rationing Constraints in Rural Credit Markets in India." *Journal of Development Economics* 53 (2): 339–71. https://doi.org/10.1016/S0304-3878(97)00020-5.

Margolis, David N. 2014. "By Choice and by Necessity: Entrepreneurship and Self-Employment in the Developing World." *European Journal of Development Research* 26 (4): 419–36. https://doi.org/10.1057/ejdr.2014.25.

Mckinnon, Ronald. 1973. *Money and Capital in Economic Development*. Washington, D.C.: Brookings Institution.

Nikaido, Yuko, Jesim Pais, and Mandira Sarma. 2015. "What Hinders and What Enhances Small Enterprises' Access to Formal Credit in India?" *Review of Development Finance* 5 (1): 43–52. https://doi.org/10.1016/j.rdf.2015.05.002.

NSSO. 2014. "Key Indicators of Debt and Investment in India (2013)." *Ministry of Statistics and Programme Implementation, Govt of India*. New Delhi.

Paulson, Anna L., and Robert Townsend. 2004. "Entrepreneurship and Financial Constraints in Thailand." *Journal of Corporate Finance* 10 (2): 229–62. https://doi.org/10.1016/S0929-1199(03)00056-7.

Rajeev, Meenakshi, and B P Vani. 2011. "Farm Sector in Karnataka: Farmers' Indebtedness and Risk Management. Project Report No. CESP/93." Bangalore: ISEC.

Rajeev, Meenakshi, and B.P. Vani. 2017. *Financial Access of the Urban Poor in India: A Story of Exclusion*. New Delhi: Springer India. https://doi.org/10.1007/978-81-322-3712-9.

Rajeev, Meenakshi, B. P. Vani, and Manojit Bhattacharjee. 2012. "Nature and Dimensions of Farmers' Indebtedness in India." 267. ISEC Working Paper. Bangalore: ISEC

Rajeev, Meenakshi, B.P. Vani, and Veerashekharappa. 2017. "Self-Help Groups for India's Financial Inclusion: Do Effective Cost of Borrowing Limit Their Operation?" *ICDD Working Paper No. 19*. Kassel: Kassel University press GmbH.

Rakesh, Mohan. 2006. "Agricultural Credit in India—Status, Issues and Future Agenda." *Economic And Political Weekly* 41 (11): 1013–23.

Schumpeter, Joseph A. 1934. *The Theory of Economic Development: An Inquiry into Profits, Capital, Credit, Interest, and the Business Cycle*. Cambridge: Harvard University Press

Stiglitz, Joseph E, and Andrew Weiss. 1981. "Credit Rationing in Markets with Imperfect Information." *The American Economic Review* 71 (3): 393–410.

Tambunan, Tulus. 2009. "Women Entrepreneurship in Asian Developing Countries : Their Development and Main Constraints." *Journal of Development and Agricultural Economics* 1 (2): 27–40.

CHAPTER 6

Financial Inclusion and Formal Savings

6.1 Introduction

After studying the first major aspect of financial inclusion, viz., access to credit, we next take-up the issue of savings in the context of Financial Inclusion. Before the launch of the financial inclusion drive, a large section of the population in India did not even have a bank account. However, this scenario has improved since 2014, as the RBI has progressively worked to reduce the costs associated with opening savings accounts. This has improved bank account registration substantially; however, the active usage of the bank accounts thus opened has become a concern.

According to Findex 2021, 78% of adults above 15 years of age have an account in a financial institution, yet around 27% of these accounts remain inactive, showing no deposits or withdrawals. Further, the percentage of respondents who report saving or setting aside any money at a bank or any type of financial institution is only 14%. Other studies also raise these concerns (Goedecke et al. 2018; Morawczynski et al. 2010). This chapter, therefore, aims to provide useful insights into the savings behaviour of households (savings through formal banks) and the various factors leading to low savings in spite of the efforts by the Government.

There are several reasons why people save. Commonly cited reasons include the precautionary motive, life-cycle motive, inter-temporal substitution motive, improvement motive, independence motive, enterprise

S. Saravanabhavan and M. Rajeev, *Moving Beyond Barriers*, Palgrave Studies in Impact Finance,
https://doi.org/10.1007/978-981-95-1066-5_6

motive, and bequest motive (Keynes, 1936; Coleman, 1998). Most often, a typical household's reason for saving is a combination of some of these motives (Browning and Lusardi 1996). However, for low-income individuals and households, the precautionary motive is most important, as they usually save to reduce future vulnerability in the face of disruptions in the flow of income.

It is usually seen that even individuals with the lowest incomes do not spend all of their income, but a small portion is always saved for some future emergencies. However, the methods used for saving are rudimentary and mostly informal in nature, which indicates a latent demand among the poor for efficient formal savings instruments(Collins et al. 2010; Aportela 1999; Banerjee and Duflo 2007). Unfortunately, due to several reasons, this demand remains unfulfilled (Karlan et al. 2014).

One prevailing misconception among people is that formal financial institutions cater only to individuals with large sums of money to deposit, discouraging low-income households from engaging with banks. At the same time, banks tend to be reluctant to maintain small accounts, as the administrative costs are similar to those for larger accounts, making them less attractive from a profitability standpoint. The Government has tried to address these problems through the financial inclusion drive, which prioritises both improving financial awareness and simplifying the process of opening bank accounts. Initiatives such as the Jan Dhan Yojana have helped increase savings among low-income households to some extent; however, there remains considerable scope for further improvement in both account usage and financial participation.

It is well-established that education plays a vital role in enhancing both access to and the effective use of financial services. Similarly, greater penetration of bank branches within a region can improve awareness and accessibility, thereby encouraging financial engagement. However, the extent of this awareness and its impact on saving behaviour may vary across individuals with different educational backgrounds. In this context, the present chapter investigates how the density of bank branches influences household savings and whether this effect differs according to households' educational attainment. In addition, the chapter explores other socio-economic factors that may influence saving behaviour. This is particularly relevant in rural areas, where socio-cultural and economic disadvantages often limit engagement with formal financial institutions. Understanding these constraints is essential for designing policies to encourage formal savings among underserved populations.

Moreover, there is a limited body of research examining formal savings within the broader context of financial inclusion. Most available research is regional in scope, often based on small-scale primary surveys with limited sample sizes (Mowl 2013; Ramji 2009). While there are several macro-level studies on aggregate household savings in India, recent demand-side studies using nationally representative household-level data are scarce. This chapter seeks to address that gap by exploring access to formal savings using household-level data from the NSSO-AIDIS, with a distinct focus on rural and urban sectors.

Given this backdrop, the chapter is organised as follows. Section 6.2 outlines the theoretical perspectives on formal savings. Section 6.3 provides a brief review of the relevant literature. Section 6.4 describes the data sources and methodology employed in the analysis. Section 6.5 presents a comparative overview of household savings in India between 2013 and 2019. Section 6.6 presents the econometric analysis and results. Section 6.7 offers concluding observations and policy implications.

6.2 Theoretical Perspectives: Motivations for Savings in Low-Income Households

This section discusses the key theoretical perspectives relevant to our study. To begin with, it is important to emphasise that savings behaviour in low-income countries is different from that of high-income countries (Rosenzweig 2001). In a developing country like India, the incomes of the poor are often irregular, as the majority are engaged in self-employment, primarily within the agricultural or informal sectors. Given the sporadic nature of their incomes and the high uncertainty that they face, regular savings are crucial to smooth consumption and maintain basic living standards during difficult times (Deaton 1990). Thus, savings as a precautionary measure are critical for these households. Additionally, the lack of adequate security nets in developing countries amplifies the risks and vulnerabilities faced by them, making personal savings even more important.

Thus, in the case of poor households, when income is highly uncertain, consumption equalling permanent income (neo-classical–life-cycle models) may not hold (Deaton 1990; Bernheim and Scholz 1993; Rosenzweig 2001). Also, these models make unrealistic assumptions such as perfect knowledge about future income and individual rationality, which may not be applicable in the case of poor-income households (Beverly and Sherraden 1999). Hence, for low-income households in developing economies, it is more realistic to assume savings to be "high-frequency intertemporal smoothing saving, not life-cycle hump or intergenerational saving" (Deaton 1990).

Apart from the different motives attributed as reasons for saving, access to financial institutions can also influence the savings behaviour of low-income households. One of the biggest challenges they face is the distance to bank branches, which makes saving in formal institutions time-consuming and costly (Giannatale and Roa 2016; Bertrand et al. 2006; Dupas et al. 2012; Honohan 2007; S. Ghosh 2020). These costs are difficult for the poor, who often earn irregular incomes and may lose a day's wage just to visit a bank. These transaction costs can be overcome by improving banking infrastructure-by increasing the number of bank branches, ATMs, and other services closer to where people live.

6.3 Brief Background: Necessity and Role of Household Savings

There is a wide range of empirical literature that deals with the need and importance of household savings. In this review, we categorise relevant studies under key themes. First, we discuss the importance of household savings in formal banking institutions. Second, we look at the level of access and use of bank accounts in India. Third, we discuss the need for interventions to enhance savings rates.

6.3.1 The Importance of Household Savings in Banks

In developing countries, a large portion of the savings is held in the form of physical property such as buildings, land, and livestock (Collins et al. 2010), while only a small proportion is saved as financial assets. However, unlike financial assets, physical property cannot easily be converted into cash in an emergency. This makes it crucial for households to have accessible and liquid forms of savings. In the absence of such resources during financial distress, households are often forced to adopt harmful coping strategies such as withdrawing children from school to contribute to household income, reducing expenditure on health and nutrition, cutting back on investments in productive activities, and resorting to the distress sale of assets-losses that may take years to recover from (Murdoch and Sharma, 2002).

For low-income households, savings are particularly important, as their access to credit is often limited and constrained by high costs or lack of collateral. Consequently, relying solely on credit to manage financial emergencies is often unreliable and unsustainable. (Aportela 1999). In such situations, maintaining adequate savings becomes a critical strategy for low-income households to cope with contingencies and plan for future needs. Additionally, holding savings in bank accounts helps prevent frequent dissaving, a common issue when money is kept in hand, thus encouraging more consistent saving behaviour (Prina 2015).

6.3.2 *Access and Use of Bank Accounts in India*

The RBI has progressively reduced the costs involved in opening savings accounts since 2005, with the help of various financial drive policies. Even though this has resulted in improved access to bank accounts, formal savings have not improved much. Studies show that a significant percentage of the bank accounts opened as part of the financial inclusion drive are not active (Demirguc-Kunt et al. 2022; Demirguc-Kunt et al. 2018; Sharma et al. 2016). Findex 2021 reveals that around 78% of adults above 15 years of age have a bank account in India, however, 27% of these people show no active usage. It was also observed that bank accounts are used mainly for receiving Government cash transfers. Though this itself marks an improvement, the narrow use of bank accounts in such a manner hardly helps in fully achieving the broader goals of financial inclusion.

6.3.3 *Need for Interventions*

Introducing low-cost financial products is a necessary step, but not sufficient on its own to promote formal savings. Along with this, these products must be complemented by targeted interventions that actively encourage and nudge individuals to save regularly. A growing body of research has explored various behavioural and institutional strategies to increase formal savings. For instance, a study from the Philippines found that appointing deposit collectors not only increased the adoption of savings accounts by households but also resulted in higher savings levels compared to households without the service of deposit collectors. This study also observed a decrease in borrowing among households that were actively saving (Ashraf et al. 2006a). In another study, sending regular reminder messages encouraging individuals to deposit money proved to be an effective, low-cost strategy for enhancing savings rates (Karlan et al. 2016).

Other Studies from Kenya and the Philippines show that the adoption of saving products and savings was higher for "commitment-based savings instruments", which restrict access to funds for a specific period, preventing impulsive spending(Dupas and Robinson 2013; Ashraf 2006b). Similarly, a study in Nepal found that reducing cost-related barriers significantly improved access to savings accounts, particularly among female-headed households (Prina 2015). Another study conducted in Kenya's Western Province revealed that when free bank accounts with simplified opening procedures were made available, 60% of the target population opened accounts (Dupas et al. 2012). These findings emphasise the importance of behavioural nudges and accessible institutions in deepening financial inclusion.

6.4 Data and Methodology

The launch of the Pradhan Mantri Jan Dhan Yojana (PMJDY) has significantly transformed the financial inclusion landscape in India by expanding account ownership and improving access to financial services. To assess the impact of these changes, this chapter draws on data from the NSSO-All-India Debt and Investment Survey (AIDIS) for the years 2013 and 2019. Further details about this dataset have been discussed in earlier chapters.

The methodology adopted in this chapter combines both descriptive and econometric approaches. We begin with a descriptive overview using tables and graphs to highlight key trends and patterns in household savings behaviour over time. To gain deeper insights, we then apply the double-hurdle model, which enables us to analyse separately the factors affecting both access to formal savings and the extent of usage. A detailed explanation of the model is provided in Sect. 6.6.

6.5 Understanding Savings Behaviour: An Analysis of NSSO Household Survey Data

For this analysis, we utilise data from two rounds of the All-India Debt and Investment Survey (AIDIS). The 70th Round (AIDIS-2013) offers a snapshot of household savings behaviour in India before the launch of the Pradhan Mantri Jan Dhan Yojana (PMJDY), while the 77th

Round (AIDIS-2019) captures the scenario five years after the program's implementation.

According to AIDIS-2019, we observe that around 85% of the population above the age of 18 has a bank account either in commercial banks, regional rural banks, or a cooperative bank. Also, we don't find much difference in individual account ownership between the rural and urban sectors, as 84% of the adult population in the rural sector and 85% of the adult population in the urban sector own deposit accounts. Additionally, we find that around 98% of the households own a bank account, implying that access to deposit accounts has reached near-universal household coverage in the country. However, the real issue lies in the limited use of these bank accounts, whether for saving or for conducting transactions.

As shown in Fig. 6.1, in 2019, 92% of rural households reported having savings in banks, slightly higher than the 90% among urban households. In 2013, households in the lowest asset class were the least likely to save in banks, showing a sharp contrast with households in higher asset classes. This difference has, however, evened out in the 2019 data.

Though the primary focus of this chapter is on savings through banks, we have also examined other formal avenues of savings such as Government deposits, National Savings Certificates, Kisan Vikas Patra, and Post office deposits. We observe that savings through these avenues remain consistently low, with no significant change observed over the period. The percentage of households saving through these instruments declined from 10% in 2013 to 8% in 2019. These schemes were targeted at low-income households, particularly in rural areas, where commercial bank penetration has historically been limited. However, the increased availability and accessibility of commercial banking services following the launch of the Pradhan Mantri Jan Dhan Yojana (PMJDY) may have reduced the reliance on these alternative savings instruments, as more households have transitioned to mainstream banking channels (Table 6.1).

In 2019, around 92% of rural households and 90% of urban households had savings in a bank, but the real issue is the amount of savings in the accounts. Around 8% of rural households had less than Rupees 500 in their accounts, while 9% had between Rupees 500 and 1000 (See Table 6.2). This implies low savings for 17% of the households in the rural sector. Similarly, 9% of urban households had less than Rupees 500 and 11% had between Rupees 500 and 1000 as savings in banks. However, when compared to 2013, this is a considerable improvement,

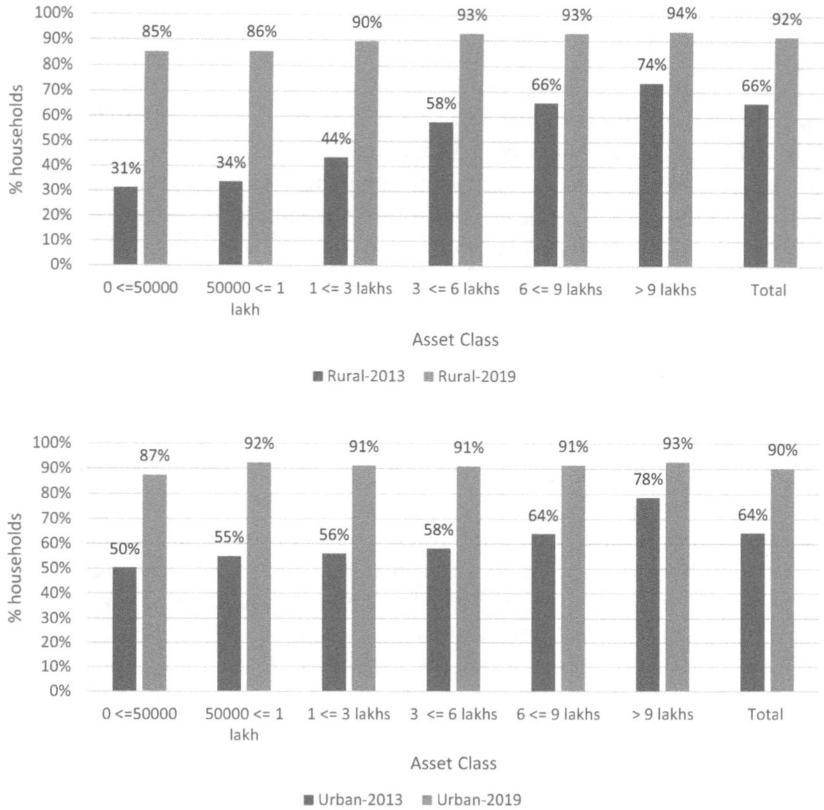

Fig. 6.1 Change in the percentage of households with bank savings across asset classes, 2013–2019
(*Source* Authors' calculations using 70th and 77th Rounds of NSSO-AIDIS data)

as the number of households having less than Rupees 1000 has reduced substantially.

Though the aggregate savings rate (at the macro level) in India is relatively high and can be compared to even developed countries,[1] it is the composition of savings that differs. From our data, we observe that bank deposits as a percentage of the total assets of the households are low, and

[1] https://data.worldbank.org/indicator/ny.gds.totl.zs

Table 6.1 Change in percentage of households having savings in a bank, classified according to the amount in the account

	Amount of Savings (% of households)						
	< ₹500	*₹500–1000*	*₹1000–3000*	*₹3000–5000*	*₹5000–10,000*	> *₹10,000*	*Total*
Rural-2013	23	17	26	10	9	16	100
Rural-2019	8	9	24	13	16	25	100
Urban-2013	9	11	18	11	12	39	100
Urban-2019	5	6	16	10	14	49	100

Source Authors' calculations using 70th and 77th Rounds of NSSO-AIDIS data

people prefer investing in physical property rather than financial assets, across states. As discussed in the review, a key limitation of saving in material or physical assets is their illiquidity in times of emergency. In contrast, banks provide a safe place for depositing money while earning interest, and they also keep the savings in an easily accessible form.

The above analysis reveals that over the period of study, the use of financial institutions for savings has substantially improved in India. Most importantly, our comparative analysis indicates that the Jan Dhan Yojana, initiated in 2014, has played a pivotal role in improving the use of formal financial services for household savings. Given these promising changes, the subsequent section undertakes an in-depth analysis of the various factors influencing the extent of bank savings, aiming to identify the key socio-economic and institutional determinants that shape household saving behaviour.

6.6 Econometric Analysis: Factors Influencing Savings Behaviour

To explore the determinants of savings behaviour, we employ a double-hurdle model, with details provided in the following sections. The discussion begins with a description of the econometric methodology used in the analysis, followed by an overview of the explanatory variables

Table 6.2 Double-hurdle model for the determinants of formal savings in the financial institutions: Rural sector

Rural sector			
	Model 1		*Model 2***
Variables	(Stage 2) Amount of savings(log)	(Stage 1) Access	(Stage 2) Amount of savings(log)
Banking infrastructure	7.4348***	0.7502*	9.7399***
	(0.543)	(0.384)	(1.152)
(Base-Below primary)			
Primary	0.2039***	0.3102***	0.4344***
	(0.045)	(0.037)	(0.119)
Secondary	0.5586***	0.5824***	0.7418***
	(0.057)	(0.040)	(0.113)
Tertiary	1.0730***	0.7821***	1.1508***
	(0.079)	(0.060)	(0.148)
Primary # Banking infrastructure			-3.3353**
			(1.459)
Secondary # Banking infrastructure			-2.6244**
			(1.318)
Tertiary # Banking infrastructure			-1.1569
			(1.647)
Log of asset value	0.2788***	0.1066***	0.2779***
	(0.029)	(0.014)	(0.029)
Female head	0.2098***	-0.0121	0.2077***
	(0.066)	(0.041)	(0.066)
(Base-SCST)			
OBC	0.1503***	0.0440	0.1501***
	(0.043)	(0.032)	(0.043)
General	0.2400***	0.0604	0.2401***
	(0.052)	(0.038)	(0.052)
Self-employed agricultural households	-0.1668***	0.0067	-0.1678***
	(0.040)	(0.029)	(0.040)
Age of hh head	-0.0269***	0.0249***	-0.0271***
	(0.010)	(0.006)	(0.010)
Age of hh head squared	0.0003***	-0.0002***	0.0003***
	(0.000)	(0.000)	(0.000)
Household size	-0.0240**	-0.0027	-0.0238**
	(0.010)	(0.008)	(0.010)
Ratio of children	0.1717*	0.0788	0.1743*
	(0.100)	(0.080)	(0.100)
(Base-North)			

(continued)

Table 6.2 (continued)

Rural sector

	Model 1		*Model 2***
North-East	1.7059***	−0.3522***	1.7010***
	(0.073)	(0.061)	(0.073)
East	0.4846***	−0.4568***	0.4829***
	(0.075)	(0.053)	(0.075)
Central	0.2921***	−0.0673	0.2918***
	(0.059)	(0.050)	(0.059)
West	0.5646***	−0.6399***	0.5626***
	(0.077)	(0.056)	(0.077)
South	−0.2944***	−0.4954***	−0.2982***
	(0.063)	(0.050)	(0.063)
Sigma	0.3040***		0.3038***
	(0.010)		(0.010)
Constant	3.3661***	−1.8485***	3.2252***
	(0.469)	(0.227)	(0.481)
Observations	56,130		56,130

Robust standard errors in parentheses
*** $p < 0.01$, ** $p < 0.05$, * $p < 0.1$

expected to influence the use of formal savings. This is then followed by a presentation and interpretation of the empirical findings.

6.6.1 *Methodology*

Saving in a bank involves two decisions, first, a household must decide whether to save in a bank and if yes, they must then determine how much to save. Problems such as these, where a decision happens in two stages, can be modelled using a double-hurdle model (Cragg 1971). In this study, the dependent variable is the amount of bank savings, which is a continuous variable characterised by a large number of zero observations (households with no bank savings) and a distribution of positive values for the rest. The double-hurdle model is estimated in two stages to account for the two-part decision-making. In the first stage, we model the probability of saving in a bank using a binary dependent variable that takes the value 1 if the household saves in a bank and 0 otherwise, representing access or the decision to save. In the second stage, for those households that report positive savings, we model the amount saved, allowing us to examine the extent of formal savings usage. Further details about this model have already been provided in Chapter 4.

6.6.2 *Variables*

Our dependent variable of interest is the amount of total savings in bank accounts (usage of bank accounts) owned by households. The data gives us the total value of the financial assets held as deposits in banks, and we use this variable to represent formal savings in bank accounts.

One of the key objectives of this analysis is to examine how access to financial institutions influences the extent of household savings in formal financial institutions. To represent access, we use the variable demographic penetration of banks/banking infrastructure, defined as the number of rural bank branches per adult population. This indicator is measured at the state level, capturing the regional variation in banking infrastructure availability across states.

Another variable that we have included is the wealth of the household, which is the total value of all physical assets, financial assets (minus the value of deposits in banks), and gold owned by a household. We also control for household type by introducing a binary variable that takes the value 1 for self-employed households and 0 otherwise. Though savings are important for all types of households, self-employed households often face greater constraints in accessing loans and generally have fewer financial resources to fall back on.

Education plays a critical role in enhancing an individual's ability to understand and engage with financial products and services. In our analysis, we account for this by including the maximum level of education attained by any member of the household as a key explanatory variable. This is a categorical variable with four levels: below primary, primary, secondary, and tertiary. Accordingly, we expect that households with higher levels of education are more likely to use formal savings.

In the Indian context, the influence of caste on financial inclusion is particularly significant and is said to impact almost every aspect of economic life (Munshi 2019). Given this, we include caste as an explanatory variable. Households are classified into three broad social groups: Scheduled Castes and Scheduled Tribes (SC/ST), Other Backward Classes (OBC), and General (Others).

Other household characteristics, such as the gender of the household head, age of the household head, ratio of children in the household, and household size, are also included in the models to rule out alternative explanations. Furthermore, regional variations may have an influence on households' savings in financial institutions. Hence, we have controlled for the different geographical zones, namely North, South, East, West, and North-East. The summary statistics are provided in Appendix Tables A10 and A11.

6.6.3 *Results and Analysis*

Tables 6.2 and 6.3 present the results of the double-hurdle model, which examines the factors influencing household savings in formal financial institutions in rural and urban sectors. The first tier of the model estimates the access to savings products in banks, and the second tier models the extent of savings in banks.

As expected, we observe that better institutional access leads to better utilisation (as well as access) of banking services both in rural and urban regressions (See Model 1 in Tables 6.2 and 6.3). When financial institutions are accessible at a reasonable distance, transaction costs such as time, effort, and travel expenses are significantly reduced and therefore usage increases. Next, we look at the impact of education on formal household savings. Across rural and urban models, we find that the estimated coefficients for education increase with higher levels of educational attainment (See Model 1 in Tables 6.2 and 6.3). This suggests a strong positive relationship between education on both access to and usage of formal savings.

The main objective of this chapter is to examine how the use of financial infrastructure differs across households with different levels of educational attainment. To explore this relationship, we introduce interaction terms between banking infrastructure and education in our econometric models (see Model 2 in Tables 6.2 and 6.3). When we examine the rural sector in particular, we observe that the interaction terms primary# banking infrastructure and secondary#banking infrastructure are negative and significant. The negative coefficient suggests that the positive effect of banking infrastructure on savings is reduced for those with primary and secondary education as compared to those with below-primary education. In other words, this means that the returns

Table 6.3 Double-hurdle model for the determinants of the extent of savings in financial institutions—Urban sector

Urban sector			
	Model 1		*Model 2*
	(Stage 2)	*(Stage 1)*	*(Stage 2)*
Variables	Amount of savings(log)	Access	Amount of savings(log)
Banking infrastructure	0.5696** (0.290)	1.0083*** (0.247)	−1.1673 (0.908)
(Base-Below primary)			
Primary	0.3160*** (0.064)	0.3911*** (0.047)	0.1439 (0.268)
Secondary	0.8692*** (0.064)	0.7326*** (0.047)	0.4031 (0.260)
Tertiary	1.6804*** (0.066)	1.0519*** (0.052)	1.1325*** (0.257)
Primary # Banking infrastructure			0.6709 (1.029)
Secondary # Banking infrastructure			1.8403* (1.017)
Tertiary # Banking infrastructure			2.1675** (0.980)
Log of asset value	0.1428*** (0.012)	0.0144** (0.007)	0.1429*** (0.011)
Female head	−0.2183*** (0.056)	−0.0863* (0.049)	−0.2188*** (0.056)
(Base-SCST)			
OBC	0.1651*** (0.047)	-0.0133 (0.041)	0.1644*** (0.047)
General	0.5558*** (0.047)	0.1373*** (0.044)	0.5515*** (0.047)
Self-employed	−0.1263*** (0.035)	0.0143 (0.030)	−0.1275*** (0.035)
Age of hh head	−0.0320*** (0.007)	0.0204*** (0.007)	−0.0322*** (0.007)
Age of hh head squared	0.0004*** (0.000)	−0.0002** (0.000)	0.004*** (0.000)
Household size	−0.0772*** (0.009)	−0.0310*** (0.007)	−0.0771*** (0.009)
Ratio of children	0.0986 (0.092)	−0.1740** (0.084)	0.0941 (0.092
(Base-North)			

(continued)

Table 6.3 (continued)

Urban sector

	Model 1		*Model 2*
	(Stage 2)	*(Stage 1)*	*(Stage 2)*
North-East	0.5870***	–0.0674	0.5845***
	(0.092)	(0.074)	(0.092)
East	0.1196*	–0.2087***	0.1125
	(0.068)	(0.060)	(0.068)
Central	–0.0868	–0.0703	–0.0893
	(0.060)	(0.057)	(0.061)
West	0.1766***	–0.3955***	0.1772***
	(0.061)	(0.062)	(0.061)
South	–0.8541***	–0.4935***	–0.8577***
	(0.061)	(0.056)	(0.061)
Sigma	0.4226***		0.4222***
	(0.008)		(0.008)
Constant	6.5358***	–0.7265***	6.9859***
	(0.235)	(0.198)	(0.346)
Observations	45,248		45,248

Robust standard errors in parentheses
*** $p < 0.01$, ** $p < 0.05$, * $p < 0.1$;
We include interaction terms in stage 2 of the model as we are interested in understanding these effects on the amount of savings. Stage 1 remains the same as in model 1

to improved banking infrastructure are highest for those with the lowest education levels.[2]

On the other hand, for the urban sector, we find differing results. The interaction terms, secondary# banking infrastructure and tertiary#banking infrastructure, are positive and are statistically significant. The positive coefficients indicate that as education increases, the marginal effect of banking infrastructure on savings also increases, implying that the effect of banking infrastructure on savings is enhanced for those with secondary and tertiary education compared to those with below-primary education. The returns to improved banking infrastructure are highest for

[2] These results have been visually verified by plotting the predicted values from the models with the interaction terms. For more details please refer- Saravanabhavan and Rajeev (2025)

those with the highest education levels in urban areas. To understand this better, we plotted the predicted values from the two regressions.[3]

Other control variables—As expected, the wealth of the household is a strong positive determinant of access to savings in banks, as well as the extent of savings in banks for both rural and urban regressions. Additionally, the caste of the household plays a significant role in influencing household saving behaviour. Our results indicate that households belonging to Other Backward Castes (OBC) and the general category are likely to have higher formal savings as compared to the SCST households. Supporting this, descriptive analysis of data reveals that a larger proportion of SC/ST households have bank savings below ₹500, highlighting persistent disparities across caste groups. The impact of caste on access to savings is mostly insignificant, implying that access to bank accounts may have become more or less universal as a result of the financial inclusion drive, and even the disadvantaged groups are not finding it difficult to access bank accounts. Other control variables produce expected results.

6.7 Concluding Observations

There are only very few studies that focus on understanding the determinants of the extent of savings in banks, especially in the context of the financial inclusion drive. This chapter seeks to address that gap by documenting and analysing the current state of formal savings in India.

From the comparative analysis over two points of time, 2013 and 2019, we observe that there is considerable improvement in the use of bank accounts for savings. According to AIDIS-2019, we observe that 85% of the adult population has a bank account either in commercial banks, regional rural banks, or a cooperative bank. Also, we don't find much difference in deposit account ownership across the rural and urban sectors from the latest data, indicating substantial progress in financial access across geographies. Additionally, the amount of savings in banks has also improved. For instance, from our data, we find that around 40% of the households had less than Rupees 500 as savings in banks in 2013, while in 2019 only 17% of households had less than Rupees 500 as savings in their account (This is only an indicative result, as one could argue that the real value of money has decreased).

[3] Figures not provided in the chapter. For more details please refer- Saravanabhavan and Rajeev (2025)

Despite notable improvements, significant challenges remain in enhancing the level of formal household savings in India. In response, this study undertakes an in-depth econometric analysis to explore the various factors that influence the amount of savings held in banks, with a particular focus on educational attainment and banking infrastructure.[4] The findings bring out several interesting insights. Most importantly, we observe that education has a stronger influence on the extent of savings than other determinants in our analysis.

Furthermore, it also shows that in rural areas, when rural bank penetration increases, the increase in savings is much higher for households with only below-primary education, as compared to households with primary or secondary education. This suggests that improved physical access to banking infrastructure can significantly benefit the least educated in rural settings by lowering access barriers. In contrast, the urban sector presents a different pattern. Here, we do not find similar improvement for the lower-educated households; rather, as urban bank penetration increases, the gap in savings widens between households with higher educational attainment (secondary and tertiary) and those with below-primary education. This implies that in urban areas, households with higher levels of education benefit more from the increased bank penetration, while lower-educated households remain relatively underserved.

This brings out an important insight. Merely expanding physical access to banking services is not sufficient. Banks must actively engage with less-educated populations, particularly in urban areas, by creating a more inclusive and user-friendly environment, with simple procedures, use of local language, and ensuring non-condescending, respectful interactions with clients, especially those from disadvantaged backgrounds (Rajeev and Vani 2017). Our results further indicate that socially disadvantaged groups, such as Scheduled Castes and Scheduled Tribes (SC/ST), tend to have lower levels of savings in banks compared to households in the general category. However, the impact of caste on access to savings accounts is insignificant, suggesting that initiatives under the financial inclusion drive have successfully expanded account ownership across social groups.

[4] Usage of banks for savings and other purposes can be enhanced by developing products depending on the behavioural pattern of the households. However, this needs detailed behavioural data and analysis—which is beyond the scope of the present thesis.

Appendix

Table A10 Summary statistics—Rural sector: formal savings

Variable	*Description of variables*	*Mean*	*Std. Dev*	*Min*	*Max*
Amount of savings	Amount of savings in banks	5.301	3.922	0	15.65
Banking infrastructure	Number of rural banks/rural adult population	0.077	0.055	0.028	0.789
Base-Below primary	= 1 if the maximum education in the household is below the primary level	0.236		0	1
Primary	= 1 if the maximum education in the household is at least primary	0.308		0	1
Secondary	= 1 if the maximum education in the household is at least secondary	0.351		0	1
Tertiary	= 1 if the maximum education in the household is at least tertiary	0.104		0	1
Wealth	Total value of assets (not including bank deposits)	13.008	1.674	0	19.339
SE in agriculture	= 1 if the household is self-employed in agriculture	0.478		0	1
Female head	= 1 if the head of the household is female	0.118		0	1
Base-SCST	= 1 if the household belongs to scheduled caste//tribe	0.372		0	1
OBC	= 1 if the household belongs to Other backward castes	0.391		0	1

(continued)

Table A10 (continued)

Variable	*Description of variables*	*Mean*	*Std. Dev*	*Min*	*Max*
General	= 1 if the household belongs to the general caste	0.237		0	1
Age of household head	Age of the household head	47.547	13.564	4	110
Ratio of children	Number of children to total household size	0.264	0.229	0	1
Household size	Number of members in the household	4.818	2.333	1	38
Base-North	= 1 if the household belongs to the Northern region	0.126		0	1
North-East	= 1 if the household belongs to the North-Eastern region	0.136		0	1
East	= 1 if the household belongs to the Eastern region	0.214		0	1
Central	= 1 if the household belongs to the central region	0.220		0	1
West	= 1 if the household belongs to the Western region	0.117		0	1
South	= 1 if the household belongs to the Southern region	0.186		0	1

Table A11 Summary statistics—Urban sector: formal savings

Variable	*Description of variables*	*Mean*	*Std. Dev*	*Min*	*Max*
Amount of savings	Amount of savings in banks	6.530	4.200	0	17.297
Banking infrastructure	Number of urban banks/urban adult population	0.088	0.074	0.028	0.790
Base-Below primary	= 1 if the maximum education in the household is below the primary	0.090		0	1
Primary	= 1 if the maximum education in the household is at least primary			0	1
Secondary	= 1 if the maximum education in the household is at least secondary	0.379		0	1
Tertiary	= 1 if the maximum education in the household is at least tertiary	0.333		0	1
Wealth	Total value of assets (not including bank deposits)	13.040	2.814	0	21.338
Female head	= 1 if the head of the household is female	0.1244		0	1
Base-SCST	= 1 if household belongs to scheduled caste//tribe			0	1
OBC	= 1 if the household belongs to Other backward castes	0.384		0	1
General	= 1 if the household belongs to general castes	0.396		0	1
Self-employed	= 1 if the household is self-employed	0.368		0	1
Age of household head	Age of household head	47.169	13.517	6	102

(continued)

Table A11 (continued)

Variable	*Description of variables*	*Mean*	*Std. Dev*	*Min*	*Max*
Ratio of children	Number of children to total household size	0.222	0.219	0	1
Household size	Number of members in the household	4.525	2.285	1	32
Base-North	= 1 if the household belongs to the Northern region	0.159		0	1
North-East	= 1 if the household belongs to the North-Eastern region	0.105		0	1
East	= 1 if the household belongs to the Eastern region	0.165		0	1
Central	= 1 if the household belongs to the central region	0.182		0	1
West	= 1 if the household belongs to the Western region	0.147		0	1
South	= 1 if the household belongs to the Southern region	0.243		0	1

References

Aportela, Fernando. 1999. "Effects of Financial Access on Savings by Low-Income People."*MIT Department of Economics Dissertation Chapter 1.*

Ashraf, Nava, Dean Karlan, and Yin Wesley. 2006a. "Deposit Collectors." *Advances in Economic Analysis & Policy* 6 (2): 1–24. https://doi.org/10.2202/1538-0637.1483.

Ashraf, Nava, Dean Karlan, and Wesley Yin. 2006b. "Tying Odysseus to the Mast: Evidence from a Commitment Savings Product in the Philippines." *Quarterly Journal of Economics* 121 (2): 635–72. https://doi.org/10.1162/qjec.2006.121.2.635.

Banerjee, Abhijit V, and Esther Duflo. 2007. "The Economic Lives of the Poor." *Journal of Economic Perspectives* 21 (1): 141–68. https://doi.org/10.1257/jep.21.1.141

Bernheim, B Douglas, and John Karl Scholz. 1993. "Private Saving and Public Policy." *Tax Policy and the Economy* 7: 73–110. https://doi.org/10.1086/tpe.7.20060630.

Bertrand, Marianne, Sendhil Mullainathan, and Eldar Shafir. 2006. "Behavioral Economics and Marketing in Aid of Decision Making Among the Poor." *Journal of Public Policy & Marketing* 25 (1): 8–23. https://doi.org/10.1509/jppm.25.1.8

Browning, Martin, and Annamaria Lusardi. 1996. "Household Saving: Micro Theories and Micro Facts." *Journal of Economic Literature* 34 (4): 1797–1855. https://doi.org/10.2307/2729595.

Beverly, Sondra G, and Michael Sherraden. 1999. "Institutional Determinants of Saving: Implications for Low-Income Households and Public Policy." *The Journal of Socio-Economics* 28 (4): 457–73. https://doi.org/10.1016/S1053-5357(99)00046-3.

Coleman, Andrew. 1998. "Household Savings: A Survey of Recent Microeconomic Theory and Evidence." 98/08. *New Zealand Treasury Working Paper Series*. http://hdl.handle.net/10419/205402.

Collins, Daryl, Jonathan Morduch, Stuart Rutherford, and Orlanda Ruthven. 2010. *Portfolios of the Poor: How the World's Poor Live on $2 a Day*. Princeton: Princeton University Press.

Cragg, John G. 1971. "Some Statistical Models for Limited Dependent Variables with Application to the Demand for Durable Goods." *Econometrica* 39 (5): 829–44.

Deaton, Angus. 1990. "Savings in Developing Countries Theory and Review." In *Proceedings of the World Bank Annual Conference on Development Economics 1989, World Bank Economic Review Supplement*, 61–96. Washington,D.C.: The World Bank.

Demirguc-Kunt, Asli, Leora Klapper, Dorothe Singer, Saniya Ansar, and Jake Hess. 2018. "The Global Findex Database 2017: Measuring Financial Inclusion and the Fintech Revolution." Washington, D.C.: World Bank Group.

Demirguc-Kunt, Asli, Leora Klapper, Dorothe Singer, and Saniya Ansar. 2022. "The Global Findex Database 2021: Financial Inclusion, Digital Payments, and Resilience in the Age of COVID-19." Washington,D.C.:World Bank. https://doi.org/10.1596/978-1-4648-1897-4.

Dupas, Pascaline, and Jonathan Robinson. 2013. "Why Don't the Poor Save More? Evidence from Health Savings Experiments." *American Economic Review* 103 (4): 1138–71. https://doi.org/10.1257/aer.103.4.1138.

Dupas, Pascaline, Sarah Green, Anthony Keats, and Jonathan Robinson. 2012. "Challenges in Banking the Rural Poor: Evidence from Kenya's Western Province." 17851. NBER Working Paper Series. Cambridge, MA: National Bureau of Economic Research. https://doi.org/10.3386/w17851.

Ghosh, Saibal. 2020. "Financial Inclusion in India: Does Distance Matter?" *South Asia Economic Journal* 21 (2): 216–38. https://doi.org/10.1177/139156 1420961649.

Giannatale, Sonia di, and María José Roa. 2016. "Formal Saving in Developing Economies-Barriers, Interventions, and Effects." IDB-WP-766. Washington, DC: Inter-American Development Bank.

Goedecke, Jann, Isabelle Guérin, Bert D'espallier, and Govindan Venkatasubramanian. 2018. "Why Do Financial Inclusion Policies Fail in Mobilizing Savings from the Poor? Lessons from Rural South India." *Development Policy Review* 36 (s1): O201–19. https://doi.org/10.1111/dpr.12272.

Honohan, Patrick. 2007. "Cross Country Variation in Household Access to Financial Services." Journal of Banking & Finance 32 (11): 2493–2500. https://doi.org/10.1016/j.jbankfin.2008.05.004.

Karlan, Dean, Margaret McConnell, Sendhil Mullainathan, and Jonathan Zinman. 2016. "Getting to the Top of Mind: How Reminders Increase Saving." *Management Science* 62 (12): 3393–3411. https://doi.org/10.1287/mnsc.2015.2296.

Karlan, Dean, Aishwarya Lakshmi Ratan, and Jonathan Zinman. 2014. "Saving by and for the Poor: A Research Review and Agenda." *Review of Income and Wealth* 60 (1): 36–78. https://doi.org/10.1111/roiw.12101.

Keynes, J. M. (1936). The general theory of employment, interest and money. London: Macmillan. https://www.hetwebsite.net/het/texts/keynes/gt/gtcont.htm

Morawczynski, Olga, David Hutchful, Nimmy Rangaswamy, and Edward Cutrell. 2010. "The Bank Account Is Not Enough: Examining Strategies for Financial Inclusion in India." In *Proceedings of the 4th ACM/IEEE International Conference on Information and Communication Technologies and Development. ACM, 2010*. London: IEEE. https://www.microsoft.com/en-us/research/publication/the-bank-account-is-not-enough-examining-strategies-for-financial-inclusion-in-india/.

Mowl, Amy Jensen. 2013. "The Role of Transaction Costs in Access to Savings and Credit." NSE Working Paper Series. Chennai: NSE-IFMR.

Murdoch, Jonathan, and Manohar Sharma. 2002. "Strengthening Public Safety Nets from the Bottom Up." Development Policy Review 20 (5): 569–588. https://doi.org/10.1257/jel.20171307.

Munshi, Kaivan. 2019. "Caste and the Indian Economy." Journal of Economic Literature 57 (4): 781–834. https://doi.org/10.1111/1467-7679.00190

Prina, Silvia. 2015. "Banking the Poor via Savings Accounts: Evidence from a Field Experiment." *Journal of Development Economics* 115: 16–31. https://doi.org/10.1016/j.jdeveco.2015.01.004.

Rajeev, Meenakshi, and B.P. Vani. 2017. *Financial Access of the Urban Poor in India: A Story of Exclusion*. New Delhi: Springer India. https://doi.org/10.1007/978-81-322-3712-9.

Ramji, Minakshi. 2009. *Financial Inclusion in Gulbarga: Finding Usage in Access*. Institute for Financial Management and Research Working Paper Series. Chennai: IFMR

Rosenzweig, Mark R. 2001. "Savings Behaviour in Low-Income Countries." *Oxford Review of Economic Policy* 17 (1): 40–54

Saravanabhavan, S., and Meenakshi R. (2025). Spatial Impact of Education on Formal Savings in India: A Household-level Analysis. *Global Journal of Emerging Market Economies*, 0(0). https://doi.org/10.1177/09749101251364587

Sharma, Manoj, Anurodh Giri, and Sakshi Chadha. 2016. "Pradhan Mantri Jan Dhan Yojana Wave III Assessment." Microsave. https://www.microsave.net/files/pdf/PMJDY_Wave_III_Assessment_MicroSave.pdf.

CHAPTER 7

Financial Inclusion and Insurance: A Case of Crop Insurance

7.1 Introduction

In the preceding chapters, we examined two fundamental components of financial inclusion, namely, credit and savings, identifying the various challenges that impede access to these services and suggesting possible remedial measures to improve the low access and use of these services. In the current chapter, we shift our focus to the third aspect of financial inclusion, namely, insurance. Insurance serves as a vital ex-ante risk management mechanism, enabling individuals and households to protect themselves against future financial risks by paying a small amount as a premium at regular intervals to the insurance provider. It is particularly useful for the poor, who often lack other resources, to overcome a financial emergency (Ray 1998).

Insurance plays a crucial role in mitigating a wide range of household-level risks such as the death of an earning member, unexpected health issues, accidents, and crop failures. Beyond its micro-level impact, the adoption of insurance also has certain macro-level benefits. It mobilises private savings, which in turn increases public expenditure (UNDP 2007). Such expenditure contributes to the larger development goals of a country, such as strengthening food security and improving health and education (Martínez et al. 2019). Thus, insurance not only strengthens

S. Saravanabhavan and M. Rajeev, *Moving Beyond Barriers*, Palgrave Studies in Impact Finance,
https://doi.org/10.1007/978-981-95-1066-5_7

individual resilience but also plays a strategic role in advancing national development goals.

In the Indian scenario, it is to be noted that access to any kind of insurance is low. According to the NABARD Rural Financial Inclusion Survey (2017), only 25% of rural households report using any form of insurance, with life insurance being the most commonly held product. While there are several other types of insurance available, including health insurance, crop insurance, and vehicle insurance, the uptake of these products remains relatively low. Studying all these insurance-related instruments in detail, however, is beyond the scope of this book. Therefore, in this chapter, we begin by providing a broad picture of the overall access to insurance in both rural and urban sectors, using data from the 77th Round of the NSSO-All-India Debt and Investment Survey. In the latter part of the chapter, we narrow our focus to crop insurance, and this segment of the analysis is based on data from the 70th and 77th Rounds of the NSSO-Situation Assessment Survey.

We give special emphasis on crop insurance given its critical role in improving the lives of low-income agricultural households. By protecting farmers against crop losses, crop insurance contributes to poverty reduction and supports agricultural productivity and GDP growth (World Bank 2008). This focus is particularly relevant in the Indian context, where the majority of the households are still dependent on agriculture and related activities. However, much of Indian agriculture is rain-fed and susceptible to weather-related uncertainties. Around 73.2 million hectares out of the 141.4 million hectares of net sown area in the country is non-irrigated and rain-fed (GOI 2018a). Due to this dependence on rain and the increasing impact of climate change, crop losses have become a common occurrence for Indian farmers. In such situations, crop insurance can provide the much-needed financial support to ensure that households maintain their usual level of consumption and avoid distress-driven decisions.

Despite the importance of crop insurance, Indian farmers generally do not insure their crops, and their adoption levels are not comparable to supply-side efforts by the Government. One of the key initiatives in this area is the Pradhan Mantri Fasal Bima Yojana (PMFBY), launched in 2016. The PMFBY aims to provide financial support to farmers facing crop loss due to unforeseen events, stabilise their income, and promote the adoption of modern farming practices.[1] To assess the impact of such initiatives, this chapter presents a comparative analysis of the pre-yojana period (using data from the 2013 Situation Assessment Survey, SAS) and the post-yojana period (based on SAS 2019), highlighting the evolving trends in crop insurance adoption and evaluating the effectiveness of the PMFBY.

Additionally, it is important to acknowledge that a lack of awareness is one of the main reasons for the low adoption of crop insurance (NABARD 2017). To delve deeper into this issue, this chapter uses appropriate econometric techniques to explore the impact of different information channels in raising awareness and improving access to crop insurance. The econometric analysis uses data from the 70th Round NSSO-Situation Assessment Survey (SAS).

The chapter is organised as follows. Section 7.2 provides a brief literature review. Section 7.3 outlines the data used. Section 7.4 provides a short descriptive analysis. Section 7.5 presents the econometric analysis and results. Finally, Sect. 7.6 concludes.

7.2 Challenges in the Adoption of Crop Insurance—A Brief Review

Similar to other financial markets, insurance markets also face the problem of asymmetries of information (Gunnsteinsson 2020). This imbalance in information between the insurer and the insured leads to underdevelopment in insurance markets, a problem that is more pronounced in the case of non-life insurance (Samuel 2004). This trend is evident in India as well, where the life insurance sector is significantly more developed than the non-life sector, including crop insurance (NABARD 2017; NSSO 2019). In the context of crop insurance, such information asymmetries, where farmers possess more information about their risks than insurers, can prevent the market from reaching a competitive equilibrium (Rothschild and Stiglitz 1976). This may lead to a moral hazard problem, where insured farmers may engage in riskier agricultural practices, knowing they are adequately covered, thereby undermining the effectiveness of the insurance system.

[1] https://pib.gov.in/PressReleasePage.aspx?PRID=2104175.

The insurance companies also cannot increase their premiums too high to cover the increased risk, as that may lead to the exclusion of good customers (low-risk customers) from the market. In addition, the high value of insurance may lead to adverse selection, where only risky customers choose to purchase the insurance. So, companies need to price their products appropriately to attract a healthy mix of customers, encouraging enough participation and responsible customers (Rothschild and Stiglitz 1976). Such characteristics of insurance markets, like pricing problems and possible risky behaviour of customers, create hindrances for the market mechanism to work freely.

Existing studies indicate that farmers rely on informal risk management methods such as on-farm and off-farm diversification, restricting their production activities to producing only safe crops, accumulating savings by cutting down on current consumption, and sharecropping arrangements (Wright and Hewitt 1994; Hazell et al. 1986). While these coping mechanisms may offer some degree of protection, research shows that they often come at a high cost to long-term productivity and growth. These methods discourage investment and prevent farmers from adopting new technology and innovations (Binswanger-Mkhize 2012; Dercon 2002). Furthermore, they may also lead to compromises with regard to health, nutrition, and education, leading to perpetuation of poverty and vulnerability (Dercon 2002).

Despite the benefits and the availability of state-supported insurance schemes in India, the adoption of crop insurance is low. The lack of adoption is primarily due to a lack of adequate information. The Comptroller and Auditor General of India (CAG) surveyed 5933 farmers in selected villages in selected states, and they found that only 37% of the farmers were aware of crop insurance schemes, including details like the rates of premium, coverage, and claims (GOI 2017). Therefore, creating awareness is relevant for India, where large parts of the rural areas are still characterised by high poverty and low levels of education.

7.3 Data

For our main analysis, we have used the 70th and 77th Rounds of the NSS—Situation Assessment Survey (SAS) of Agricultural Households. These surveys are carried out to understand the agricultural situation in rural India. The survey is done in two visits to obtain information about the two major agricultural seasons without the problem of recall error.

The 70th Round collected information for the agricultural year, July 2012–June 2013. A sample of 35,200 households was surveyed during visit one, and 34,907 households out of this were surveyed in visit two. The 77th Round collected information for the agricultural year, July 2018 to June 2019. In visit-1, information was collected for July to December 2018, and in visit-2, information was collected for January to June 2019. A sample of 58,035 households was surveyed during visit-1, and 56,894 households were surveyed in visit-2.

In our study, an agricultural household is said to have access to insurance if it adopts crop insurance for any crop. As per the 77th Round Survey, an agricultural household is defined as one that is receiving "some value of produce more than Rs. 4000 from agricultural activities (e.g. cultivation of field crops, horticultural crops, fodder crops, plantation, animal husbandry, poultry, fishery, piggery, bee-keeping, vermiculture, sericulture, etc.) and having at least one member self-employed in agriculture either in principal status or in subsidiary status during last 365 days". The income cut-off was earlier Rs. 3000 in the 70th Round; the latest Round has updated it to Rs. 4000 to account for inflation.

Our econometric analysis utilises data from the NSS 70th Round Situation Assessment Survey, and we consider only five major crops-paddy, maize, green gram, sorghum, and groundnut. We restrict our analysis to states in which these crops are insurable. And we do so because only a few specific crops are insurable in a state, and this list is different for each state. Hence, including all the crops (both insurable and non-insurable) is meaningless, as households may not be adopting insurance, because the crops they are cultivating are not insurable within the particular state.

7.4 Access to Insurance—Descriptive Analysis

We start our analysis with a brief comparison of India with other emerging Asian countries to see where India stands relative to countries in the region at similar stages of economic development. Table 7.1 shows that the overall insurance penetration of India is only 3.7%. Here, insurance penetration is the total insurance premium as a percentage of Gross Domestic Product. This is the most common measure to assess the development of the insurance sector of a country. The measure for India is almost equal to the average insurance penetration of the Asian countries that we have listed in the table, and half of the average world measure, implying low penetration in the entire region. In the selected region,

Table 7.1 Insurance penetration (premium as a per cent of GDP) in emerging Asia-Pacific countries—2019

Country	*Total*	*Life*	*Non-life*
THA	5.27	3.59	1.68
MYS	4.77	3.32	1.45
CHN	4.22	2.3	1.92
IND	3.7	2.74	0.97
VNM	2.42	1.58	0.85
IDN	1.95	1.49	0.47
PHL	1.82	1.26	0.56
LKA	1.15	0.54	0.62
BGD	0.57	0.41	0.17
Total	3.83	2.25	1.58
World	6.09	3.31	2.78

Note THA—Thailand, MYS—Malaysia, CHN—China, IND—India, VNM—Vietnam, IDN—Indonesia, PHL—Philippines, LKA—Sri Lanka, BGD—Bangladesh
Source Swiss Re-sigma No 3/2019

though Thailand and Malaysia have the highest penetration levels, it is still lower than the world average.

7.4.1 Indian Scenario: Access to Life and Non-life Insurance

We now turn our attention to India-specific analysis using the 77th Round NSSO-All-India debt and investment survey. Table 7.2 shows the percentage of households in India having access to different types of insurance. Here, non-life insurance includes vehicle insurance, health insurance, fire insurance, etc.

We observe that 47% of the households have life insurance and 76% have non-life insurance. However, within the non-life insurance category, vehicle insurance predominates, indicating limited coverage in other areas. It is also evident that the Scheduled Caste (SC) and Scheduled Tribe (ST) households have the lowest uptake of both life and non-life insurance adoption.

Among the non-life insurance services, crop insurance is particularly significant, as a large portion of the rural population in India is engaged in agriculture. Given this context, we will focus our analysis on access to crop insurance for rural farmers. Our discussion begins with an examination of

Table 7.2 Percentage of households having access to different types of insurance (life and non-life)

	Life-insurance			*Non-life insurance**		
	Rural(%)	*Urban(%)*	*All(%)*	*Rural(%)*	*Urban(%)*	*All(%)*
SC	47	51	48	14	71	69
ST	43	46	44	71	75	72
OBC	44	45	45	75	81	77
General	49	52	50	71	80	76
All	45	48	47	72	80	76

Note *Non-life insurance includes vehicle, crop, and other agricultural insurance, health, marine, fire, and other miscellaneous
Source Author's calculations using 77th Round of NSSO-AIDIS data

the Pradhan Mantri Fasal Bima Yojana (PMFBY), a key initiative designed to provide crop insurance to farmers and safeguard their livelihoods against agricultural risks.

7.4.2 Pradhan Mantri Fasal BhimaYojana

In 2016, the Pradhan Mantri Fasal Bhima Yojana (PMFBY) was formed by merging and modifying the existing schemes, the National Agricultural Insurance Scheme (NAIS), the National Crop Insurance Programme (NCIP), and the Weather-based Crop Insurance Scheme (RWBCIS). Apart from covering unavoidable risks to standing crops, the insurance also covers the insured farmers if they are unable to sow, experience post-harvest losses (up to 14 days), or suffer damages due to localised calamities.

This scheme introduced a standardised premium charging 2% for Kharif crops, 1.5% for Rabi crops, and 5% for commercial and horticultural crops. These rates are notably lower than previous schemes and also, unlike earlier schemes, PMFBY does not impose an upper limit on the subsidy. The government provides low rates with the assurance that it will pay the remaining amount, thereby providing the farmer full insurance against any natural disasters. In earlier schemes, there was a cap on the premium that insurance companies could charge, and this resulted in lower sums being insured by the companies and therefore smaller claims (GOI 2016).

Under the PMFBY, the adoption of technology is encouraged to streamline processes and prevent delays in the payment of claims to farmers. The Government encourages the use of smartphones to capture and transmit data from crop-cutting experiments in real time, which enables reliable estimates of crop yields. Also, the scheme mandates that the claim amount will be transferred to the claimant's bank account, ensuring efficient payment of funds (GOI 2016). This scheme also places special emphasis on the coverage of Scheduled castes/Scheduled Tribes and women farmers, to improve the inclusion of vulnerable populations.

Table 7.3 presents the number of farmers insured in 2020 and 2024 across a few major states, covering both the kharif and rabi seasons in a year. The table shows a decline in coverage of farmers from 2020 to 2024 for many states for the Kharif season. Particularly, a considerable decline is observed in states like Karnataka, Madhya Pradesh, Assam, and Haryana during the kharif season. Several reasons are ascribed to this decrease, for instance, debt waivers, farmers' perception of risk mitigation and deduplication as a result of the mandatory requirement of Aadhar for insurance.[2] Other non-price issues, such as lack of trust, lack of awareness about the product, deficiency of adequate money, and unsuitability of available products, are often cited as reasons for low adoption (Cole et al. 2013).

This brief review emphasises the importance of insurance and highlights the slow growth in its adoption in India. To delve deeper into this issue, we will analyse data from the 70th and 77th Rounds of the National Sample Survey Office (NSSO) Situation Assessment Survey (SAS). This comparative analysis will provide insights into the factors affecting the adoption of insurance and the change in adoption during the study period.

7.4.3 Access to Crop Insurance—A State-Level and Disaggregated Analysis

As mentioned earlier in this chapter, crop loss is a common phenomenon in the Indian agricultural scene, as a large majority of the farmers depend on the monsoon rains for irrigation. As a result, one of the major reasons

[2] Decline in number of beneficiaries under PMFBY, Press Information Bureau, http://pib.nic.in/newsite/PrintRelease.aspx?relid=181469.

Table 7.3 Number of farmers insured under the PMFBY—A few major states

States	*Kharif* 2020	*Kharif* 2024	*Rabi* 2020	*Rabi* 2024	*Growth rate (%)* 2017–2018	*Growth rate (%)* 2018–2019
AS	596,530	351,996	237,240	235,664	−41	−1
HR	644,027	251,612	565,507	234,902	−61	−58
HP	85,587	95,581	84,817	96,574	12	14
KA	1,344,763	1,085,154	161,072	297,799	−19	85
MP	2,824,644	2,432,748	2,154,680	2,027,429	−14	−6
MH	4,277,762	7,882,844	566,533	3,590,242	84	534
OR	1,586,110	2,263,156	52,328	133,595	43	155
RJ	3,044,992	3,061,944	2,142,672	2,326,759	1	9
UP	1,867,881	1,815,027	1,731,577	1,223,834	−3	−29
Total	18,001,919	23,358,231	9,959,822	13,033,666	30	31

Note AS—Assam, HR—Haryana, HP—Himachal Pradesh, KA—Karnataka, MP—Madhya Pradesh, MH—Maharashtra, OR—Orissa, RJ—Rajasthan, UP—Uttar Pradesh
Source PMFBY Administrative Dashboard, https://pmfby.gov.in/adminStatistics/dashboard

for crop loss, both in the Kharif as well as Rabi seasons, is drought. Additionally, plant diseases, infestation by insects, and destruction by wild animals are other major contributors to crop failure. Given the frequent occurrence of crop loss due to these events, access to crop insurance is beneficial for farmers to protect their livelihoods. In this section, we will conduct a disaggregated analysis of crop insurance in India, utilising data from two rounds of the Situation Assessment Survey (SAS) conducted in 2013 and 2019.

To begin with, we examine access to crop insurance across different states (In the SAS survey, data on crop insurance is collected for the crops harvested by agricultural households during the reference period). As illustrated in Fig. 7.1, the average percentage of households accessing crop insurance in India is just 13%, marking a 6% increase from the 70th Round survey. Haryana, Tamil Nadu, and Maharashtra have the highest adoption of crop insurance, while states such as Bihar, Uttar Pradesh, and Assam have the lowest adoption rates.

Table 7.4 reveals that the majority of crop insurance policies are acquired as a compulsory requirement when receiving loans, while

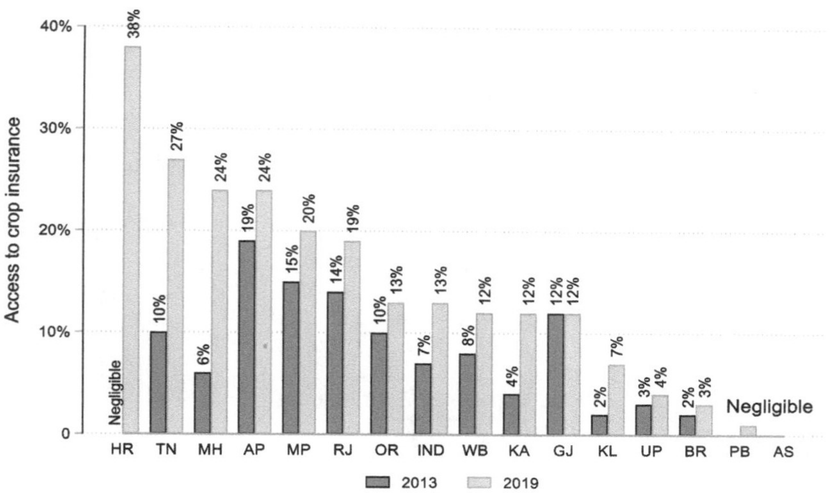

Fig. 7.1 Percentage of agricultural households having access to crop insurance across various states

Note A household is said to have access to crop insurance if it has taken crop insurance anytime during the agricultural year

(*Source* Author's calculations using 70th and 77th Rounds of NSSO-SAS data)

the proportion of households that voluntarily purchase crop insurance remains very low. Additionally, the percentage of medium and large farmers insuring their crops is significantly higher, at 23% and 34% respectively, compared to small and marginal farmers.

Furthermore, the problem of socio-economic discrimination continues to be a significant issue. Analysis of our data reveals that a large portion of the SC and ST households belong to the lower economic classes, compared to Other Backward Castes and General castes. For these disadvantaged groups, access to insurance is generally low, and it is particularly severe for those in the lowest economic classes. Thus, being socially backward, combined with a disadvantageous economic position, makes these caste groups especially vulnerable to agricultural risks in the absence of crop insurance adoption.

The low adoption of crop insurance, despite significant efforts by the government, makes us probe into the reasons why people do not insure their crops. We find that the primary reason for the lack of crop insurance adoption is the widespread lack of awareness about insurance

Table 7.4 Percentage of households accessing crop insurance across farmer categories (based on size of landholdings)

Land classification (hectares)	*Insured only when receiving a loan (%)*	*Insured additionally (%)*	*Insured either way (%)*
<0.01	Negligible (%)	Negligible (%)	Negligible (%)
0.01–0.40	1	1	2
0.41–1.00	2	1	3
1.01–2.00	5	2	7
2.01–4.00	9	4	13
4.01–10.00	17	6	23
>10.01	26	8	34
Total	8	3	11

Source Author's calculations using 77th Round of NSSO-SAS data

programmes. From the data, we find that 51% of the households cite "not aware" as the reason for not insuring. Another 13% say that they are not aware of the facility. This implies that a lack of awareness (about the service as well as the specific scheme) is one of the main reasons for people not insuring their crops, a situation often linked to financial illiteracy. Awareness can be improved through different channels, including government institutions, private agents, and progressive farmers (progressive peers). Networking with such entities can play an important role in influencing farmers' decisions regarding the adoption of new methods and programmes. These institutions, both private and public, can act as channels for the flow of information within the community. Identifying the most effective avenues through which information can flow is important in creating awareness about crop insurance and could enable wider adoption of crop insurance.

Another significant issue regarding crop insurance is the irregularity in the payment of claims. A delay in payments can diminish the farmers' trust in insurance schemes, discouraging future adoption. From the data, we find that 80% of the households that have been insured additionally and have experienced crop losses reported not receiving the settlement. To resolve the issue of delayed payment of claims, new Government guidelines have introduced stricter timelines and penalty provisions. Accordingly, a 12% interest rate has to be paid by the Insurance Company to farmers for delays in settlement claims beyond 10 days from the prescribed cut-off date for payment. States are also required to pay 12% interest for delay in the release of the State share of Subsidy beyond three months from the prescribed cut-off date/submission of requisition by Insurance Companies (GOI 2018b). Thus, there are sufficient efforts from the state to improve delivery.

In spite of the government's efforts, we observe that access to insurance is low in India, which is indeed a cause for concern. The descriptive analysis indicates that several socio-economic factors are responsible for the low adoption, particularly the lack of awareness. In the subsequent section, we further investigate these issues related to low access to insurance using appropriate econometric techniques.

7.5 Factors Determining the Extent of Crop Insurance Adoption: Econometric Analysis and Results

7.5.1 *Econometric Method Used*

The extent of crops insured is used as the dependent variable, which is measured as the number of crops insured divided by the total number of crops cultivated by the household. This proportion allows us to understand, to what extent crops cultivated are insured, and this variable ranges between values of 0 and 1. Due to the proportional nature and the significant number of zero values, a standard linear regression or log odds transformation would be unsuitable, as it would be difficult to interpret the coefficients (Wooldridge 2010). In such cases, Papke and Woolridge (1996) recommend the implementation of a fractional model, where $E(y/x)$ can be modelled as a logit or a probit function.

According to the fractional probit model, the conditional mean of a fractional outcome (y) given the explanatory variables (x) can be written as

$$E(y/x) = \Phi(x\beta)$$

where Φ is the standard cumulative distribution function and β is the vector of unknown parameters. This allows the predicted values to be between 0 and 1, and the effect of any of the x variables on $E(y/x)$ diminishes as $x\beta \to \infty$. The model is estimated using Bernoulli quasi-maximum likelihood estimation.

7.5.2 *Variables Used*

In our regression analysis, the variable of interest is the proportion of crops insured, which is calculated as the number of crops insured divided by the total number of crops cultivated by the household. This measure is important for understanding financial inclusion, as it provides information on the extent of insurance coverage, as opposed to a binary variable that only tells us whether the household has insurance or not. While it is important to examine whether a farmer adopts crop insurance or not, it is more relevant to assess the degree to which they insure all their crops, to shield against risk. Therefore, unlike other existing studies (Rajeev and Nagendran 2019; Rajeev et al. 2015), we use the extent of crop insurance adoption as our dependent variable.

For this analysis, we have identified several variables that may influence the extent of crop insurance coverage. One key factor is the lack of awareness, which is a primary reason for the non-adoption of crop insurance. Awareness can be improved through various agents, who can inform households about available programmes and schemes, increasing their understanding and participation. Some of the important agents in a rural setting are Government organisations (such as Krishi Vigyan Kendra, Agricultural colleges, and Extension agents), private agents (private commercial agents) and progressive farmers (advanced peers in the community). We explore how networking with these agents impacts the adoption of crop insurance.

Another important factor we consider is the effect of mass media such as television, newspapers, and radio on the adoption of crop insurance. We use the frequency of access to mass media channels as an indicator of their impact. Here, the variable is such that the values are coded from one to six, representing the frequency of access in descending order: daily, weekly, monthly, seasonal, need-based, and casual contact. A higher frequency of exposure to these channels may contribute to greater awareness and, consequently, higher adoption rates of crop insurance.

Furthermore, we include the average number of crops cultivated by the household as an indicator of informal risk diversification by the households. We expect that farmers who employ such informal methods of insurance may be less likely to adopt formal crop insurance, as they may perceive their risk as being adequately managed.

Whether a household accesses insurance also depends on the anticipated risk; the higher the anticipated risk, the more likely that a household will access insurance. We account for this by including the ratio of unirrigated land to the total cultivated land area in our regression model. Unirrigated land is especially vulnerable to excess, untimely, or insufficient rainfall, and can have a calamitous effect on the crops. Therefore, more cultivation in unirrigated land increases the risk within a farm household, and so we expect this variable to have a positive association with access to insurance.

We have also included the types of farm households in the model. For this, we categorise households based on their operational land holdings into two groups: smaller and marginal farmers operating on less than four hectares of land holdings and larger farm households operating on more than four hectares of land holdings. Among other explanatory variables, we included consumption expenditure as an indicator of the household's economic status and a proxy for the income of household. We expect that households with higher-income levels may be more capable of affording insurance premiums, leading to a positive correlation between income and access to crop insurance.

Among the household characteristics, we include the gender of the household head, caste, the highest educational level of household members, household size, and the ratio of child dependents. Summary statistics are provided in Appendix Table A12. A fractional probit model has also been done to affirm the analysis (See Appendix A13).

7.5.3 Results and Discussion

As mentioned in the data section, this analysis considers only households cultivating any of the five major crops -paddy, maize, groundnut, jowar, and gram. These crops are insurable in the selected states. Consequently, the dependent variable is calculated as a proportion of the number of crops insured (out of the five selected crops) divided by the total number of insurable crops (out of the five selected crops) cultivated by the household. This measure provides a better understanding of the extent of crop insurance coverage among households growing these specific crops.

Table 7.5 shows that households with access to Government organisations and private agents are likely to have a larger number of crops insured compared to those without such access. This result highlights the importance of networking with Government organisations and private agents to improve crop insurance adoption. Additionally, crop diversification is a popular risk-reducing mechanism followed by farmers. We find from the analysis that the more the number of crops cultivated, the lesser the extent of adoption of crop insurance. In this case, perhaps the farmers have already adopted an informal risk-mitigating strategy through crop diversification, and hence they do not feel the necessity to adopt formal crop insurance. However, it has been argued in the literature that these informal methods of risk mitigation can be inefficient, as they may encourage farmers to cultivate less profitable crops and discourage specialising in a single crop, which could improve their productivity and income (Binswanger-Mkhize 2012; Dercon 2002).

Next, we find that the ratio of unirrigated land to total cultivated land area has a positive and significant effect on the extent of access to insurance, as expected. Generally, as the ratio of unirrigated land to total cultivated land area increases for a household, the risk also increases, leading to a higher demand from these farmers to insure against their risks.

We also find that larger farm households are likely to have more number of crops insured as compared to other smaller farmers. Similarly, as income increases, the extent of crops insured also increases. When income rises, the agricultural households can afford the cost of the premium and still manage their average level of consumption.

Other household characteristics, such as education and caste, show expected results. Households with better-educated members are more likely to insure a greater number of crops. Similarly, we see that the general castes and Other Backward Castes are more likely to insure more crops as compared to SC/ST.

Table 7.5 Fractional logit model—factors determining the extent of crop insurance

Variables	*Extent of crops insured*
Govt organisations	0.2936**
	(0.143)
Private agencies	0.2688**
	(0.125)
Frequency of access to media	0.0128
	(0.049)
The average number of crops	−3.0604***
	(0.214)
Ratio of unirrigated land	0.8504***
	(0.149)
Income	0.0000**
	(0.000)
Large farmers	1.0500***
	(0.201)
Education (base-below primary)	
Primary	−0.1406
	(0.192)
Secondary	0.3428**
	(0.154)
Tertiary	0.3623*
	(0.209)
Caste (base-SCST)	
OBC	0.7321***
	(0.112)
General	0.6456***
	(0.155)
Household size	0.0419*
	(0.024)
Ratio of children	−0.6041**
	(0.305)
State dummies	Included
Constant	–0.7007*
	(0.374)
Observations	8920

Note Only major crops have been considered for the analysis
Standard errors in parentheses, ***$p < 0.01$, **$p < 0.05$, *$p < 0.1$

7.6 Concluding Observations

In this chapter, we explored the access and adoption of crop insurance in India, using the household-level data from the 70th and 77th Situation Assessment Surveys (SAS). Overall, we find that while the insurance market in India is growing, it remains relatively underpenetrated compared to global standards, presenting significant expansion opportunities. While there is a considerable uptake of non-life insurance, particularly vehicle insurance, perhaps due to regulation, the adoption of crop insurance has much to improve.

The analysis of the Pradhan Mantri Fasal Bima Yojana (PMFBY) reveals that despite the government's efforts to make crop insurance more accessible and affordable, there is still a significant coverage gap, indicating much scope for improvement. From the analysis of the PMFBY data (data from administrative sources), though we see there has been some increase, it needs to be noted that the targeted adoption rate has not yet been met.

To examine the low adoption of crop insurance further, we undertook a comparative analysis of the 70th and 77th Rounds Situational Assessment Survey of farmer households. From this analysis, we find the average percentage of households accessing crop insurance in India is just 13%, marking only a 6% increase from the 70th Round survey. Our analysis also shows the wide disparity across the states, with states such as Haryana, Tamil Nadu, and Maharashtra having the highest crop insurance adoption rates, while states such as Bihar, Uttar Pradesh, and Assam have the lowest adoption rates. The analysis also reveals that one of the main reasons for not insuring is a lack of awareness.

We also employed a fractional logit model to examine the factors influencing crop insurance uptake. Access to government agencies and private agents is positively associated with adoption, highlighting the important role these intermediaries play in disseminating information and raising awareness about insurance schemes. Additionally, socio-economic factors such as caste, education and household income significantly impact crop insurance adoption, with wealthier households, forward castes, and more educated households showing higher adoption rates.

Appendix

See Tables A12 and A13.

Table A12 Summary statistics—Crop insurance

Variables	*Description of variable*	*Mean*	*Std. Dev*	*Min*	*Max*
Extent of crops insured	Total number of crops insured/ total crops cultivated by household	0.077	0.264	0	1
Government organisation	=1 if the household has access to any Government organisation	0.234		0	1
Private agency	=1 if the household has access to any Government organisation	0.280		0	1
Frequency of access to media	Frequency at which household accesses media	1.002	2.025	0	6
Ratio of unirrigated	Ratio of unirrigated to total land owned	0.376	0.448	0	1
Income	Value of income of the household	8713.323	16,216.67	0	481,945.8
Average number of other crops cultivated	Average number of other crops cultivated by household	1.642	0.981	0	4
Large farmer	=1 if the household belongs to the large farmer category	0.088		0	1

(continued)

Table A12 (continued)

Variables	*Description of variable*	*Mean*	*Std. Dev*	*Min*	*Max*
Base-below primary	=1 if the maximum educational level in the household is below primary				
Primary	=1 if the maximum educational level in the household is primary	0.094		0	1
Secondary	=1 if the maximum educational level in the household is secondary	0.582		0	1
Tertiary	=1 if the maximum educational level in the household is tertiary	0.158		0	1
SCST	=1 if the household belongs to SC/ST category				
OBC	=1 if the household belongs to Other backward caste	0.520		0	1
General	=1 if the household belongs to the general caste	0.222		0	1
Household size	Number of members in the household	5.377	2.884	1	41
Ratio of children	Number of children to total household size	0.263	0.223	0	0.875

Table A13 Fractional probit model to explore the factors determining the extent of crop insurance

Variables	*Extent of crops insured*
Govt organisations	0.4878***
	(0.064)
Private agencies	0.2693***
	(0.064)
Frequency of access to media	0.0235*
	(0.014)
Ratio of unirrigated land	0.1158
	(0.092)
Income	0.0000**
	(0.000)
Crop number	−1.0297***
	(0.058)
Large farmers	0.6111***
	(0.081)
(Base-below primary)	
Primary	0.1775*
	(0.091)
Secondary	0.3060***
	(0.077)
Tertiary	0.3678***
	(0.108)
(Base-SCST)	
OBC	0.4343***
	(0.071)
General	0.4548***
	(0.082)
Female-headed household	0.0812
	(0.140)
Household size	0.0333***
	(0.012)
Ratio of children	−0.4089***
	(0.132)
State dummies	Included
Constant	−1.0940**
	(0.508)
Observations	31,731

Robust standard errors in parentheses, ***$p < 0.01$, **$p < 0.05$, *$p < 0.1$

References

Binswanger-Mkhize, Hans P. 2012. "Is There Too Much Hype About Index-Based Agricultural Insurance?" *Journal of Development Studies* 48 (2): 187–200. https://doi.org/10.1080/00220388.2011.625411.

Cole, Shawn, Xavier Giné, Jeremy Tobacman, Petia Topalova, Robert Townsend, and James Vickery. 2013. "Barriers to Household Risk Management: Evidence from India." *American Economic Journal: Applied Economics* 5 (1): 104–135. https://doi.org/10.1257/app.5.1.104.

Dercon, Stefan. 2002. "Income Risk, Coping Strategies, and Safety Nets." *The World Bank Research Observer* 17 (2): 141–166. https://doi.org/10.1093/wbro/17.2.141.

GOI. 2016. "Operational Guidelines of 'Pradhan Mantri Bhima Fasal Yojana'." https://pmfby.gov.in/pdf/Oprational_Guidelines.pdf.

GOI. 2017. "Performance Audit Union Government Agriculture Crop Insurance Schemes Reports of Agriculture and Farmers Welfare." https://cag.gov.in/content/report-no7-2017-performance-audit-union-government-agriculture-crop-insurance-schemes.

GOI. 2018a. "Doubling Farmers' Income." *Report of the Committee on Doubling Farmers' Income*. New Delhi.

GOI. 2018b. "Pradhan Mantri Fasal Bima Yojana." Press Information Bureau. https://pib.gov.in/Pressreleaseshare.aspx?PRID=1555569.

Gunnsteinsson, Snaebjorn. 2020. "Experimental Identification of Asymmetric Information: Evidence on Crop Insurance in the Philippines." *Journal of Development Economics* 144 (May): 102414. https://doi.org/10.1016/j.jdeveco.2019.102414.

Hazell, P., C. Pomareda, and A. Valdes. 1986. *Crop Insurance for Agricultural Development: Issues and Experience*. London: Johns Hopkins University Press.

Martínez, Christiane Ströh de, Martina Wiedmaier Pfister, Corinna Müller, and Ariane Schoen. 2019. *Inclusive Insurance in National Financial Inclusion Strategies—Survey Report*. Kuala Lumpur: Alliance for Financial Inclusion (AFI). https://www.afi-global.org/sites/default/files/publications/2018-08/afi_a2ii_report_view.pdf.

NABARD. 2017. "NABARD All India Rural Financial Inclusion Survey-2016–17." Mumbai. https://www.nabard.org/auth/writereaddata/tender/1608180417NABARD-Repo-16_Web_P.pdf.

NSSO. 2019. "Key Indicators of Social Consumption in India: Health, NSS 75th Round." New Delhi.

Papke, Leslie E., and Jeffrey M. Wooldridge. 1996. "Econometric Methods for Fractional Response Variables with an Application to 401 (k) Plan Participation Rates." *Journal of Applied Econometrics* 11 (6): 619–632. https://doi.org/10.1002/(SICI)1099-1255(199611)11:63.0.

Rajeev, Meenakshi, Manojit Bhattacharjee, and B. P. Vani. 2015. "Crop Insurance and Risk Mitigation: Experiences from India." No 15. ICDD Working Paper. Kassel: Kassel University Press GmbH.

Rajeev, Meenakshi, and Pranav Nagendran. 2019. "Crop Insurance in India-Where Do We Stand?" *Economic and Political Weekly* 54 (26–27). https://www.epw.in/journal/2019/26-27/review-rural-affairs/crop-insurance-india.html.

Ray, Debraj. 1998. *Development Economics. Princeton University Press, Princeton.* Princeton: Princeton University Press.

Rothschild, Michael, and Joseph Stiglitz. 1976. "Equilibrium in Competitive Insurance Markets: An Essay on the Economics of Imperfect Information." *Quarterly Journal of Economics* 90 (4): 355–375. https://doi.org/10.1007/978-94-015-7957-5_18.

Samuel, Achamma. 2004. "Insurance : The Indian Experience." *RBI Occational Papers* 21 (2–3). https://rbidocs.rbi.org.in/rdocs/Publications/Pdfs/33958.pdf.

UNDP. 2007. *Building Security for the Poor: Potential and Prospects for Microinsurance in India*, 2nd ed. Colombo: United Nations Development Programme.

Wooldridge, Jeffrey M. 2010. *Econometric Analysis of Cross Section and Panel Data*. Cambridge: MIT Press.

World Bank. 2008. "Growth and Poverty Reduction in Agriculture's Three Worlds." In *World Development Report 2008: Agriculture for Development*, 26–44. Washington, DC: The world Bank.

Wright, B.D., and J.A. Hewitt. 1994. "All-Risk Crop Insurance: Lessons from Theory and Experience." In *Economics of Agricultural Crop Insurance: Theory and Evidence*, edited by Darrell L. Hueth and William H. Furtan, vol. 4, 73–112. Natural Resource Management and Policy. Dordrecht: Springer. https://doi.org/10.1007/978-94-011-1386-1_4.

CHAPTER 8

Financial Inclusion and Remittances

8.1 Introduction

In the previous chapters, we examined the first three components of financial inclusion: credit, savings, and insurance. Now, in this chapter, we shift our focus to the fourth component, remittance services, which are crucial for improving the lives of migrant families, particularly those from poor backgrounds. Currently, we are at a juncture where geographic mobility is being actively promoted to open out avenues for populations who lack opportunities locally, especially rural populations who are finding it increasingly difficult to support themselves by depending only on agriculture. As a result, internal migration is on the rise. The latest rounds of census data reveal that there has been a marked surge in internal labour migration over the last two decades.

Consequently, domestic remittances have increased considerably. For instance, the economic survey of 2016–17 estimates that the domestic remittances are more than 1.5 lakh crores (GOI 2017). It is worth noting that many of the domestic migrants are working as labourers and often come from underdeveloped regions; therefore, the amount of money that they remit may be modest. This money, however, reaches a large number of households, particularly in rural areas (Deshingkar 2006). Collectively, these funds have a significant impact on the economic development of these regions (Tumbe 2011). Essentially, the flow of remittances serves as

S. Saravanabhavan and M. Rajeev, *Moving Beyond Barriers*, Palgrave Studies in Impact Finance,
https://doi.org/10.1007/978-981-95-1066-5_8

a mechanism for the redistribution of resources from developed regions to lesser developed regions.

In addition to the redistribution of resources at a macro level, remittances enhance the welfare of households in diverse ways. For poor and vulnerable households, remittances alleviate poverty and positively impact household health and children's education. In other cases, such as in more resilient households, they may use remittances to strengthen their investments (IFAD and Bank 2015). Despite the stated benefits, the topic of domestic remittances has not received sufficient attention within the financial inclusion literature.

There are several studies on internal remittances and their importance in the Indian context (Tumbe 2011; Mohanty et al. 2014); however, only very few studies address the issue of lack of access to proper formal financial channels for money transfers. Also in the Indian context, many of the existing studies are dated (Tiwari et al. 2011; Pareek et al. 2011; Garg et al. 2009). This shows the lack of attention given to this area and reveals an important lacuna in financial inclusion literature that needs to be addressed.

When it comes to formal remittance channels, two types are of significance for financial inclusion: the traditional banking channel and the digital channel (which uses mobile technology). The Findex 2018 data shows that of those who received remittances, around 40% still send money through informal agents/friends/families in cash. This indicates that even the traditional banking channel is not used by many. Recently, the Government has given special emphasis on digital financial inclusion, as it reduces transaction costs for the customer and lowers the overheads for financial institutions (Bachas et al. 2018). This aspect of financial inclusion is of considerable importance to migrants for sending remittances.

Given this background, this chapter examines the remittance component of financial inclusion through traditional and digital channels. As mentioned before, there is limited literature on the subject, and the lack of studies may be due to scarcity of relevant data. We find that government sources such as National Sample Surveys do not gather any information on formal remittance channels as yet. Therefore, this chapter examines the issue of access to formal remittance channels, using the Findex database, which is a cross-country database published by the World Bank. This is the only database available currently which provides information on the channels of remittance transmission.

Using descriptive statistics and an analytical review of the existing research, we aim to shed light on the key factors influencing the adoption of formal remittance channels. We examine whether there exist any population groups that need special attention. Such groups may include the aged population, women, the unemployed, or lesser-educated people who usually remain at home and receive remittances. Additionally, we aim to explore the effectiveness of digital remittance methods, especially via mobile technology, in overcoming the challenges associated with insufficient banking infrastructure. Through this chapter, we aim to derive valuable insights for policymakers on the adoption and utilisation of formal money transfer channels.

The rest of the chapter unfolds as follows. Section 8.2 provides a brief literature review. Section 8.3 presents the data and methodology used. Section 8.4 provides an analysis of domestic remittances and the various transaction channels. In Sect. 8.6, we provide the concluding observations.

8.2 Remittance Channels: A Brief Background

In this section, we present a brief review of the literature, organised into four sections. The first and second parts discuss the significance of remittances and the challenges in accessing formal transaction channels. The third section explores the growing role of mobile banking across various developing countries. Finally, in the fourth part, we review the prevalence of informal channels of money transfer, outlining the continued appeal despite the improvements in formal systems.

8.2.1 Importance of Remittances

Understanding the context of domestic migration is crucial to appreciate the need for remittance channels. For some households, migration is a way of diversifying risk by sending members to places with better employment opportunities, allowing them to earn higher incomes. These higher incomes can act as a buffer in times of need for such families (Lucas and Stark 1985). For some others, migration is a coping mechanism, a necessity rather than a choice, in times of financial constraint.

This is especially true for the agricultural households in India whose incomes are uncertain and heavily dependent on climatic factors. Notably, it is the poorest agricultural households, unable to sustain their livelihoods by depending solely on agriculture, who are usually compelled to migrate (Deshingkar 2006; Viswanathan and Kumar 2015). Also, in cases where not all members of a household can sustainably work on a small landholding, some must look for opportunities elsewhere (Dodd et al. 2017). An important reason leading to this migration pattern is the lack of alternative employment opportunities in rural areas.

8.2.2 *Low Usage of Formal Channels of Money Transfer*

Given the aforementioned benefits of remittances, people must have access to reliable formal channels for remitting money. Banks provide convenient and efficient means for remitting funds, and for many households, sending or receiving money could be the first interaction with a financial institution, marking an important initial step towards further financial inclusion (IFAD and Bank 2015). Studies also note that when households receive money through bank transfer, the recipients do not immediately utilise the entire amount, instead, they leave some amount as savings, thus enhancing the household reserves for future emergencies (IFAD and Bank 2015; Tiwari et al. 2011). Despite the evident benefits, the use of formal channels is low in India and most developing countries. While the use of UPI has improved the scenario to a great extent, the poor in rural regions continue to use cash.

Low usage is due to several reasons. Most internal migrants lack adequate skills and education and are usually involved in low-income jobs. For them, prolonged waiting time to access banking services may impose costs in the form of lost income (Garg et al. 2009). Moreover, in rural areas, bank outreach is limited, necessitating long travel to reach banking facilities (Gopinath et al. 2010; Tiwari et al. 2011). In addition, inconvenient working hours, long queues at the bank, unhelpful behaviour of bank officials, and lack of appropriate financial knowledge also discourage migrants and their families from using formal services (ibid.).

As a consequence, they prefer to transfer money through informal ways (Agarwalla et al. 2016). This trend is observed even in the case of households that have bank accounts (Bakshi et al. 2014). These migrants send money through friends and relatives, even though it is inefficient and time-consuming (CDFI 2020). The risks involved are also higher as the money could get stolen or lost during transit, which could be a huge setback for poor migrants already struggling with their limited incomes.

8.2.3 *Relevance of Mobile Banking in Promoting Development*

Mobile banking is gaining popularity in several developing countries as the most efficient means of improving financial inclusion. It serves as a transformative model, and there are several examples of developing countries that have taken advantage of the high penetration of mobile phones.

One of the well-known examples is the case of M-PESA, which is a mobile phone-based financial payment service in Kenya that was launched in 2007 by Safaricom. It was seen that within four years of initiation, around 70 per cent of the population was using M-PESA, and it soon replaced cash remittances (Mas and Morawczynski 2009; Jack and Suri 2016). Similarly, several other African countries such as Uganda, Tanzania, and Ghana are also taking advantage of the improved access to mobile phones and encouraging mobile banking as a platform for social and economic development.

Households that use mobile banking are more likely to receive financial assistance during emergencies from a broader network of relatives and friends, making them better equipped to manage financial shocks compared to those without access to mobile banking (Jack and Suri 2016). Furthermore, access to mobile money has been linked to poverty reduction. It can also influence financial behaviour, leading to outcomes such as increased savings, particularly among women-headed households, who often face greater financial vulnerability (Suri and Jack 2016).

8.2.4 *Informal Channels of Money Transfer*

A popular way of sending money in India is through "courierwallahs", a system that has long existed in villages (Garg et al. 2009). The dependence on courier wallahs may also be because many of the migrants lack verifiable papers that are necessary for opening a bank account. While the charges may be higher for these informal services, their appeal lies in the high degree of trust they have built over years of service. This trust, rooted in familiarity, discourages most migrants from transitioning to formal financial products. Another characteristic that makes the courier wallahs attractive to the migrants is the doorstep delivery of services, an invaluable feature for migrants, as visiting a branch may lead to loss of precious time, in turn leading to loss of income (Tiwari et al. 2011; Pareek et al. 2011; IFAD and Bank 2015).

It is essential to note that many of these informal services now use the core banking solutions of banks to facilitate faster money transfers. Typically, a representative at the sender's village withdraws the money and delivers it to the recipient, charging a fee for the intermediation services provided (Gopinath et al. 2010). Thus, these informal businesses are built on the constraints and inconveniences faced by the remitter. The banks could absorb this clientele; however, the bank products need to have attributes that make the products and services cost-effective and convenient for the poor migrants.

Summing up our review, the introduction of core banking solutions and the expansion of mobile phones have all made transactions easier through the bank route. These advancements allow remitting money without the inconvenience of physical payment procedures. Sending money has now become efficient, timely, and less expensive. Nevertheless, many still do not access or are unaware of or are unable to access, these new services, and many are still dependent on informal means for sending and receiving money.

8.3 Data and Methodology

In the previous chapters, we used NSSO household-level data to analyse various components of financial inclusion. NSSO data gives comprehensive information on the social and economic condition of the household, as well as their access to financial services such as credit, savings, and insurance. To address the issues related to these financial services, NSSO data was appropriate and provided reliable state-level estimates of different indicators of interest. However, for this chapter, we are unable to use NSSO data as it does not capture information regarding the channels used for money transfers.

For the analysis in this chapter, we use the Findex database 2017 and Findex database 2021, which provide respondent-level data, unlike the NSSO surveys used in previous chapters, where the unit of analysis is the household. The target participants of these surveys are adults who are above the age of 15. The 2017 edition of the Findex survey is a cross-country study that covers around 150,000 people in 144 economies, and the 2021 edition of the Findex survey is a cross-country study that covers around 128,000 people in 123 economies. We use data for India, which includes 3000 respondents (in both surveys).

We have also used information from several other databases, such as the Reserve Bank of India database, the various issues of the Economic Survey of India, Employment and unemployment survey Reports, and the Migration Survey Report (NSSO 64th Round), for enriching our narrative. As mentioned earlier, we mainly use descriptive statistics and analytical reviews of studies to present a comprehensive understanding of the topic.

8.4 Analysis

In this section, we first look at the level of access to transaction channels across different global regions and also across specific South Asian countries. This is followed by a focused discussion on India, where we conduct a comparative analysis over two time periods, utilising data from the latest two rounds of the Findex surveys—Findex 2017 and Findex 2021. The Findex database gives us information on whether the respondent has engaged in sending/receiving money to/from a relative or friend residing in a different city or area within the country. It also provides us with information on what channels have been used for the transactions.

8.4.1 Domestic Remittances and Use of Formal Transaction Channels: A Global Analysis

We begin by analysing the percentage of individuals who have sent or received remittances through any channel (formal or informal) and whether any changes have occurred over the past few years. The latest Findex survey was conducted in 2021, which is a COVID year. Comparing this data with Findex 2017 also allows us to capture the changes brought about by the pandemic.

Figure 8.1 shows the percentage of respondents who have sent or received remittances in different regions of the world. The respondents from low-income countries send/receive remittances much more than the Organisation for Economic Co-operation and Development (OECD) or other higher-income countries. Within developing countries, there are pockets of underdevelopment which compel people from such regions to migrate to more developed areas in search of employment. These people need to send money to their homes and their dependent families who stay behind. Such situations are less common in developed countries. Accordingly, we observe from Fig. 8.1 that the poorest region, Sub-Saharan

Africa, records the highest percentage of respondents sending or receiving remittances. This highlights the role of remittances in supporting families in economically disadvantaged regions.

Using Fig. 8.1, we examined the flow of remittances, now, we will specifically look at the use of formal channels for sending and receiving remittances across regions. As shown in Fig. 8.2, the use of banks/mobiles for remittance is highest for High-income OECD countries, sub-Saharan African countries, and East Asia and Pacific countries. The latest Findex survey-2021 does not provide separate data on money transfers made through banks and those made via mobile phones. There is only one category, "send received money through banks or mobiles". However, the 2017 data includes this information, and when we examine this edition of the data, we see that the use of banks is high for high-income OECD countries, East Asia and the Pacific, and Latin America and the Caribbean. On the other hand, the use of mobiles as a remittance channel is high in Sub-Saharan Africa (See Saravanabhavan and Rajeev 2023).

Further, upon closer examination of major South Asian Countries using Findex 2021, it is revealed that, of the people who received remittances, only 3 per cent of respondents from Afghanistan, 40 per cent of respondents from India, 41 per cent of respondents from Sri Lanka, and

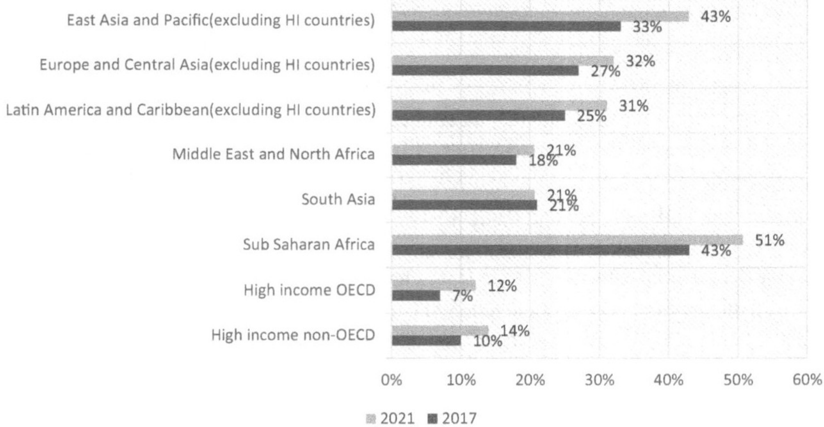

Fig. 8.1 Percentage of respondents who have sent/received remittances (in the last year)—Comparison across different regions (2017 and 2021) (*Source* Saravanabhavan and Rajeev (2023))

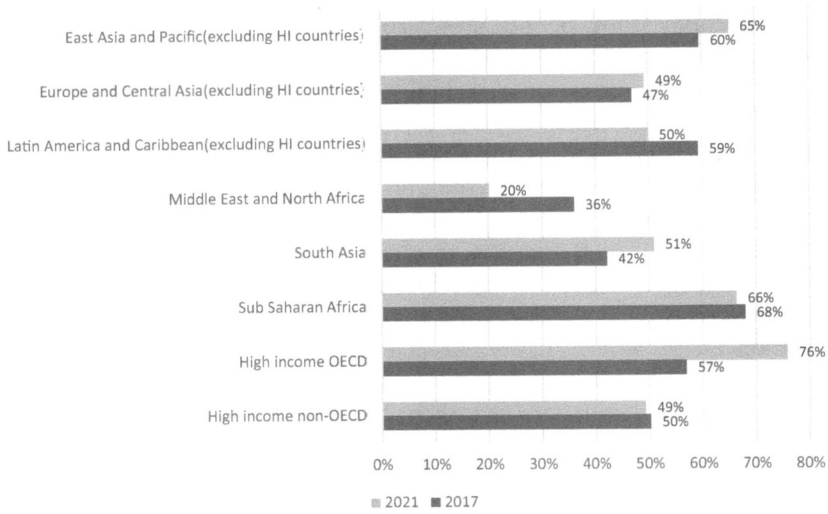

Fig. 8.2 Percentage of respondents who have sent/received remittances through banks and mobiles (Of the people who received remittances in the last year)—Comparison across different regions (2017 and 2021)
(*Source* Saravanabhavan and Rajeev (2023))

59 per cent of respondents from Pakistan used the bank/mobile channel for sending/receiving remittances. In stark contrast, if we compare these estimates with China, we see that 90 per cent of respondents in China reported using formal channels, which is far above any of the South Asian nations.

Further, to gain a more comprehensive understanding of the situation in India, we present the following analysis.

8.4.2 *Channels of Money Transfer in India*

In India, domestic remittances mainly happen through three important channels—money transfer through banks, sending cash through people, and thirdly, through over-the-counter services. The people who send money through over-the-counter services (OTC) do not have accounts, but pay cash at a financial service provider counter, and the respective service provider does the online transaction on behalf of the person for a fee.

During the study period, from 2017 to 2021, there was minimal change in remittances sent/received. Similarly, the use of formal channels for remittance transmission also shows no substantial increase or decrease from 2017 to 2021 (see Table 8.1).

Overall, 18 per cent of the respondents from the latest survey have reported sending or receiving remittances, which is one per cent lower than the previous survey year. The latest survey was conducted during the COVID-19 pandemic, a period characterised by widespread loss of jobs, which could account for the decrease in the percentage of respondents sending/receiving remittances. Of the total people sending or receiving remittances, 39 per cent have used financial institutions, while 37 per cent have sent cash directly. We see that during 2017–2021, the percentage of people sending remittances as cash has decreased. We also note that the

Table 8.1 Percentage of respondents in India who have sent/received domestic remittances through different transaction channels across different income quintiles

			Of those who sent/received remittances		
	Income quintile	*Sent/received (%)*	*Financial institutions (%)*	*In-person: cash (%)*	*Money transfer service(%)*
2017	Poorest 20%	13	6	66	2
	Second 20%	17	29	62	1
	Middle 20%	14	35	52	5
	Fourth 20%	22	39	47	4
	Richest 20%	30	63	39	2
	Total	19	40	51	3
2021	Poorest 20%	14	28	53	3
	Second 20%	9	31	37	3
	Middle 20%	18	26	39	4
	Fourth 20%	17	45	36	8
	Richest 20%	31	52	29	11
	Total	18	39	37	7

Source Saravanabhavan and Rajeev (2023)

use of money transfer operators has increased by four percentage points (Table 8.1).

Table 8.1 also shows the percentage of respondents who have sent/ received domestic remittances through various transaction channels across different income quintiles. Here, the respondents are categorised into five equal quintiles based on their income (Findex data does not provide the level of income but only the income quintile to which the respondent belongs). We observe that the poorest 20 per cent of the respondents show low usage of financial institutions for sending and receiving money (sending remittances through financial institutions includes transactions at a branch, at an automated teller machine (ATM), or through direct deposit into an account). Not surprisingly, the respondents in the poorest income quintiles show the highest dependence on sending cash in person. Around 53 per cent of the individuals (in 2021) in the poorest quintile send money in cash.

From the 2017[1] data, we observe that (not shown in the table) sending or receiving money through mobile phones is drastically low in India for all income quintiles. The Government is encouraging online banking as it can reduce administrative costs and indirect overheads considerably, as well as make the processes easier for the user. However, India has a lot of progress to make on this front. Even though mobile transactions are increasingly used in India for point-of-sale payments, utility bills, etc., their potential for sending remittances has not been realised.

Further, a gender-wise analysis of the use of banks and mobile phones as remittance channels across rural and urban areas in India shows there are significant disparities across the genders. For instance, in rural areas, only 27 per cent of the females who have sent/received remittances have used the bank/ mobile channel as compared to 38 per cent of males. Similarly, in urban areas, only 36 per cent of females have used the bank/ mobile channel as compared to 50 per cent of males (see Fig. 8.3). Overall, from Fig. 8.3, we observe that 45% of the urban respondents and 33% of the rural respondents who sent/received any remittances have used banks/mobile phones.

Next, we examine whether the respondents who have access to bank accounts and have sent/received money in 2021 use the formal channels

[1] Findex 2021 does not provide separate information on remittances through the mobile channel, it offers aggregate data on remittances through both financial institutions and mobile channels combined.

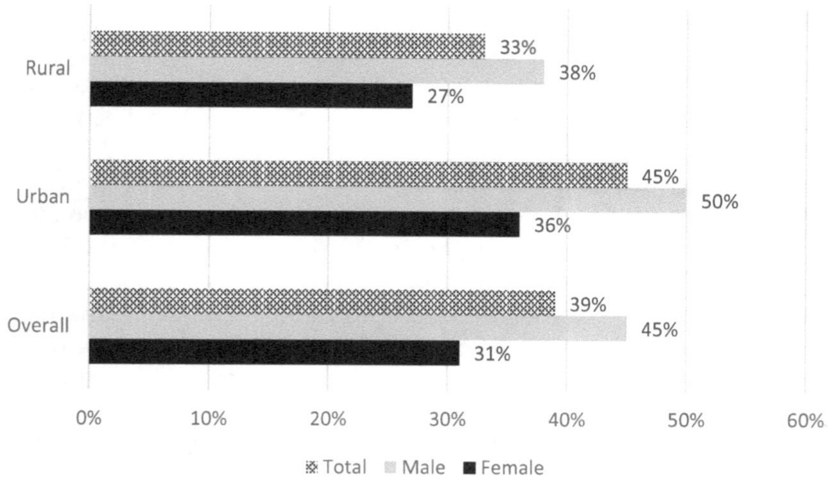

Fig. 8.3 Percentage of respondents who have Sent/Received Remittances through banks/mobile phones across rural and urban regions—2021
Note Here, we consider only the respondents who have sent/received any remittances in the past year through any channel
(*Source* Authors' calculations using the Findex database 2021) Here, we consider only the respondents who have sent/received any remittances in the past year through any channel)

(see Table 8.2). This analysis is crucial as the non-use of bank accounts is one of the major challenges faced by the financial inclusion drive in India. Therefore, understanding how many account holders still rely on cash transactions can provide valuable insights into this issue.

From Table 8.2, we observe that only 42 per cent of respondents with bank accounts who have sent or received remittances in the past year have used formal means of remittances. This implies that a significant portion of account holders still prefer to send remittances as cash. Specifically, around 35 per cent of those who own a bank account have relied on informal ways to send cash. These figures highlight the lack of use of bank accounts and affirm that many with bank accounts still prefer to send remittances in cash.

Table 8.2 Percentage of respondents who have a bank account and have sent/received remittances through financial institutions (or as cash)-2021

	Poorest 20%(%)	*Second 20%(%)*	*Middle 20%(%)*	*Fourth 20%(%)*	*Richest 20%(%)*	*Total(%)*
Sent/received through financial institutions/ Mobile phones	30	30	25	50	55	42
Sent/received as cash	50	36	39	29	28	35

Source Authors' calculations using the Findex databas 2021

8.5 Role of Different Institutions and Technology and Their Effect on Domestic Remittances in India

Advances in the banking system have been rapid in recent times, with technology playing a crucial role in driving these changes. "Fintech" has become the watchword in the financial inclusion drive, with financial agents continually devising innovative products to attract new customers. The payment system, in particular, has seen significant improvements in recent years. However, despite these improvements in banking technologies, such services have not yet been widely adopted by the majority of the population.

8.5.1 Relevance of Banking Technology for Remote Payment

The advent of National Electronic Funds Transfer (NEFT), the spread of ATMs, and the introduction of the United Payments Interface (UPI) have been important for facilitating remote payments. NEFT allows account-to-account money transfers, and to use this service, the user must submit the NEFT form with the beneficiary's name, account number, and IFSC code. Even a person with no bank account can deposit money at the bank for an NEFT transfer.[2] Once the recipient receives the money in their

[2] Reserve Bank of India, https://rbi.org.in/Scripts/FAQView.aspx?Id=60.

account, they can withdraw the funds from an ATM or directly from the bank.

Furthermore, the introduction of the United Payments Interface (UPI) has significantly simplified payments. UPI is a platform that integrates bank accounts into a mobile application, enabling users to remit money and make other payments. Porteous (2006) distinguishes between two types of mobile banking: the additive model, where mobile banking is an add-on to an existing bank account, and the transformative model, which aims to improve financial inclusion for the unbanked and poor. The UPI is designed to be transformative, and it is also user-friendly, requiring minimal information for money transfers. After a one-time registration process, the remitter only needs to remember their user PIN and the recipients' user ID to make a transaction. If the beneficiary does not have a virtual user ID, the money can also be transferred to their account using the IFSC code and account number. Anyone with a mobile phone and a bank account can use this, making it an easily accessible system.

Additionally, the Government has launched the BHIM (Bharat Interface for Money) application, which facilitates money transfers from any commercial bank account, making it accessible to people across all economic strata. BHIM works on both smartphones as well as on ordinary feature phones, ensuring usability even for those without access to a smartphone. While mobile penetration is high in India, the use of mobile banking remains low compared to several other countries that have used the telecommunication revolution to their advantage. However, with the increasing number of mobile phone users and the introduction of new and convenient platforms for financial transactions, mobile banking in India is expected to grow. Notably, Findex data from 2021 indicates that 66% of the respondents owned mobile phones.

8.5.2 Business Correspondent Model

To address the challenges associated with bank usage, one of the key models encouraged by the Government is the Business Correspondent Model (branchless banking). Under this model, banks appoint Business correspondents, who facilitate the receipt and delivery of small-value remittances using mobile banking or internet banking (Gupta 2011). This service is just one among a range of services performed by Business correspondents such as processing loan applications, disbursal of small credit, creating awareness of products, processing and submitting applications to banks, post-sanction monitoring, following up and recovery of loans, collecting and depositing small savings, and delivery of other payment instruments.

According to RBI guidelines, owners of Kirana shops, well-run Self-Help Groups, NGOs, MFIs (Microfinance Institutions), and Postal services are eligible to become business correspondents (RBI 2011). Banks provide the necessary technology and equipment for these agents to function effectively. Transactions are done on POS (point-of-sale) devices or mobile phones, which are connected to the bank's core banking systems. This allows immediate confirmation of the transactions, and payment slips are instantly provided to the customers. The business correspondents are compensated through commissions paid by the banks, and their services are usually free or nominal for certain services. While similar models have been successful in other developing countries, the business correspondent model has not reached its potential in the case of India.

Tapping into the domestic remittances market through business correspondents offers significant market opportunities for the banks. Especially, advances such as core banking solutions and Immediate Payment Service (IMPS) have drastically lowered operational costs for banks, as well as decreased both the financial and time-related expenses for customers. As a result, a large number of small transactions could actually be profitable for the banks.

8.5.3 Role of Post Offices

Post offices remain a popular and conventional channel for money transfer. A large number of people still use post offices for remitting money due to their extensive reach and the trust associated with the institution. Studies, however, indicate that this channel is relatively expensive due to the service charges as well as the customary tips that have to be paid to the delivery personnel (Gopinath et al. 2010). India Post discontinued the traditional Money order Service in 2015 and has introduced three types of money orders: Electronic Money Order (eMO), Smart Money Order, and Instant Money Order (IMO).

In all three types of money orders offered by India Post, the charges are higher compared to those of banks. For both eMO and Smart Money order the charge is 5 per cent of the amount transferred, with a maximum transfer limit of Rupees 5,000. For the Instant Money Order (IMO), the transfer amount ranges from a minimum of Rupees 1,000 to a maximum of Rupees 50,000. Here, the commission fee is between Rupees 150 and 330, depending on the amount of money transferred.[3] Thus, in all three cases, the charges are much higher than those of banks. Studies show that, for this reason, people are likely to switch from using post offices to banks for remitting money if given a choice (Thorat et al. 2009; Gopinath et al. 2010).

8.6 Concluding Observations

In this chapter, we examined the use of formal channels for remittance in a context where opportunities are declining in rural areas, and migration is on the rise. As migrants seek efficient and secure ways to transfer money back home, the accessibility and use of formal remittance channels have become crucial. However, the access and use of formal remittance channels, as part of financial inclusion, have not received much attention in existing studies. This chapter addresses this gap by examining the use of banks and mobiles as remittance channels, drawing on data from the 2017 and 2021 Findex data.

There have been notable advances in the use of financial institutions and mobile phones as remittance channels among lower-income groups from 2017 to 2021. In rural India, for example, only 6% of the poorest group (those belonging to the poorest income quintile) used financial institutions for sending or receiving remittances in 2017. By 2021, this figure had increased to 28%, indicating a significant rise in the use of financial institutions for remittances among economically disadvantaged groups. Over the same period, the practice of sending money as cash through intermediaries declined. Around 37 per cent of the people sending or receiving remittances have sent cash directly, which is a substantial decline from 51 per cent in 2017. This could be the effect of increased UPI uptake during the COVID-19 pandemic; whether this shift is permanent remains to be seen.

One solution proposed by the RBI to enhance financial inclusion is payment banks. Since 2015, the RBI has been issuing licenses to "profit only" companies to function as payment banks. According to RBI guidelines, the primary objective for setting up payment banks is to provide savings accounts and "payments/remittance services to the

[3] India Post, https://www.indiapost.gov.in/Financial/Pages/Content/Money-Order.aspx.

migrant labour force, low-income households, small businesses, unorganised sector entities, and other users".[4] These institutions are heavily reliant on technology, making them scalable and, therefore, capable of handling large volumes of small transactions sustainably. However, because these specialised institutions are profit-driven, reaching out to the poorest migrants may not be so much in their interest, limiting their services to the neediest populations. To address this, targeted incentives could be offered to these banks to enhance outreach and awareness among underserved populations.

References

Agarwalla, Sobhesh Kumar, Samir K. Barua, Joshy Jacob, and Jayanth R. Varma. 2016. "Savings, Borrowings and Remittance Behaviour of Migrant Workers in Urban India, IIMA Report." Ahmedabad.

Bachas, Pierre, Paul Gertler, Sean Higgins, and Enrique Seira. 2018. Digital Financial Services Go a Long Way: Transaction Costs and Financial Inclusion. *AEA Papers and Proceedings* 108 (May): 444–448. https://doi.org/10.1257/pandp.20181013.

Bakshi, Ishan, Anil Kumar Sharma, Preeti Kakkar, and Amit Sharma. 2014. *National Remote Payments Survey*. New Delhi: National Council of Applied Economic Research. http://www.ncaer.org/publication_details.php?pID=238.

CDFI. 2020. "How Migrants Send Money Home?" CDFI Migrant Remittance Study Report. Bangalore.

Deshingkar, Priya. 2006. Internal Migration, Poverty and Development in Asia: Including the Excluded. *IDS Bulletin* 37 (3): 88–100. https://doi.org/10.1111/j.1759-5436.2006.tb00272.x.

Dodd, Warren, Sally Humphries, Kirit Patel, Shannon Majowicz, and Cate Dewey. 2017. "The Internal Migration-Development Nexus: Evidence from Southern India." *Asian and Pacific Migration Journal* 26 (1): 56–83. https://doi.org/10.1177/0117196816684349.

Garg, Nitin, Krishna Thacker, N.A. Venkata, Sachin Bansal, and Graham A.N. Wright. 2009. "MicroSave India Focus Note 29, Potential for E/M-Banking Enabled Migrant Remittances." Microsave. https://www.microsave.net/wp-content/uploads/2018/10/IFN_29_Potential_for_E_M-Banking_Enabled_Migrant_Remittances.pdf.

GOI. 2017. "India on the Move and Churning: New Evidences." In *Economic Survey 2016–17*. New Delhi.

[4] Reserve Bank of India, https://rbi.org.in/scripts/bs_viewcontent.aspx?Id=2900.

Gopinath, Shreyas, Justin Oliver, Ajay Tannirkulam, Supriyo Bhattacharya, and R.R. Kulkarni. 2010. *Putting Money in Motion: How Much Do Migrants Pay for Domestic Transfers?* Chennai: Centre for Micro Finance at IFMR Research.
Gupta, Sanjeev Kumar. 2011. "Financial Inclusion—IT as Enabler." *Reserve Bank of India Occasional Papers* 32 (2).
IFAD, and World Bank. 2015. "The Use of Remittances and Financial Inclusion, A Report by the International Fund for Agricultural Development and the World Bank Group to the G20 Global Partnership for Financial Inclusion." IFAD and World Bank. https://www.ifad.org/documents/38714170/40187309/gpfi.pdf/58ce7a06-7ec0-42e8-82dc-c069227edb79.
Jack, William, and Tavneet Suri. 2014. Risk Sharing and Transactions Costs:Evidence from Kenya's Mobile Money Revolution. *American Economic Review* 104 (1): 183–223. https://doi.org/10.1257/aer.104.1.183.
Lucas, Robert E B., and Oded Stark. 1985. Motivations to Remit: Evidence from Botswana. *Journal of Political Economy* 93 (5): 901–918. https://doi.org/10.1086/261341.
Mas, Ignacio, and Olga Morawczynski. 2009. "Designing Mobile Money Services Lessons from M-PESA." *Innovations:Technology,Governance,Globalisation* 4 (2): 77–91.
Mohanty, Sanjay K., Manisha Dubey, and Jajati K. Parida. 2014. Economic Well-Being and Spending Behaviour of Households in India: Does Remittances Matter? *Migration and Development* 3 (1): 38–53. https://doi.org/10.1080/21632324.2014.886905.
Pareek, Abhay, Akhand Tiwari, Akhilesh Singh, Anirban Roy, Ghiyazuddin A Mohammad, Madhurantika Moulick, Mukul Singh, et al. 2011. "Understanding Remittance Networks in Punjab and Uttar Pradesh." Microsave Report. http://www.microsave.net/wp-content/uploads/2011/06/Understanding_Remittance_Networks_In_Punjab_and_Uttar_Pradesh.pdf.
Porteous, D. (2006). The enabling environment for mobile banking in Africa. Bankable Frontier Associates for the UK Department for International Development (DFID). https://www.gsma.com/mobilefordevelopment/wp-content/uploads/2012/06/theenablingenvironmentformobilebankinginafrica.pdf
RBI. 2011. "Financial Inclusion by Extension of Banking Services—Use of Business Correspondents (BCs)." RBI Notification. Mumbai. https://www.rbi.org.in/scripts/NotificationUser.aspx?Mode=0&Id=6017.
Saravanabhavan, Shika, and Meenakshi Rajeev. 2023. "Financial Inclusion and Remittance Services." *Economic And Political Weekly* 58 (20). https://www.epw.in/journal/2023/20/special-articles/financial-inclusion-and-remittance-services.html.

Suri, Tavneet, and William Jack. (2016). The long-run poverty and gender impacts of mobile money. Science, 354(6317), 1288–1292. https://doi.org/10.1126/science.aah5309

Thorat, Y. S. P., N. V. Ramana, R. V. Ramakrishna, Anne Koshy, and Therese Zak. 2009. *Remittance Needs in India, NABARD-GTZ Technical Study*. New Delhi.

Tiwari, Akhand, Akhilesh kumar Singh, Anurodh Giri, Minakshi Ramji, Sachin Bansal, and Alphina Jos. 2011. "Understanding Remittance Networks In Gujarat, Orissa and Bihar." Microsave. http://www.microsave.net/files/pdf/Understanding_Remittance_Networks_In_Gujarat_Orissa_and_Bihar.pdf.

Tumbe, Chinmay. 2011. *Remittances in India: Facts & Issues*. No. 331. IIMB Working Papers. Bangalore: Indian Institute of management.

Viswanathan, Brinda, and K. S. Kavi Kumar. 2015. "Weather, Agriculture and Rural Migration: Evidence from State and District Level Migration in India." *Environment and Development Economics* 20 (4): 469–92. https://doi.org/10.1017/S1355770X1500008X.

CHAPTER 9

Summary, Concluding Remarks and Policy Implications

India has come a long way in expanding access to financial inclusion, particularly through recent financial inclusion initiatives that have substantially improved the overall financial inclusion landscape. However, challenges remain, such as less than optimal usage of financial services and persistent disparities in access across regions and socio-economic groups.

The Rangarajan committee (RBI 2008b) emphasised that financial inclusion is truly meaningful only when it provides access to a wide range of suitable financial services. Drawing on this perspective, this book provides an in-depth analysis of key aspects of financial inclusion—credit, savings, insurance, and remittance services, as emphasised in the report. In doing so, this book documents the level of access and usage of different financial services across Indian states and explores the various factors influencing it.

The book is structured around two levels of analysis with the aim of providing a comprehensive understanding of financial inclusion in India. At the macro level, we examine the extent of financial inclusion across various Indian states using supply-side data from banks. At the micro level, we delve into household-level data to investigate the access to and usage of key financial services, namely credit, savings, insurance, and remittances. This approach allows us to capture both the broad trends and the demand-side realities faced by households. For the analyses, we draw

S. Saravanabhavan and M. Rajeev, *Moving Beyond Barriers*, Palgrave Studies in Impact Finance,
https://doi.org/10.1007/978-981-95-1066-5_9

on a range of data sources such as the Reserve Bank of India, NSSO-All-India debt and investment Surveys, NSSO-Situation assessment surveys, and the Findex database

This chapter summarises the key results and discusses the policy implications derived from the study.

9.1 A Historical Overview

The book begins with a historical overview of financial sector development in India, tracing its development from the pre-independence era to the present day. In doing so, we categorised the financial inclusion initiatives as belonging to three major periods: pre-independence, pre-liberalisation, and post-liberalisation. The review chapter reveals significant changes in the key players within the system across these periods.

In the pre-independence era, India's financial sector was dominated by private banks and joint stock companies, which operated with a profit-oriented approach and had little incentive to serve the poor. This situation, however, started to change after independence as the government recognised the need to improve access for the underserved. During the initial decades, policy efforts focussed on the agricultural sector, where a majority of the population was employed. The state of the agricultural sector was bad, with small and marginal farmers struggling to finance their agricultural activities. To make matters worse, the farmers were also highly dependent on moneylenders, who charged exorbitant interest rates.

To address these issues, the Government undertook several initiatives, with the nationalisation of major commercial banks in 1969 marking a turning point in India's financial landscape. This move significantly expanded financial access, particularly in rural areas. The expansion of rural bank branches, combined with the introduction of priority sector lending norms, played a crucial role in directing credit to agriculture and other underserved sectors, thus improving access to formal finance substantially.

However, these socially oriented banking policies, while promoting inclusion, gradually began to erode the profitability of commercial banks by the 1980s. In response, financial sector reforms were introduced as part of the economic reforms of 1991. Policies following these reforms prioritised banking efficiency, leading to a period when financial inclusion took a back seat. However, this phase did not last long. By the early 2000s, financial inclusion became a policy priority in most developing countries, with India actively aligning its policies with this global development.

The financial inclusion drive brought a significant shift in approach. Earlier initiatives were largely credit-centric, focusing mainly on providing loans to the agricultural sector. However, since 2006, the financial inclusion drive has aimed at providing access to a wider range of financial services, while also emphasising the importance of universal bank account ownership. Furthermore, the launch of PMJDY in 2014 marked a major milestone, introducing an ambitious and inclusive strategy compared to earlier financial inclusion programmes, and as a result, led to a remarkable transformation in the financial inclusion scenario.

The analysis of the PMJDY scheme reveals that India's financial inclusion landscape has made significant progress, particularly in providing basic banking services to the unbanked population. For instance, according to Findex 2011, bank account ownership was only 35 per cent, whereas the latest 2021 edition shows this has risen to around 78 per cent—a significant improvement from the pre-PMJDY period. Thus, this scheme has laid a strong framework for advancing financial inclusion across the country.

Understanding both the historical and current policies provides a foundation for analysing financial inclusion. Building on this, in the subsequent chapter, we developed a comprehensive financial inclusion index to examine the trend of financial inclusion over time and to evaluate how different policies have affected financial inclusion in India.

9.2 Financial Inclusion Index—The State of Financial Inclusion Across Indian States

A reliable and comprehensive index is a critical first step in assessing the state of financial inclusion in the country. In Chapter 3, we address this need by developing a comprehensive financial inclusion index using indicators from both commercial and cooperative banks to gain a clearer understanding of the status of financial inclusion across states and between rural and urban areas.

Prior works on financial inclusion, which focussed mostly on commercial banks, have largely ignored the role of cooperative banks that operate at the grassroots level and play a crucial role in extending financial services to the underserved in rural areas. In our index formulation, we have introduced indicators from the cooperative banks along with scheduled commercial banks to arrive at a more representative measure of financial inclusion. Furthermore, given the fact that financial inclusion has historically been low in rural areas, the rural and urban indices serve as crucial tools in examining whether financial inclusion drive policies have been effective in closing the persistent rural–urban gap or not. Through this exercise, we assess the progress and identify areas that still need attention.

To develop the index, we arrived at the weighting scheme for aggregation, using factor analysis, following the method by Nicoletti et al.(1999). Using this method variables are statistically grouped into intermediate composite indicators, and these intermediate indicators are further aggregated to form the final measure. First, we constructed the rural index, where the intermediate indices are the Rural Banks Index and the Rural Cooperatives Index. The bank indicators statistically grouped together to form the Rural Banks Index, and the PACSs indicators formed the Rural Cooperatives Index. Secondly, we constructed the urban index using the indicators from urban scheduled commercial banks. Both the rural and urban indices were calculated using a weighted geometric mean.

The analysis of the indices shows a significant improvement in financial inclusion across most states during the post-2005 financial inclusion drive. However, the data also reveal a widening rural–urban gap, with rural areas consistently lagging behind. While urban indicators have improved markedly, rural progress has been more modest, even after the launch of the Jan Dhan Yojana in 2014. While the urban financial inclusion index shows a sharp rise post-2014, the rural index does not reflect a comparable increase. This disparity can be partly attributed to the lower level of economic activity in rural regions, which tends to result in smaller volumes of deposits and credit, which are key components of the index. Notably, only Goa and Gujarat exhibit comparable improvements in both rural and urban indices. In all other states, the rural index remains below the urban.

In this chapter, we provided a macro-level view of financial inclusion by studying state-level indicators using supply-side data. To further complement this broad perspective, we delve into the micro-level foundations of financial inclusion in the following chapters. Specifically, we will explore the key aspects of financial inclusion-credit, savings, insurance, and remittance services—using household-level data from NSSO.

9.3 Financial Inclusion and Rural Credit Access

In a country where a large percentage of the population is self-employed across both agricultural and non-agricultural sectors, access to credit plays a critical role in sustaining livelihoods. This chapter examines access to credit at the household level, with emphasis on the agriculture sector, which still remains the backbone of the rural economy. The agricultural sector is predominantly composed of small and marginal farmers who face not only low but also highly volatile incomes, largely due to unpredictable weather patterns and fluctuating market conditions. Moreover, these small farmers lack adequate savings to rely on in case of an emergency, making them particularly vulnerable to any kind of financial shocks. Consequently, they require regular loans not just to fund their fixed capital needs but also to finance their working capital expenditure, such as buying seeds and fertilisers, hiring labour, and leasing farming equipment like tractors and tillers. Without regular access to external finance, these households will face difficulties in maintaining and improving their productivity. Given this, Chapter 4 of this book delves into the credit constraints faced by rural cultivator households and examines the specific factors influencing their access to credit.

Initially, we examined the change in access to agricultural credit by comparing data from two time points (years 2013 and 2019) using the 70th and the 77th Rounds of the NSSO-All-India Debt and Investment Surveys. To further explore the factors influencing access to production credit for agricultural households, we applied a double-hurdle model. Here, the dependent variable is the amount of credit for production purposes. Using this model, we examined the effect of various socio-economic variables such as caste, income, and education on the likelihood of accessing credit as well as the volume of credit accessed.

The state-level analysis reveals the existence of disparities in access to rural production credit for cultivator households across different states. When comparing the access to production credit in 2013 and 2019, we find that the overall percentage of households accessing production credit has not improved much. Especially, states such as Bihar, Jharkhand, and Assam show very low levels of access.

Our analysis also reveals that informal sources of credit are still relevant, however, reliance on non-institutional credit sources has declined since 2013. Specifically, the share of rural households borrowing from moneylenders or input traders at the all-India level dropped from 20 per cent in 2013 to 13 per cent in 2019. While most states have seen a decline in reliance on moneylenders, states like Punjab, Uttar Pradesh, Odisha, Maharashtra, and Kerala have experienced an increase. Notably, Southern states such as Andhra Pradesh, Karnataka, Kerala, Tamil Nadu, and Odisha report particularly high dependence on non-institutional credit sources (excluding friends and relatives), highlighting a significant unmet demand for formal credit. Again, from the descriptive analysis, we observe that the number of households accessing informal loans for non-income-generating purposes, especially for consumption expenditure, has increased from 2013 to 2019. The problem with the informal lenders is that they charge very high interest rates. We find that the majority of the households borrow at rates above 12 per cent. Also, around 18 per cent of those who borrowed from non-institutional sources borrowed at rates which are more than 36 per cent.

In the econometric analysis examining the factors influencing access to agricultural production credit, we observe that marginal farmers are less likely to secure formal production credit as compared to larger farmers. Additionally, socially disadvantaged caste groups have a lower probability of accessing formal credit, and when they do, they tend to receive smaller amounts of loans than those belonging to the general castes. This suggests that government affirmative policies have not yet succeeded in fully bridging the gap in formal financial access for agricultural households.

In addition to the agricultural sector in the rural areas, another crucial segment requiring regular access to credit is non-agricultural self-employed households in urban areas. Though facing significant issues in accessing formal credit (Saravanabhavan and Rajeev 2020), the urban self-employed have received relatively scant attention in the existing financial inclusion literature. In the next chapter, we turn our focus to issues related to credit access for urban self-employed households.

9.4 Financial Inclusion and Urban Credit Access

Urban self-employed households face different challenges compared to rural households, and banking norms developed for rural beneficiaries often fall short of meeting their needs. The self-employed in rural areas are primarily farmers who benefit from defined priority sector lending norms for agriculture. In contrast, the urban self-employed households usually are own-account enterprises, and most of them lack any external support. These household enterprises are small in scale, with little or no savings, necessitating a constant requirement for external funds to cover even their working capital requirements (Rajeev et al. 2017).

For the analysis in this chapter, we used the 70th and 77th Rounds of NSSO-AIDIS data. We began with a state-wise comparative analysis to examine changes in access to production credit for self-employed households in the urban sector, allowing us to identify regional disparities and trends in credit availability. Further, to gain deeper insights into the different factors that may influence access to production loans to urban self-employed households, we employed a probit regression model with correction for selection bias.

From the comparative analysis of the 70th and 77th Rounds of NSSO data, we find that access to production loans is low for both years. Nationally, the rate improved marginally from 8% in 2013 to 9% in 2019. Only a few states—such as Maharashtra, Jharkhand, and West Bengal—showed above-average improvements during this period, while most states experienced only minimal changes. Notably, the Southern states, despite having a higher percentage of self-employed households accessing production loans from formal sources, show a decrease in access during the study period.

From the regression analysis, examining the different factors influencing access to production loans for self-employed households, several key results emerge. First, the analysis confirms the importance of financial infrastructure in improving credit access. However, we find a non-linear relationship between financial infrastructure and access to production credit. The coefficient of bank infrastructure is negative, and the coefficient of its squared term is positive, indicating a non-linear relationship. This implies that in regions where the number of bank branches is low, it has a negative impact on access to production loans; however, in regions where the number is higher, access improves.

In regions where the Bank infrastructure is low, banks may focus on serving large borrowers, which can result in smaller borrowers being crowded out. It is possible that the banking institutions primarily serve larger borrowers, leading to a crowding out of smaller borrowers. However, in regions with extensive networks of branches, larger borrowers are spread across multiple institutions, potentially encouraging banks to lend to small household enterprises.

Education and gender also play a significant role in determining access to urban production credit. Households with members who have attained secondary or higher levels of education are more likely to access production credit compared to households with illiterate members. Furthermore, the analysis reveals that women-owned enterprises and socially deprived castes are relatively less likely to become self-employed, but we do not find any evidence of bias in terms of access to credit in the case of those women-owned enterprises and socially backward caste households who become self-employed.

After examining credit access, we now shift our focus to household savings within formal financial institutions. While the number of bank accounts has significantly increased, the active utilisation of these accounts has not kept pace with the rate at which they are being opened. In the following chapter, we focus on this issue, exploring formal savings patterns and the various factors that influence them.

9.5 Financial Inclusion and Savings in Banks

For low-income individuals and households, savings are necessary to reduce vulnerability in the case of disruptions in the flow of income. Banks provide a secure option for storing money in easily cashable form, allowing individuals to access their savings when necessary. Despite the several benefits, the usage of bank savings remains relatively low in India.

While 78 per cent of the Indian population now has a bank account, according to Findex 2021 (98 per cent of households according to AIDIS-2019), some of these accounts show no activity, indicating that people are not taking full advantage of financial inclusion policies. To understand this issue, we examine important factors such as financial infrastructure and educational attainment of the household. We conduct this analysis separately for the rural and urban sectors as the problems and challenges to financial access differ significantly across rural and urban areas. Specifically, we examine how bank infrastructure influences the extent of household savings and whether this impact differs across households with different levels of educational attainment. Additionally, this chapter also explores socio-economic characteristics that influence the savings behaviour of households. For the analyses, we have used the 70th and 77th Rounds of NSSO-AIDIS data, which provide information on household savings in banks. The methodology includes both descriptive analysis and a double-hurdle model to explore the determinants in greater depth.

It is well-established that increasing savings in banks helps households to smooth consumption during emergencies and contribute to overall financial stability. The descriptive analysis, however, reveals that even though a majority of the households claim that they have savings in banks, the amount of savings is negligible in many cases. For instance, the 2019 data reveal that around 17 per cent of rural households have less than Rupees 1000 as savings in banks.

The econometric analysis, which identifies the various determinants influencing access to and usage of formal savings, reveals the importance of bank infrastructure and educational attainment. Higher bank infrastructure leads to higher amounts of savings. Interestingly, in rural areas, we find that the returns to improved banking infrastructure are highest for those with the lowest education levels compared to those with primary, secondary, or tertiary education. In contrast, in urban areas, as education increases, the marginal effect of banking infrastructure on savings also increases. This indicates that the effect of banking infrastructure on savings is enhanced for those with secondary and tertiary education compared to those with below-primary education. The returns to improved banking infrastructure are highest for those with the highest education levels in urban areas.

Additionally, the econometric analysis reveals that the households belonging to Other Backward Castes (OBC) and General category are more likely to have higher amounts of savings in banks, both in rural and urban areas, compared to Scheduled Caste (SC) and Scheduled Tribe (ST) households. The descriptive results also highlight that a disproportionately larger percentage of SC/ST households report bank savings of less than ₹500, compared to other social groups. This suggests significant disparities in formal savings behaviour across different social strata, with SC/ST households being particularly disadvantaged in terms of using formal savings. These differences persist even after controlling for income. Interestingly, caste variables are found to be statistically insignificant in the first stage of the double-hurdle model, suggesting that access to bank accounts has become nearly universal, likely due to the financial inclusion drive. Even disadvantaged groups such as SC and ST households appear to face fewer barriers to opening bank accounts, although disparities remain in usage and savings volume.

Another critical component of financial inclusion, beyond credit and savings, is access to insurance. In a developing country like India, where households frequently face various risks and uncertainties, insurance can serve as a vital tool for mitigating financial shocks. In Chapter 6, we have documented the status of access to insurance in India and have studied the key factors that may influence households' adoption of crop insurance.

9.6 Financial Inclusion and Insurance

The insurance sector provides financial instruments that individuals and households save formally to overcome adverse economic situations. While the insurance market in India is growing, the current penetration of insurance services remains relatively low compared to global standards, presenting significant expansion opportunities for the insurance sector.

The insurance sector offers financial tools that enable individuals and households to save in a structured manner and manage economic shocks effectively. Although the insurance market in India has been expanding, overall penetration remains low by global standards, highlighting substantial scope for growth. Non-life insurance, particularly vehicle insurance, has seen relatively high adoption, largely due to regulatory mandates and urban demand. In contrast, the uptake of crop and health insurance remains considerably low, especially among rural populations.

In Chapter 7, we explore the scenario of insurance adoption in India, with special emphasis on the accessibility and uptake of crop insurance among agricultural households. The analysis of the Pradhan Mantri Fasal Bima Yojana (PMFBY) shows that despite government efforts, significant coverage gaps remain. While adoption has increased, the programme has not met its target, and several states have seen a decline in participation. Examining the 77th Round Situation Assessment Survey data, we see that the average percentage of households accessing crop insurance in India stands at just 13 per cent, reflecting a modest 6 per cent increase from the 70th Round survey. This slow growth highlights the ongoing challenges in expanding crop insurance coverage. The analysis also uncovers significant disparities in adoption rates across states. States like Haryana, Tamil Nadu, and Maharashtra have the highest rates of crop insurance uptake, whereas states such as Bihar, Uttar Pradesh, and Assam lag far behind.

One of the primary reasons for low adoption, as indicated by our findings, is the lack of awareness about crop insurance. According to the data, 51 per cent of households that do not have crop insurance cite "not aware" as the reason for opting out. This suggests that despite government efforts in promoting schemes like the Pradhan Mantri Fasal Bima

Yojana, a substantial portion of the population remains uninformed about the availability and benefits of crop insurance. Addressing this awareness gap is crucial for increasing adoption rates and providing more comprehensive risk protection for rural households. This calls for a closer examination of the factors driving the low adoption of crop insurance.

We use the 70th Round NSSO—Situation Assessment survey to explore the different factors influencing the extent of crop insurance adoption among Indian households. For this analysis, we employed a fractional logit model, where the dependent variable is the proportion of crops insured to the total crops cultivated by the household. This variable gives a measure of the extent to which households insure their crops.

The results reveal that households with access to both Government organisations, as well as private agencies, are likely to have a larger number of crops insured. Additionally, we find that small and marginal farmers, who typically have lower incomes, insure fewer crops than larger, wealthier farmers. Similarly, households with lower levels of education, belonging to disadvantaged castes, or in lower-income brackets are more likely to have a lesser number of crops insured. These findings reflect trends seen in other financial services, where socio-economic disadvantages limit access and utilisation.

So far, we have explored three key dimensions of financial inclusion: credit, savings, and insurance. Next, we turn our attention to the fourth critical aspect—access to remittance services. This is especially important for migrant workers, as it enables them to send remittances home, playing a vital role in supporting their families and contributing to local economies.

9.7 Financial Inclusion and Remittance Services

The issue of lack of access to proper formal channels for money transfer is of relevance as geographic mobility in search of better opportunities is on the rise in India. This increase in migration has led to a surge in internal remittances, making access to formal institutions and reliable money transfer channels essential for individuals and households. Despite its importance, this area remains under-researched, largely due to the limited availability of relevant data. In Chapter 88, we address this gap by examining the use of various money transfer channels, such as financial institutions and mobile phones, and their role in facilitating remittances for migrant households.

In this chapter, we have analysed data from the Global Findex Database for the years 2017 and 2021, using both descriptive methods and an analytical review of existing research. The findings reveal significant improvements in the use of financial institutions and mobile phones as remittance channels for lower-income groups between 2017 and 2021. For instance, in rural India in 2017, only 6% of the poorest group (those belonging to the poorest income quintile) used financial institutions for sending or receiving remittances. By 2021, this figure had risen to 28%, indicating a significant increase in the use of formal channels for remittances among the poorest households. Additionally, in 2021, 37 per cent of the total people sending or receiving remittances sent cash directly, which is a substantial decline from 51 per cent in 2017. This shift may be an immediate consequence of increased adoption of UPI during the COVID-19 pandemic.

9.8 Conclusion

Summing up, FI has significantly improved over the years, especially following the launch of the PMJDY. However, our analysis reveals that regional disparities, the availability of banking infrastructure, and specific household characteristics continue to influence access to and use of financial services.

Certain states such as Bihar, Odisha, and Assam have low rural access to all financial services, while states such as Bihar, Rajasthan, and Uttar Pradesh have the lowest urban access (See Appendix Table A14 for the list of states having the lowest and highest access for each financial service). Most of these are low-income states and rank low in other development indicators too. The states having the highest access to financial services are Himachal Pradesh, Kerala, Karnataka, and Andhra Pradesh. Overall, we find that the southern regions have fared much better compared to other regions.

An examination of household characteristics reveals a disparity in the use and access to financial services, with low-income and disadvantaged groups facing significant barriers. For instance, our results reveal that caste is still an important feature that determines access. For instance, the disadvantaged castes are less likely to have access to rural production credit when compared to the general castes. In the urban case, however, we do not find any significant evidence of the caste of the household having an impact on access to production loans. As regards insurance too, we find that the disadvantaged categories are likely to have lower access. Further, concerning access to bank accounts, we do not find any significant difference in effects across the caste variables, both in the rural as well as urban regions, implying that bank account access has become more or less universal.

9.9 Policy Implications

A few policy suggestions can be derived from this research.

In constructing the FI index, we have included indicators for both commercial and cooperative banks, unlike most other studies that focus solely on scheduled commercial banks. We emphasise the critical role played by cooperative banks in reaching out to disadvantaged groups and the unique advantage they hold because of their wide network, strong local presence, and inclusive nature of functioning. Therefore, it is essential that cooperative banks play a larger role in the government's financial inclusion strategy.

However, the cooperative banks in the country face several challenges, including high levels of non-performing loans and systemic issues. To revive the cooperative system, the Vaidyanathan committee, which was the designated task force on the revival of rural cooperative credit institutions (2004), recommended several measures. Based on these recommendations, the Government introduced a revival package that included financial support, infrastructural reforms, and management improvements[1]. Even after these reforms, cooperatives in many states in India still struggle with inefficiencies and operational challenges. The RBI must continue to strengthen the regulatory framework with comprehensive structural and managerial reforms to ensure the long-term stability and efficiency of cooperative banks.

Our analysis of urban self-employed households reveals that many of them have low levels of assets, which essentially means that these sample households belong to the lowest income groups. Many such households may lack suitable property documents, which are essential to gain access to formal finance. In this context, credit bureaus can play a crucial role by offering reliable information on an individual's creditworthiness, thereby reducing the information asymmetry between lenders and borrowers. A

[1] https://pib.gov.in/PressReleasePage.aspx?PRID=1578809

strong credit history can help compensate for the lack of collateral, lower perceived lending risk, and ultimately reduce borrowing costs (Sinha 2012). Thus, developing a reliable credit information system is in the interests of the financial institutions as it reduces the risk involved, as well as enables customers to obtain reasonably priced loans.

There is a Central Repository of Information on Large Credits (CRILC) that was set up by the RBI in 2014. A new system for small borrowers, known as Unified Lending Interface (ULI), was launched in pilot mode in 2023 and is aimed at enabling credit delivery to small and rural borrowers, including farmers. Currently under development, it aims to streamline lending for small-scale and rural borrowers by consolidating land records, financial data, and identity records on a single platform to enable lenders to have a complete view of the borrower's creditworthiness. Such a system also holds promise for the landless and tenant farmers.

Our analysis reveals that many low-income households, both rural agricultural and urban self-employed, face significant challenges in obtaining loans from formal financial institutions. For such low-income households, diversifying assets into savings instruments could serve as a valuable alternative to improve their financial security. Following the nationalisation of banks in India, the focus has been mainly on improving credit access to special groups such as farmers, while access to savings options for low-income urban households has received less attention. Although the government has made notable progress in increasing bank account registrations in recent years, our analysis of supply-side indicators shows that the usage of financial services, measured as deposit volume per capita, has not seen a corresponding improvement. To address this gap, it is essential to educate individuals about the importance of formal savings and the various savings instruments that are available to them.

Additionally, our household-level analysis of formal savings reveals that in both urban and rural sectors, the proportion of financial assets to total assets is hardly of any significance. Many low-income-individuals resort to risky informal savings channels, such as chit funds or saving at home, which may lead to a loss of savings. To encourage the poor to save formally, focused institutional policies and mechanisms are essential. A viable strategy could be leveraging local banking correspondents as intermediaries in regions where there is a lack of brick-and-mortar branches.

Furthermore, learning from the successful examples of other developing countries, short-term seasonal savings products for farmers (commitment-type savings) is an initiative that could prove appropriate for the Indian farmer too (Dupas and Robinson 2013; Ashraf et al. 2006a). Relatedly, another initiative that has been observed to work in other developing countries is the use of deposit collectors to facilitate and increase savings (Ashraf et al. 2006b). Given the approachability and awareness issues that India is facing, the implementation of innovations such as deposit collectors and similar other ideas could help in improving savings. Local kiosk-based business correspondents can also be helpful, especially in urban regions (Rajeev et al. 2017).

Another development under the Digital India programme is the Common Services Centres (CSCs), under which local village-level entrepreneurs (VLEs) are providing access to various government schemes using the online platform. Some of these CSC-VLEs also provide banking services, and given their proximity to the local population, they can enable the underbanked people to get the full benefit of financial inclusion. The potential of the CSC-VLE programme has not been fully utilised by the banking sector, and leveraging this initiative could significantly enhance the usage of financial services.

The analysis of formal savings brings out another important insight: when bank penetration improves in the urban sector, it is the more educated who benefit, as compared to the lower educated. Since in the urban sector, there are large numbers of educated customers, the poor and the less educated get crowded out. Hence, special attention is needed for this group in urban regions. A financial literacy programme specifically tailored for low-income, low-educated households and individuals will be beneficial in this regard.

Furthermore, we find that a large majority of those who remit money still do so using non-formal methods. In this regard, we need to understand that banks and informal transaction channels have different strengths, and if the banks are to attract more people (especially migrants) to use their transaction channels, they have to imbibe certain characteristics of the informal sector, such as approachability, convenient timings, and home delivery. We also find that a large majority of those who have a bank account also remit money as cash, highlighting the low levels of awareness regarding money transfers through banks and mobile banking. Therefore, we reiterate the need for parallel financial literacy programmes. Without educating the customers about the potential uses of their newly opened accounts, the accounts could remain underutilised, ultimately becoming a burden on the financial sector. Engaging local NGOs to give training to certain special segments, such as poor migrants, can be effective. Additionally, Common Services Centres, in alignment with Bank Mitras, can also play an important role in facilitating this education and outreach.

In recent years, there has been a significant increase in digital transactions facilitated by the Unified Payments Interface (UPI). India's UPI now handles the highest volume of daily transactions on any comparable platform globally. In FY 2022, UPI accounted for nearly 52 per cent of the overall 8.84 billion digital financial transactions (GOI 2022). However, India has a lot more progress to make in this area. Even though such transactions over mobile phones are increasingly used in India for point-of-sale payments and for paying utility bills, their potential for transmitting remittances has not been realised. In contrast, many low-income African countries with poor infrastructure are leveraging digital/mobile services to remit money. By learning from this, India has the opportunity to expand UPI's capabilities to support remittance flows (Findex, 2021). With the foundational infrastructure already in place, the next crucial step is to raise awareness among low-educated domestic migrants.

Furthermore, our analysis of insurance reveals that a lack of awareness is a primary reason for the low adoption of insurance schemes. We find that households that have access to government institutions and private agents are more likely to adopt crop insurance as opposed to those who do not have access, highlighting the critical role these institutions play in improving awareness. To improve insurance adoption, mandatory information disbursal through Government agencies such as Krishi Vigyan Kendra and extension agents should be done, to ensure that farmers receive information on insurance options. An important point to be discussed in this respect is that, in 2020, crop insurance was made optional[2](earlier, crop insurance was mandatory while taking crop loans), and therefore in the new context, non-awareness of the benefits of insurance could further reduce the number of farmers opting for crop insurance in India. There is also the issue of irregularity in payment

[2] https://pib.gov.in/newsite/PrintRelease.aspx?relid=200215

of claims, as evident from the analysis, which could further discourage farmers from using crop insurance. We find that a substantial percentage of households that faced crop loss and were insured additionally did not receive a settlement for the losses suffered. Even though measures have been introduced recently to tighten the timelines of settlement[3], there are still delays in the payment of claims. This is another issue that needs to be addressed.

Finally, we also observe that the use and access of certain financial services are lower for socially disadvantaged categories, necessitating focused support for these populations. As far as access to financial services by women is concerned, a large percentage access bank credit through self-help groups. Thus, encouraging the formation of SHGs can be a good strategy to enhance access to financial services for women. In India, there is an uneven distribution of SHGs with the northeastern region having a relatively lower presence, and hence, these bank-linked self-help groups should be more popularised across states to enable borrowing (Rajeev et al. 2017). Additionally, such joint liability groups are less prevalent among male members, and efforts should be made to form groups among them to provide access to credit, especially for landless labourers.

Appendix

Table A14 States with the highest and lowest access in rural India

	Rural		*Urban*
	Production loans—for farmers	*Crop Insurance—for farmers*	*Production loans for Self-employed*
Highest	Andhra Pradesh	Haryana	Andhra Pradesh
	Maharashtra	Tamil Nadu	West Bengal
	Punjab	Maharashtra	Kerala
	Karnataka	Andhra Pradesh	Jharkhand
Lowest	Assam	Assam	Punjab
	Bihar	Bihar	Uttar Pradesh
	Uttar Pradesh	Uttar Pradesh	Rajasthan
	Kerala	Kerala	Gujarat

Source Author's compilation based on analysis in various chapters

[3] https://loksabha.nic.in/Members/QResult16.aspx?qref=78477

References

Ashraf, Nava, Dean Karlan, and Yin Wesley. 2006a. Deposit Collectors. *Advances in Economic Analysis & Policy* 6 (2): 1–24. https://doi.org/10.2202/1538-0637.1483.

Ashraf, Nava, Dean Karlan, and Wesley Yin. 2006b. Tying Odysseus to the Mast: Evidence from a Commitment Savings Product in the Philippines. *Quarterly Journal of Economics* 121 (2): 635–672. https://doi.org/10.1162/qjec.2006.121.2.635.

Dupas, Pascaline, and Jonathan Robinson. 2013. Why Don't the Poor Save More? Evidence from Health Savings Experiments. *American Economic Review* 103 (4): 1138–1171. https://doi.org/10.1257/aer.103.4.1138.

GOI. 2022. "The Economic Survey of India 2021-22." https://www.indiabudget.gov.in/budget2022-23/economicsurvey/doc/eschapter/echap09.pdf.

Nicoletti, Giuseppe, Stefano Scarpetta, and Olivier Boyland. 1999. *Summary Indicators of Product Market Regulation with an Extension to Employment Protection Legislation. OECD Economics Department Working Papers.*

Rajeev, Meenakshi, B.P. Vani, and Veerashekharappa. 2017. "Self-Help Groups for India's Financial Inclusion:Do Effective Cost of Borrowing Limit Their Operation?" *ICDD Working Paper No. 19*. Kassel: Kassel university press GmbH.

Saravanabhavan, Shika, and Meenakshi Rajeev. 2020. The Urban Self-Employed: Is Access to Financial Services Adequate? In *Deciphering India's Service Sector Growth-Forthcoming*, ed. V. N. Shashanka Bhide, Balasubramanya, and K. L. Krishna. New Delhi: Routledge.

Sinha, Anand. 2012. "Striking a Balance: Credit Penetration and NPA Management—Role of Information Sharing, Address by Shri Anand Sinha, Deputy Governor, Reserve Bank of India at the Fourth Annual Credit Information Conference on March 7, 2012." RBI Monthly Bulletin. Mumbai.

References

Adams, Dale W. 1992. Taking a Fresh Look at Informal Finance. In *Informal Finance in Low Income Countries*, ed. Dale W. Adams and Delbert A. Fitchett, 5–23. Colorado: Westview Press.

Agarwalla, Sobhesh Kumar, Samir K. Barua, Joshy Jacob, and Jayanth R. Varma. 2016. "Savings, Borrowings and Remittance Behaviour of Migrant Workers in Urban India, IIMA Report." Ahmedabad.

Ahluwalia, M. S. 2000. "Reforming Indias Financial Sector: An Overview." Planning Commission.

Alonso, Cristian, Tanuj Bhojwani, Emine Hanedar, Dinar Prihardini, Gerardo Una, and Kateryna Zhabska. 2023. "Stacking Up the Benefits Lessons from India's Digital Journey e." 23/78. IMF Working Paper No. 23/78. IMF Working Paper. Washington, DC.

Alonso, Cristian, Tanuj Bhojwani, Emine Hanedar, Dinar Prihardini, Gerardo Uña, and Kateryna Zhabska. 2023. "Stacking up the Benefits: Lessons from India's Digital Journey." *IMF ELibrary* 202 (78). https://doi.org/10.5089/9798400240416.001.

Amjad, Shehla, and Saf Hasnu. 2007. Small Holders' Access to Rural Credit: Evidence from Pakistan. *The Lahore Journal of Economics* 12 (2): 1–25.

Anzoategui, Diego, Asli Demirgüç-Kunt, and María Soledad Martínez. Pería. 2014. Remittances and Financial Inclusion: Evidence from El Salvador. *World Development* 54 (February): 338–349. https://doi.org/10.1016/j.worlddev.2013.10.006.

Aportela, Fernando. 1999. "Effects of Financial Access on Savings by Low-Income People." *MIT Department of Economics Dissertation Chapter 1.*

S. Saravanabhavan and M. Rajeev, *Moving Beyond Barriers*, Palgrave Studies in Impact Finance, https://doi.org/10.1007/978-981-95-1066-5

Arora, Rashmi Umesh. 2012. Financial Inclusion and Human Capital in Developing Asia: The Australian Connection. *Third World Quarterly* 33 (1): 177–197. https://doi.org/10.1080/01436597.2012.627256.

Ashraf, Nava, Dean Karlan, and Yin Wesley. 2006a. Deposit Collectors. *Advances in Economic Analysis & Policy* 6 (2): 1–24. https://doi.org/10.2202/1538-0637.1483.

Ashraf, Nava, Dean Karlan, and Wesley Yin. 2006b. Tying Odysseus to the Mast: Evidence from a Commitment Savings Product in the Philippines. *Quarterly Journal of Economics* 121 (2): 635–672. https://doi.org/10.1162/qjec.2006.121.2.635.

Ayyagari, Meghana, Asli Demirgüç-Kunt, and Vojislav Maksimovic. 2008. How Important Are Financing Constraints? The Role of Finance in the Business Environment. *World Bank Economic Review* 22 (3): 483–516. https://doi.org/10.1093/wber/lhn018.

Ayyagari, Meghana, Asli Demirgüç-Kunt, and Vojislav Maksimovic. 2010. "Formal versus Informal Finance: Evidence from China." *Review of Financial Studies* 23 (8): 3048–3097. https://doi.org/10.1093/rfs/hhq030.

Bachas, Pierre, Paul Gertler, Sean Higgins, and Enrique Seira. 2018. Digital Financial Services Go a Long Way: Transaction Costs and Financial Inclusion. *AEA Papers and Proceedings* 108 (May): 444–448. https://doi.org/10.1257/pandp.20181013.

Bakshi, Ishan, Anil Kumar Sharma, Preeti Kakkar, and Amit Sharma. 2014. *National Remote Payments Survey.* New Delhi: National Council of Applied Economic Research. http://www.ncaer.org/publication_details.php?pID=238.

Banerjee, Abhijit, Emily Breza, Esther Duflo, and Cynthia Kinnan. 2018. "Do Credit Constraints Limit Entrepreneurship? Heterogeneity in the Returns to Microfinance." *NBER Working Paper No. 26346.*

Banerjee, Abhijit, Shawn Cole, and Esther Duflo. 2004. "Banking Reform in India." In *India Policy Forum*, 1:277–332. Global Economy and Development Program, The Brookings Institution.

Banerjee, Abhijit V., and Esther Duflo. 2005. "Chapter 7 Growth Theory through the Lens of Development Economics." In *Handbook of Economic Growth*, 473–552. Cambridge, MA. https://doi.org/10.1016/S1574-0684(05)01007-5.

Banerjee, Abhijit V., and Esther Duflo. 2007. The Economic Lives of the Poor. *Journal of Economic Perspectives* 21 (1): 141–168. https://doi.org/10.1257/jep.21.1.141.

Banerjee, Abhijit V., and Esther Duflo. 2011. *Poor Economics: A Radical Rethinking of the Way to Fight Global Poverty*, 2011th ed. Delhi: Random House Publishers Private Limited.

Banerjee, Abhijit V., and Andrew F. Newman. 1993. "Occupational Choice and the Process of Development." *Journal of Political Economy* 101 (2): 274–298. https://doi.org/10.1086/261876.

Bartlett, M. S. 1950. Tests of Significance in Factor Analysis. *British Journal of Statistical Psychology* 3 (2): 77–85. https://doi.org/10.1111/j.2044-8317.1950.tb00285.x.

Barua, Abheek, Rajat Kathuria, and Neha Malik. 2016. "The Status of Financial Inclusion, Regulation, and Education in India." 568. ADBI Working Paper Series. Tokyo: Asian Development Bank.

Beck, Thorsten. 2013. Banking Finance for SMEs-Lessons from the Literature. *National Institute Economic Review* 225 (1): R23-38.

Beck, Thorsten, and Asli Demirguc-Kunt. 2006. Small and Medium-Size Enterprises: Access to Finance as a Growth Constraint. *Journal of Banking and Finance* 30 (11): 2931–2943. https://doi.org/10.1016/j.jbankfin.2006.05.009.

Bell, Clive. 1991. "Interactions between Institutional and Informal Credit Agencies in Rural India." *The World Bank Economic Review* 4 (3): 297–327. http://documents.worldbank.org/curated/en/160931468756339586/Interactions-between-institutional-and-informal-credit-agencies-in-rural-India.

Bernheim, B. Douglas, and John Karl Scholz. 1993. "Private Saving and Public Policy." *Tax Policy and the Economy* 7: 73–110. https://doi.org/10.1086/tpe.7.20060630.

Bertrand, Marianne, Sendhil Mullainathan, and Eldar Shafir. 2006. Behavioral Economics and Marketing in Aid of Decision Making Among the Poor. *Journal of Public Policy & Marketing* 25 (1): 8–23. https://doi.org/10.1509/jppm.25.1.8.

Besley, Timothy. 1994. How Do Market Failures Justify Interventions in Credit Markets? *The World Bank Research Observer* 9 (1): 27–47.

Beverly, Sondra G., and Michael Sherraden. 1999. Institutional Determinants of Saving: Implications for Low-Income Households and Public Policy. *The Journal of Socio-Economics* 28 (4): 457–473. https://doi.org/10.1016/S1053-5357(99)00046-3.

Bhattacharjee, Manojit, and Meenakshi Rajeev. 2013. Modeling Loan Repayment Behavior in Developing Countries. *Applied Economic Perspectives and Policy* 35 (2): 270–295.

Bhattacharjee, Manojit, and Meenakshi Rajeev. 2014. "Accessibility to Credit and Its Determinants: A State-Level Analysis of Cultivator Households in India." *Margin: The Journal of Applied Economic Research* 8 (3): 285–300. https://doi.org/10.1177/0973801014531137.

Bhavani, T. A., and N. R. Bhanumurthy. 2012. *Financial Access in Post-Reform India*. Oxford University Press. https://doi.org/10.1093/acprof:oso/9780198076650.003.0002.

Bhole, L. M. 1985. Administered Interests Rates in India. *Economic & Political Weekly* 20 (25/26): 1089–1104.

Bhowmik, Sharit K. 2005. "Street Vendors in Asia: A Review." *Economic and Political Weekly* 40 (22/23): 2256–2264. https://www.epw.in/journal/2005/22-23/review-labour-review-issues-specials/street-vendors-asia-review.html?0=ip_login_no_cache%3D970e446f652ce29bb2dcdd4b471ad5ed.

Binswanger-Mkhize, Hans P. 2012. Is There Too Much Hype about Index-Based Agricultural Insurance? *Journal of Development Studies* 48 (2): 187–200. https://doi.org/10.1080/00220388.2011.625411.

Binswanger, Hans P., and Shahidur R. Khandker. 1995. "The Impact of Formal Finance on the Rural Economy of India." *The Journal of Development Studies* 32 (2): 234–262. https://doi.org/10.1080/00220389508422413.

Bose, Pinaki. 1998. Formal—Informal Sector Interaction in Rural Credit Markets. *Journal of Development Economics* 56 (2): 265–280.

Browning, Martin, and Annamaria Lusardi. 1996. Household Saving: Micro Theories and Micro Facts. *Journal of Economic Literature* 34 (4): 1797–1855. https://doi.org/10.2307/2729595.

Burgess, Robin, and Rohini Pande. 2005. Do Rural Banks Matter? Evidence From the Indian Social Banking Experiment. *American Economic Review* 95 (3): 780–795. https://doi.org/10.1257/0002828054201242.

Camara, Noelia, Ximena Pena, and David Tuesta. 2014. "Factors That Matter for Financial Inclusion: Evidence from Peru." BBVA Bank, Economic Research Department, Working Papers: 1409, No. 14: 23. https://doi.org/10.5605/IEB.10.1.

CDFI. 2020. "How Migrants Send Money Home?" *CDFI Migrant Remittance Study Report*. Bangalore.

Chakravarthy, Tapas Kumar. 2005. "The Share of Cooperatives in Rural Credit." *RBI Publications*.

Chakravarty, Satya R, and Rupayan Pal. 2010. "Measuring Financial Inclusion: An Axiomatic Approach." WP-2010-003. Indira Gandhi Institute of Development Research Working Papers. Mumbai. http://www.igidr.ac.in/pdf/publication/WP-2010-003.pdf.

Chattopadhyay, Sadhan Kumar. 2011. "Financial Inclusion in India: A Case-Study of West Bengal." 34269. MPRA Working Paper. Munich. https://mpra.ub.uni-muenchen.de/34269/1/Financial_Inclusion_in_India.pdf.

Chowdhary, S., and M. R. Gupta. 1996. Delayed Formal Credit, Bribing and the Informal Credit Market in Agriculture: A Theoretical Analysis. *Journal of Development Economics* 51 (2): 433–449.

Cole, Shawn, Xavier Giné, Jeremy Tobacman, Petia Topalova, Robert Townsend, and James Vickery. 2013. Barriers to Household Risk Management: Evidence from India. *American Economic Journal: Applied Economics* 5 (1): 104–135. https://doi.org/10.1257/app.5.1.104.

Cole, Shawn, Thomas Sampson, and Bilal Zia. 2011. Prices or Knowledge? What Drives Demand for Financial Services in Emerging Markets? *Journal of Finance* 66 (6): 1933–1967.

Coleman, Andrew. 1998. "Household Savings: A Survey of Recent Microeconomic Theory and Evidence." 98/08. New Zealand Treasury Working Paper Series. http://hdl.handle.net/10419/205402.

Collins, Daryl, Jonathan Morduch, Stuart Rutherford, and Orlanda Ruthven. 2010. *Portfolios of the Poor: How the World's Poor Live on $2 a Day*. Princeton: Princeton University Press.

Cragg, John G. 1971. Some Statistical Models for Limited Dependent Variables with Application to the Demand for Durable Goods. *Econometrica* 39 (5): 829–844.

Das, Maitreyi Bordia. 2003. "The Other Side of Self Employment: Household Entreprises in India." 27873. Social Protection Discussion Paper Series. The World Bank.

Dasgupta, Rajaram. 2001. Priority Sector Lending-Yesterday,Today and Tomorrow. *Economic & Political Weekly* 37 (41): 4239–4245.

Deaton, Angus. 1990. "Savings in Developing Countries Theory and Review." In *Proceedings of the World Bank Annual Conference on Development Economics 1989, World Bank Economic Review Supplement*, 61–96. Washington, D.C.: The World Bank.

Deb, Sharmistha, and Meenakshi Rajeev. 2007. Banking on ' Baniyas ' for Credit. *Economic and Political Weekly* 42 (4): 280–283.

Demirgüç-Kunt, A., L. Klapper, and G. Panos. 2007. *The Origins of Self-Employment*. Washington, D.C.: Development Research Group, World Bank.

Demirgüç-Kunt, Asli, Leora Klapper, Dorothe Singer, and Saniya Ansar. 2021. "Financial Inclusion, Digital Payments, and Resilience in the Age of COVID-19." Washington, DC. https://www.worldbank.org/en/news/press-release/2022/06/29/covid-19-drives-global-surge-in-use-of-digital-payments#:~:text=In.

Demirgüç-Kunt, Asli, Leora Klapper, Dorothe Singer, and Saniya Ansar. 2022. "The Global Findex Database 2021: Financial Inclusion, Digital Payments, and Resilience in the Age of COVID-19." Washington, DC. https://doi.org/10.1596/978-1-4648-1897-4.

Demirguc-Kunt, Asli, Leora Klapper, Dorothe Singer, Saniya Ansar, and Jake Hess. 2018. *The Global Findex Database 2017: Measuring Financial Inclusion and the Fintech Revolution*. Washington, DC: World Bank Group.

Demirgüç-Kunt, Asli, Leora Klapper, Dorothe Singer, Saniya Ansar, and Jake Hess. 2018. *Asli Demirgüç-Kunt The Global Findex Database*.

Demirgüç-Kunt, Aslı, T. Beck, and P. Honohan. 2008. "Access to Finance and Development: Theory and Measurement." In *Finance for All? Policies and Pitfalls in Expanding Access—A World Bank Policy Research Report*. Washington, DC: The world Bank.

Dercon, Stefan. 2002. Income Risk, Coping Strategies, and Safety Nets. *The World Bank Research Observer* 17 (2): 141–166. https://doi.org/10.1093/wbro/17.2.141.

Deshingkar, Priya. 2006. Internal Migration, Poverty and Development in Asia: Including the Excluded. *IDS Bulletin* 37 (3): 88–100. https://doi.org/10.1111/j.1759-5436.2006.tb00272.x.

DeSoto, Hernando. 1989. *The Other Path: The Invisible Revolution in the Third World*. New York: Harper and Row.

Diagne, Aliou. 1999. Determinants of Household Access to and Participation in Formal and Informal Credit Markets in Malawi. *International Food Policy Research Institute* 67 (67): 1–62.

Dodd, Warren, Sally Humphries, Kirit Patel, Shannon Majowicz, and Cate Dewey. 2017. "The Internal Migration-Development Nexus: Evidence from Southern India." *Asian and Pacific Migration Journal* 26 (1): 56–83. https://doi.org/10.1177/0117196816684349.

Dupas, Pascaline, Sarah Green, Anthony Keats, and Jonathan Robinson. 2012. "Challenges in Banking the Rural Poor: Evidence from Kenya's Western Province." 17851. NBER Working Paper Series. Cambridge, MA: National Bureau of Economic Research. https://doi.org/10.3386/w17851.

Dupas, Pascaline, and Jonathan Robinson. 2013. Why Don't the Poor Save More? Evidence from Health Savings Experiments. *American Economic Review* 103 (4): 1138–1171. https://doi.org/10.1257/aer.103.4.1138.

Evans, David S., and Boyan Jovanovic. 1989. An Estimated Model of Entrepreneurial Choice under Liquidity Constraints. *Journal of Political Economy* 97 (4): 808–827. https://doi.org/10.1086/261629.

Feder, Gershon, Lawrence J. Lau, Justin Y. Lin, and Xiaopeng Luo. 1990. The Relationship between Credit and Productivity in Chinese Agriculture: A Microeconomic Model of Disequilibrium. *American Journal of Agricultural Economics* 72 (5): 1151–1157.

Fields, Gary S. 2013. "Self Employment in the Developing World." Background Research Paper Submitted to the High Level Panel on the Post-2015 Development Agenda, Cornell University and IZA.

Fletschner, Diana. 2009. Rural Women's Access to Credit: Market Imperfections and Intrahousehold Dynamics. *World Development* 37 (3): 618–631. https://doi.org/10.1016/j.worlddev.2008.08.005.

Gadgil, M. V. 1986. Agricultural Credit in India: A Review of Performance and Policies. *Indian Journal of Agricultural Economics* 41 (3): 282–309.

Garg, Nitin, Krishna Thacker, N. A. Venkata, Sachin Bansal, and Graham A. N. Wright. 2009. "MicroSave India Focus Note 29, Potential for E/M-Banking Enabled Migrant Remittances." Microsave. https://www.microsave.net/wp-content/uploads/2018/10/IFN_29_Potential_for_E_M-Banking_Enabled_Migrant_Remittances.pdf.

Ghosh, Parikshit, Dilip Mookherjee, and Debraj Ray. 2000. "Credit Rationing in Developing Countries: An Overview of the Theory." In *Readings in the Theory of Economic Development*, edited by Dilip Mookherjee and Debraj Ray, ch 11:283–301. London: Blackwell.

Ghosh, Saibal. 2020. Financial Inclusion in India: Does Distance Matter? *South Asia Economic Journal* 21 (2): 216–238. https://doi.org/10.1177/1391561420961649.

Ghosh, Saibal, and D. Vinod. 2012. Determinants Of Banking Outreach: An Empirical Assessment of Indian States. *The Journal of Developing Areas* 46 (2): 269–295. https://doi.org/10.1353/jda.2012.0034.

Ghosh, Saibal, and Dharmarajan Vinod. 2017. What Constrains Financial Inclusion for Women? Evidence from Indian Micro Data. *World Development* 92: 60–81. https://doi.org/10.1016/j.worlddev.2016.11.011.

Giannatale, Sonia di, and María José Roa. 2016. "Formal Saving in Developing Economies-Barriers, Interventions, and Effects." IDB-WP-766. IDB Working Paper Series.

Gill, Anita. 2016. Agricultural Credit in Punjab: Have Policy Initiatives Made a Dent in Informal Credit Markets? In *Economic Transformation of a Developing Economy*, ed. Lakhwinder Singh and Nirvikar Singh, 165–182. Singapore: Springer.

Goedecke, Jann, Isabelle Guérin, Bert D'espallier, and Govindan Venkatasubramanian. 2018. Why Do Financial Inclusion Policies Fail in Mobilizing Savings from the Poor? Lessons from Rural South India. *Development Policy Review* 36 (s1): O201–O219. https://doi.org/10.1111/dpr.12272.

GOI. 2011. "Key Indicators of Employment and Unemployment in India 2009–10, NSS 60th Round." New Delhi: NSSO.

GOI. 2016. "Operational Guidelines of 'Pradhan Mantri Bhima Fasal Yojana.'" https://pmfby.gov.in/pdf/Oprational_Guidelines.pdf.

GOI. 2017a. "India on the Move and Churning: New Evidences." *Economic Survey 2016–17*. New Delhi.

GOI. 2017b. "Performance Audit Union Government Agriculture Crop Insurance Schemes Reports of Agriculture and Farmers Welfare." https://cag.gov.in/content/report-no7-2017-performance-audit-union-government-agriculture-crop-insurance-schemes.

GOI. 2018a. "Doubling Farmers' Income." *Report of the Committee on Doubling Farmers' Income*. New Delhi.

GOI. 2018b. "Pradhan Mantri Fasal Bima Yojana." Press Information Bureau. https://pib.gov.in/Pressreleaseshare.aspx?PRID=1555569.

GOI. 2022. "The Economic Survey of India 2021–22." https://www.indiabudget.gov.in/budget2022-23/economicsurvey/doc/eschapter/echap09.pdf.

Gonzalez-Vega, Claudio. 1984. "Cheap Agricultural Credit:Redistribution in Reverse." In *Undermining Rural Development with Cheap Credit*, edited by Dale W. Adams, Douglas H. Graham, and J. D. Von Pischke, 1984th ed., 120–143. Colorado: Westview Press.

Gopinath, Shreyas, Justin Oliver, Ajay Tannirkulam, Supriyo Bhattacharya, and R. R. Kulkarni. 2010. *Putting Money in Motion: How Much Do Migrants Pay for Domestic Transfers?* Chennai: Centre for Micro Finance at IFMR Research.

Greene, William H. 2003. *Econometric Analysis*, 5th ed. London: Pearson Education.

Gunnsteinsson, Snaebjorn. 2020. Experimental Identification of Asymmetric Information: Evidence on Crop Insurance in the Philippines. *Journal of Development Economics* 144 (May): 102414. https://doi.org/10.1016/j.jdeveco.2019.102414.

Gupta, Sanjeev Kumar. 2011. "Financial Inclusion—IT as Enabler." *Reserve Bank of India Occasional Papers* 32 (2).

Gurtoo, Anjula, and Colin C. Williams. 2009. Entrepreneurship and the Informal Sector. *The International Journal of Entrepreneurship and Innovation* 10 (1): 55–62. https://doi.org/10.5367/000000009787414280.

Harttgen, Kenneth, and Stephan Klasen. 2011. A Human Development Index by Internal Migrational Status. *Journal of Human Development and Capabilities* 12 (3): 393–424. https://doi.org/10.1080/19452829.2011.576819.

Hazell, P., C. Pomareda, and A. Valdes. 1986. *Crop Insurance for Agricultural Development: Issues and Experience*. London: Johns Hopkins University Press.

Honohan, Patrick. 2006. "Household Financial Assets in the Process of Development." WPS 3965. World Bank Policy Research Working Paper. Washington, DC.

Honohan, Patrick. 2007. Cross Country Variation in Household Access to Financial Services. *Journal of Banking & Finance* 32 (11): 2493–2500. https://doi.org/10.1016/j.jbankfin.2008.05.004.

IFAD, and World Bank. 2015. "The Use of Remittances and Financial Inclusion, A Report by the International Fund for Agricultural Development and the World Bank Group to the G20 Global Partnership for Financial Inclusion." IFAD and World Bank. https://www.ifad.org/documents/38714170/40187309/gpfi.pdf/58ce7a06-7ec0-42e8-82dc-c069227edb79.

Jack, William, and Tavneet Suri. 2014. Risk Sharing and Transactions Costs:Evidence from Kenya's Mobile Money Revolution. *American Economic Review* 104 (1): 183–223. https://doi.org/10.1257/aer.104.1.183.

Lucas, Robert E B., and Oded Stark. 1985. Motivations to Remit: Evidence from Botswana. *Journal of Political Economy* 93 (5): 901–918. https://doi.org/10.1086/261341.

Margolis, David N. 2014. By Choice and by Necessity: Entrepreneurship and Self-Employment in the Developing World. *European Journal of Development Research* 26 (4): 419–436. https://doi.org/10.1057/ejdr.2014.25.

Martínez, Christiane Ströh de, Martina Wiedmaier Pfister, Corinna Müller, and Ariane Schoen. 2019. *Inclusive Insurance in National Financial Inclusion Strategies—Survey Report*. Kuala Lumpur: Alliance for Financial Inclusion (AFI). https://www.afi-global.org/sites/default/files/publications/2018-08/afi_a2ii_report_view.pdf.

Mas, Ignacio, and Olga Morawczynski. 2009. "Designing Mobile Money Services Lessons from M-PESA." *Innovations: Technology, Governance, Globalisation* 4 (2): 77–91.

Massally, Keyzom Ngodup, Rahul Matthan, and RUDRA Chau. 2023. "What Is the DPI Approach?". https://carnegieindia.org/2023/05/15/what-is-dpi-approach-pub-89721.

Mckinnon, Ronald. 1973. *Money and Capital in Economic Development*. Washington, D.C.: Brookings Institution.

Mehrotra, N., V. Puhazhendhi, G. Nair, and B. B. Sahoo. 2009. "Financial Inclusion: An Overview." 48. NABARD Occasional Papers. Mumbai: NABARD.

Mohanty, Sanjay K., Manisha Dubey, and Jajati Parida. 2014. Economic Well-Being and Spending Behaviour of Households in India: Does Remittances Matter? *Migration and Development* 3 (1): 38–53. https://doi.org/10.1080/21632324.2014.886905.

Mohieldin, Mahmoud S., and Peter W. Wright. 2014. Formal and Informal Credit Markets in Egypt. *Economic Development and Cultural Change* 48 (3): 657–670.

Morawczynski, Olga, David Hutchful, Nimmy Rangaswamy, and Edward Cutrell. 2010. "The Bank Account Is Not Enough: Examining Strategies for Financial Inclusion in India." In *Proceedings of the 4th ACM/IEEE International Conference on Information and Communication Technologies and Development. ACM, 2010*. London: IEEE. https://www.microsoft.com/en-us/research/publication/the-bank-account-is-not-enough-examining-strategies-for-financial-inclusion-in-india/.

Morsy, Hanan. 2020. Access to Finance—Mind the Gender Gap. *The Quarterly Review of Economics and Finance* 78 (November): 12–21. https://doi.org/10.1016/j.qref.2020.02.005.

Mowl, Amy Jensen. 2013. "The Role of Transaction Costs in Access to Savings and Credit." NSE Working Paper Series. Chennai: NSE-IFMR.

Munshi, Kaivan. 2019. Caste and the Indian Economy. *Journal of Economic Literature* 57 (4): 781–834. https://doi.org/10.1257/jel.20171307.

Muranjan, S. K. 1952. *Modern Banking in India. Third Edit*. Bombay: Kamal Publishing House.

NABARD. 2017. "NABARD All India Rural Financial Inclusion Survey-2016–17." Mumbai. https://www.nabard.org/auth/writereaddata/tender/1608180417NABARD-Repo-16_Web_P.pdf.

Nicoletti, Giuseppe, Stefano Scarpetta, and Olivier Boyland. 1999. "Summary Indicators of Product Market Regulation with an Extension to Employment Protection Legislation." OECD Economics Department Working Papers.

Nicoletti, Giuseppe, Stefano Scarpetta, and Oliver Boylaud. 2000. "Summary Indicators of Product Market Regulation with an Extension to Employment Protection Legislation." 226. OECD Economics Department Working Papers. Paris. https://doi.org/10.2139/ssrn.201668.

Nikaido, Yuko, Jesim Pais, and Mandira Sarma. 2015. What Hinders and What Enhances Small Enterprises' Access to Formal Credit in India? *Review of Development Finance* 5 (1): 43–52. https://doi.org/10.1016/j.rdf.2015.05.002.

NSSO. 2014. "Key Indicators of Debt and Investment in India (2013)." *Ministry of Statistics and Programme Implementation, Govt of India*. New Delhi.

NSSO. 2019. "Key Indicators of Social Consumption in India: Health, NSS 75th Round." New Delhi.

Pal, R., and R. Vaidya. 2011. "Outreach of Banking Services across Indian States: 1981–2007 Converging or Diverging?" In *India Development Report*. New Delhi: Oxford University Press.

Pal, Sarmistha. 2002. Household Sectoral Choice and Effective Demand for Rural Credit in India. *Applied Economics* 34 (14): 1743–1755. https://doi.org/10.1080/00036840210121228.

Pareek, Abhay, Akhand Tiwari, Akhilesh Singh, Anirban Roy, Ghiyazuddin A. Mohammad, Madhurantika Moulick, Mukul Singh, et al. 2011. "Understanding Remittance Networks in Punjab and Uttar Pradesh." *Microsave Report*. http://www.microsave.net/wp-content/uploads/2011/06/Understanding_Remittance_Networks_In_Punjab_and_Uttar_Pradesh.pdf.

Patra, Michael Debabrata, and Sunando Roy. 2000. "Financial Stability: A Survey of the Indian Experience." *Reserve Bank of India Occasional Papers* 21 (1).

Paulson, Anna L., and Robert Townsend. 2004. Entrepreneurship and Financial Constraints in Thailand. *Journal of Corporate Finance* 10 (2): 229–262. https://doi.org/10.1016/S0929-1199(03)00056-7.

Pawar, Jagannathrao, and Subhash R. Sutar. 1982. Impact of Lower Interest Rate Finance on Economic Conditions of Rural Weaker Section. *Indian Journal of Agricultural Economics* 37: 265–272.

Pitt, Mark M., and Shahidur Khandkar. 1998. The Impact of Group-Based Credit Programs on Poor Households in Bangladesh: Does the Gender of Participants Matter? *The Journal of Political Economy* 106 (5): 958–996.

Pradhan, Narayan Chandra. 2013. "Persistence of Informal Credit in Rural India: Evidence from 'All-India Debt and Investment Survey' and beyond. WPS (DEPR): 05/2013." RBI Working Paper Series, Reserve Bank of India.

Prina, Silvia. 2015. Banking the Poor via Savings Accounts: Evidence from a Field Experiment. *Journal of Development Economics* 115: 16–31. https://doi.org/10.1016/j.jdeveco.2015.01.004.

Quach, M., and A. Mullineux. 2007. The Impact of Access to Credit on Household Welfare in Rural Vietnam. *Research in Accounting in Emerging Economies* 7: 279–307.

Rajan, Raghuram G. 2009. *A Hundred Small Steps: Report of the Committee on Financial Sector Reforms.* http://eprints.cscs.res.in/141/%5Cnhttp://scholar.google.com/scholar?hl=en&btnG=Search&q=intitle:A+hundred+small+steps:+Report+of+the+Committee+on+Financial+Sector+Reforms#0%5Cnhttp://books.google.com/books?hl=en&lr=&id=HGhjfUa_EukC&oi=fnd&pg=PP1&dq=A+Hun.

Rajan, Raghuram G. 2014. "Financial Inclusion: Technology, Institutions and Policies'Keynote Address at NASSCOM India Leadership Forum, Mumbai." In *RBI Documents*. Mumbai: Reserve Bank of India.

Rajeev, Meenakshi, and Manojit Bhattacharjee. 2012. "Access to Financial Services : Are Poor Excluded ?" 808. Norwegian Institute of International Affairs Working Paper. Oslo. https://brage.bibsys.no/xmlui/handle/11250/277551.

Rajeev, Meenakshi, Manojit Bhattacharjee, and B. P. Vani. 2015. "Crop Insurance and Risk Mitigation: Experiences from India." No. 15. ICDD Working Paper. Kassel: Kassel University Press GmbH.

Rajeev, Meenakshi, and H. P. Mahesh. 2010. "Banking Sector Reforms and NPA: A Study of Indian Commercial Banks." ISEC Working Paper 252. Bangalore.

Rajeev, Meenakshi, and Pranav Nagendran. 2019. "Crop Insurance in India-Where Do We Stand?" *Economic and Political Weekly* 54 (26–27). https://www.epw.in/journal/2019/26-27/review-rural-affairs/crop-insurance-india.html.

Rajeev, Meenakshi, and Shika Saravanabhavan. 2019. "Has Access to Formal Credit Improved? A Study of Rural Cultivator Households in India." In *Contemporary Issues in Indian Agriculture*, edited by Meenakshi Rajeev. Bangalore: ISEC Monograph series.

Rajeev, Meenakshi, B. P. Vani, and Manojit Bhattacharjee. 2012. "Nature and Dimensions of Farmers' Indebtedness in India." 267. ISEC Working Paper. Bangalore: ISEC.

Rajeev, Meenakshi, and B. P. Vani. 2017. *Financial Access of the Urban Poor in India: A Story of Exclusion*. New Delhi: Springer India. https://doi.org/10.1007/978-81-322-3712-9.

Rajeev, Meenakshi, B. P. Vani, and Manojit Bhattacharjee. 2011. Credibility of Equal Access to Credit:Does Gender Matter? *Economic & Political Weekly* 46 (33): 76–79.

Rajeev, Meenakshi, B. P. Vani, and Veerashekharappa. 2017. "Self-Help Groups for India's Financial Inclusion: Do Effective Cost of Borrowing Limit Their Operation?" ICDD Working Paper No. 19. Kassel: Kassel University Press GmbH.

Rajeev, Meenakshi, and B. P. Vani. 2011. "Farm Sector in Karnataka: Farmers' Indebtedness and Risk Management. Project Report No. CESP/93." Bangalore: ISEC.

Rakesh, Mohan. 2006. Agricultural Credit in India—Status, Issues and Future Agenda. *Economic and Political Weekly* 41 (11): 1013–1023.

Rakesh, Mohan, and Partha Ray. 2016. "Indian Financial Sector: Structure, Trends, and Turns." WP/17/7. IMF Working Papers.

Ramji, Minakshi. 2009. *Financial Inclusion in Gulbarga: Finding Usage in Access*. Institute for Financial Management and Research Working Paper Series. Chennai: IFMR.

Ray, Debraj. 1998. *Development Economics. Princeton University Press, Princeton*. Princeton: Princeton University Press, Princeton.

RBI. 2007. "Report of the Task Force on Empowering RRB Boards for Operational Efficiency." Mumbai.

RBI. 2008a. *Evolution of Banking in India. RBI Publications*. Mumbai: Reserve Bank of India. https://rbidocs.rbi.org.in/rdocs/Publications/PDFs/86727.pdf.

RBI. 2008b. "Report of the Committee on Financial Inclusion-Chairman: Dr. C. Rangarajan." Mumbai: Reserve Bank of India.

RBI. 2011. "Financial Inclusion by Extension of Banking Services—Use of Business Correspondents (BCs)." RBI Notification. Mumbai. https://www.rbi.org.in/scripts/NotificationUser.aspx?Mode=0&Id=6017.

RBI. 2012. "Strengthening and Revitalising Rural Cooperative Credit Delivery System." *RBI Documents-Speech Delivered by Dr Deepali Pant Joshi, Executive Director, Reserve Bank of India*. Mumbai: Reserve Bank of India. https://rbidocs.rbi.org.in/rdocs/Speeches/PDFs/SRRCDS250314.pdf.

Rosenzweig, Mark R. 2001. Savings Behaviour in Low-Income Countries. *Oxford Review of Economic Policy* 17 (1): 40–54.

Rothschild, Michael, and Joseph Stiglitz. 1976. Equilibrium in Competitive Insurance Markets: An Essay on the Economics of Imperfect Information. *Quarterly Journal of Economics* 90 (4): 355–375. https://doi.org/10.1007/978-94-015-7957-5_18.

Samuel, Achamma. 2004. "Insurance: The Indian Experience." *RBI Occational Papers* 21 (2/3). https://rbidocs.rbi.org.in/rdocs/Publications/Pdfs/33958.pdf.

Saravanabhavan, Shika, and Meenakshi; Rajeev. 2023. "Financial Inclusion and Remittance Services." *Economic and Political Weekly* 58 (20). https://www.epw.in/journal/2023/20/special-articles/financial-inclusion-and-remittance-services.html.

Saravanabhavan, Shika, and Meenakshi Rajeev. 2020. "The Urban Self-Employed: Is Access to Financial Services Adequate?" In *Deciphering India's Service Sector Growth-Forthcoming*, edited by Shashanka Bhide, V. N. Balasubramanya, and K.L. Krishna. New Delhi: Routledge.

Saravanabhavan, Shika, and Meenakshi Rajeev. 2024. Financial Inclusion in India: How Far Do Grassroots Institutions Matter? *Journal of International Development* 36 (5): 2318–2341. https://doi.org/10.1002/jid.3897.

Sarma, Mandira. 2012. "Index of Financial Inclusion—A Measure of Financial Sector Inclusiveness." 07/2012. School of International Studies Working Paper. New Delhi.

Schumpeter, Joseph A. 1934. *The Theory of Economic Development: An Inquiry into Profits, Capital, Credit, Interest, and the Business Cycle*. Cambridge: Harvard University Press.

Sen, Kunal, and Rajendra R. Vaidya. 1997. *The Process of Financial Liberalization in India*. Delhi: Oxford University Press.

Sharma, Manoj, Anurodh Giri, and Sakshi Chadha. 2016. "Pradhan Mantri Jan Dhan Yojana Wave III Assessment." Microsave. https://www.microsave.net/files/pdf/PMJDY_Wave_III_Assessment_MicroSave.pdf.

Sinha, Anand. 2012. "Striking a Balance: Credit Penetration and NPA Management—Role of Information Sharing, Address by Shri Anand Sinha, Deputy Governor, Reserve Bank of India at the Fourth Annual Credit Information Conference on March 7, 2012." RBI Monthly Bulletin. Mumbai.

Stiglitz, Joseph E., and Andrew Weiss. 1981. Credit Rationing in Markets with Imperfect Information. *The American Economic Review* 71 (3): 393–410.

Swain, Bijay Kumar. 2018. "A Research Study Report on Evaluating Implementation of Jan Dhan Yojana." Hyderabad.

Tambunan, Tulus. 2009. Women Entrepreneurship in Asian Developing Countries: Their Development and Main Constraints. *Journal of Development and Agricultural Economics* 1 (2): 27–40.

The World Bank. 2023. "G20 Policy Recommendations for Advancing Financial Inclusion and Productivity Gains through Digital Public Infrastructure." https://www.g20.org/content/dam/gtwenty/gtwenty_new/document/G20_POLICY_RECOMMENDATIONS.pdf.

Thorat, Y. S. P., N. V. Ramana, R. V. Ramakrishna, Anne Koshy, and Therese Zak. 2009. "Remittance Needs in India, NABARD-GTZ Technical Study." New Delhi.

Tiwari, Akhand, Akhilesh Kumar Singh, Anurodh Giri, Minakshi Ramji, Sachin Bansal, and Alphina Jos. 2011. "Understanding Remittance Networks in Gujarat, Orissa and Bihar." Microsave. http://www.microsave.net/files/pdf/Understanding_Remittance_Networks_In_Gujarat_Orissa_and_Bihar.pdf.

Tiwari, Akhand, Akhilesh Kumar Singh, Anurodh Giri, Minakshi Ramji, Abhishek Lahiri, Alphina Jos, and Ritesh Dhawan. 2011. "Relative Risk to the Savings of the Poor in Rajasthan." Microsave. https://www.microsave.net/2011/01/06/relative-risk-to-the-savings-of-the-poor-in-rajasthan-2/.

Tram, Thi Xuan Huong, Tien Dinh Lai, and Thi Truc Huong Nguyen. 2023. "Constructing a Composite Financial Inclusion Index for Developing Economies." *The Quarterly Review of Economics and Finance* 87 (February): 257–265. https://doi.org/10.1016/j.qref.2021.01.003.

Tripathi, Dwijendra. 2004. *The Oxford History of Indian Business*. New Delhi: Oxford University Press.

Tripathi, Sabyasachi, and Meenakshi Rajeev. 2023. "Gender-Inclusive Development through Fintech: Studying Gender-Based Digital Financial Inclusion in a Cross-Economy Setting." 1397. ADBI Working Paper Series. https://doi.org/10.56506/ZWGS6876.

Tumbe, Chinmay. 2011. *Remittances in India: Facts & Issues*. No. 331. IIMB Working Papers. Bangalore: Indian Institute of management.

UNDP. 2007. *Building Security for the Poor: Potential and Prospects for Microinsurance in India*, 2nd ed. Colombo: United Nations Development Programme.

United Nations, Organisation for Economic Co-operation and Development. European Commission., International Monetary Fund., and World Bank. 2008. "System of National Accounts-2008."

Van, Loan, Anh The Vo, Nhan Thien Nguyen, and Duc Hong Vo. 2021. Financial Inclusion and Economic GROWTH: An International Evidence. *Emerging Markets Finance and Trade* 57 (1): 239–263. https://doi.org/10.1080/1540496X.2019.1697672.

Viswanathan, Brinda, and K. S. Kavi Kumar. 2015. "Weather, Agriculture and Rural Migration: Evidence from State and District Level Migration in India." *Environment and Development Economics* 20 (4): 469–492. https://doi.org/10.1017/S1355770X1500008X.

Weber, Olaf, and Adnan Ahmad. 2014. Empowerment through Microfinance: The Relation between Loan Cycle and Level of Empowerment. *World Development* 62: 75–87. https://doi.org/10.1016/j.worlddev.2014.05.012.

Wooldridge, Jeffrey M. 2010. *Econometric Analysis of Cross Section and Panel Data*. Cambridge: MIT Press.

Kaboski, Joseph P., and Robert M. Townsend. 2012. The Impact of Credit on Villages. *American Journal of Applied Economics* 4 (2): 98–133. https://doi.org/10.1257/app.4.3.98.

Kaiser, Henry F. 1958. The Varimax Criterion for Analytic Rotation in Factor Analysis. *Psychometrika* 23 (3): 187–200.

Kannan, Elumalai. 2011. "Relationship between Agricultural Credit Policy, Credit Disbursements and Crop Productivity: A Study in Karnataka." *Indian Journal of Agricultural Economics* 66 (3): 444–456. https://doi.org/10.22004/ag.econ.204767.

Kannan, Elumalai. 2015. "Trends in Agricultural Income: An Analysis at the Select Crop and State Levels in India." *Journal of Agrarian Change* 15 (2): 201–219. https://doi.org/10.1111/joac.12068.

Karlan, Dean, Margaret McConnell, Sendhil Mullainathan, and Jonathan Zinman. 2016. Getting to the Top of Mind: How Reminders Increase Saving. *Management Science* 62 (12): 3393–3411. https://doi.org/10.1287/mnsc.2015.2296.

Karlan, Dean, Aishwarya Lakshmi Ratan, and Jonathan Zinman. 2014. Saving by and for the Poor: A Research Review and Agenda. *Review of Income and Wealth* 60 (1): 36–78. https://doi.org/10.1111/roiw.12101.

Karlan, Dean, and Jonathan Zinman. 2010. Expanding Credit Access: Using Randomized Supply Decisions to Estimate the Impacts. *Review of Financial Studies* 23 (1): 433–464. https://doi.org/10.1093/rfs/hhp092.

Kashuliza, Anacleti, and Jonathan G. Kydd. 1996. Determinants of Bank Credit Access Forn Smallholder Farmers in Tanzania: A Discriminant Analysis Application. *Savings and Development* 20 (3): 285–304.

Khan, H. R. 2005. *Report of the Internal Group to Examine Issues Relating to Rural Credit and Microfinance*. Mumbai.

King, Robert G., and Ross Levine. 1993. "Finance and Growth: Schumpeter Might Be Right." *The Quarterly Journal of Economics* 108 (3): 717–737. https://doi.org/10.2307/2118406.

Kochar, Anjini. 1997. An Empirical Investigation of Rationing Constraints in Rural Credit Markets in India. *Journal of Development Economics* 53 (2): 339–371. https://doi.org/10.1016/S0304-3878(97)00020-5.

Kumar, Nitin. 2013a. Financial Inclusion and Its Determinants: Evidence from India. *Journal of Financial Economic Policy* 5 (1): 4–19. https://doi.org/10.1108/17576381311317754.

Kumar, Nitish. 2014. *Political Interference and Crowding out in Bank Lending*. University of Chicago.

Kumar, Sunil Mitra. 2013b. Does Access to Formal Agricultural Credit Depend on Caste? *World Development* 43 (March): 315–328. https://doi.org/10.1016/j.worlddev.2012.11.001.

World Bank. 2008. "Growth and Poverty Reduction in Agriculture's Three Worlds." In *World Development Report 2008: Agriculture for Development*, 26–44. Washington, DC: The World Bank.

Wossen, Tesfamicheal, Tahirou Abdoulaye, Arega Alene, Mekbib G. Haile, Shiferaw Feleke, Adetunji Olanrewaju, and Victor Manyong. 2017. "Impacts of Extension Access and Cooperative Membership on Technology Adoption and Household Welfare." *Journal of Rural Studies* 54: 223–233. https://doi.org/10.1016/j.jrurstud.2017.06.022.

Wright, B. D., and J. A. Hewitt. 1994. "All-Risk Crop Insurance: Lessons from Theory and Experience." In *Economics of Agricultural Crop Insurance: Theory and Evidence*, edited by Darrell L. Hueth and William H. Furtan, 4: 73–112. Natural Resource Management and Policy. Dordrecht: Springer. https://doi.org/10.1007/978-94-011-1386-1_4.

Yorulmaz, Recep. 2018. An Analysis of Constructing Global Financial Inclusion Indices. *Borsa Istanbul Review* 18 (3): 248–258. https://doi.org/10.1016/j.bir.2018.05.001.

Zeller, Manfred. 1994. Determinants of Credit Rationing: A Study of Informal Lenders and Formal Credit Groups in Madagascar. *World Development* 22 (12): 1895–1907.

Zeller, Manfred, Aliou Diagne, and Charles Mataya. 1998. Market Access by Smallholder Farmers in Malawi: Implications for Technology Adoption, Agricultural Productivity and Crop Income. *Agricultural Economics* 19: 219–229.

FSC
www.fsc.org
MIX
Papier | Fördert gute Waldnutzung
FSC® C083411

Kolibri 360 GmbH
Ferdinand-Jühlke-Straße 7
99095 Erfurt, Deutschland
produktsicherheit@kolibri360.de